Impact of Buddhism on Socio-Religious Life of the Asian People

Impact of Buddhism on Socio-Religious Life of the Asian People

— With Special Reference to Sri Lanka, China and Tibet —

(From 1st century BCE to 8th century CE)

Bhupender Heera

Decent Books
New Delhi

Cataloging in Publication Data — DK

[Courtesy: D.K. Agencies (P) Ltd. <docinfo@dkagencies.com>]

Heera, Bhupender, 1976-

Impact of Buddhism on socio-religious life of the Asian peoples : with special reference to Sri Lanka, China and Tibet, from 1st century BCE to 8th century CE/ Bhupender Heera.

xviii, 269 p., 23 cm.

Includes bibliographical references (p.)

ISBN 8186921435

1. Asia — Civilization — Buddhist influences. 2. Buddhism — Asia — History. I. Title.

DDC 294.309 5 22

ISBN 81-86921-43-5

First Published in India in 2007

Published and printed by:

Decent Books

D-36/A-1, Mohan Garden

Najafgarh Road

New Delhi - 110 059

Ph. (011) 2535-3435

Distributed by:

D.K. Printworld (P) Ltd.

Regd. office: *'Sri Kunj,'* F-52, Bali Nagar

Ramesh Nagar Metro Station

New Delhi - 110 015

Phones : (011) 2545-3975, 2546-6019; *Fax* : (011) 2546-5926

E-mail : dkprintworld@vsnl.net

Web : www.dkprintworld.com

Dedicated to
the reverent memories of my father
Late Shri Hem Raj Heera
who passed away while this work
was in progress

Preface

THE present research work aims at studying and evaluating the Impact of Buddhist Thought and Culture on Socio-Religious Life of the Asian People with Special Reference to Sri Lanka, China and Tibet. Buddhism had a tremendous civilizing influence on the socio-religious life of the Asian people since the days of Aśoka the Great when royal missionaries were sent for the propagation of the Buddhist faith to far-flung areas. Till eighth century CE, Buddhism was deeply rooted in many Asian countries and the most prominent among them were Sri Lanka, China and Tibet. The reason for limiting the scope of this thesis specifically to Sri Lanka, China and Tibet is that these countries substantially contributed towards the creation of Buddhist faith. Besides India, these three countries also served as the launching pad for the dissemination of Buddhist thought and culture to their neighbours. All these three countries kept on sending Buddhist missionaries to other countries for the propagation of this supremely sublime faith. In the monasteries and translation bureaus of these countries Buddhist *śāstra*s were not only translated and commented upon but were also created, and the entire exercise was done under royal instance and patronage. Sri Lanka became a stronghold of Theravāda Buddhism whereas China and Tibet greatly contributed to the Mahāyāna and Tantrayāna Buddhist traditions. It is also noteworthy that most of the missionary work was finished till eighth century CE in Sri Lanka and China, while it started only in the seventh century CE in Tibet. Still during seventh and eighth centuries a lot of missionary work was completed in Tibet due to the two wives of Tibetan King Srong-bstan-gam-po and two learned Indian paṇḍits — Śāntarakṣita and Padmasambhava with the establishment of Sam-ye monastery. This ambitious movement gained a momentum. In course of time Buddhism was introduced in Asian countries of the far east and south-east.

Academically, Buddhist thought and philosophy look complicated. But, otherwise, if it is understood, keeping in view the motto of *bahujana hitāya bahujana sukhāya*, it is very plain and simple. It preaches peace, brotherhood, tolerance, sympathy, friendliness, compassion, etc. It is free from the barriers of caste and creed. It comes forward with a spiritual consolation that *duḥkha* can be overcome and it also offers a remedial measure in the form of Four Noble Truths and it advises us to take to the Noble Eightfold Path. It also preaches a threefold culture of *śila, samādhi* and *prajñā*. Such sublime thoughts of the Buddha gave birth to an uncommonly altruistic culture. The ethico-spiritual thought and culture of Buddhism left an indelible imprint on the thoughts and minds of the Asian people.

In the present volume we have tried to show how Buddhist thought and culture brought about a total change in the socio-religious life of the Asian people with special reference to Sri Lanka, China and Tibet.

Buddhism is in fact *saddharma*. It is (*dharma*), culture (*saṁskṛti*), morality (*ācāra*), and practice (*sādhanā*) — all in one. As a religion or way of life it is a "light house" and as a faith it is a monument of all that is virtuous and absolutely good for the human beings, to be more precise, for the *prāṇimātra*. It is a religion of compassion, tolerance, love, sympathy, peace, universal fraternity and philanthropy. The Buddha is rightly regarded as the "Light of Asia." His *dharma* enlightened the entire human race but the continent of Asia was more fortunate to get the maximum light during the early centuries of the Christian era since the attainment of Enlightenment by the *Mahākāruṇika Śāstā*.

The Buddha blessed the human race with a unique wisdom and a spiritual culture which taught us the basics of sympathy, love and friendliness towards one and all. His message and sermons of peace and universal brotherhood were respected and practised by all those who heard and understood the underlying spirituality interwoven in his precepts. Initially Buddhism and its exalted sermons left an indelible impression on the thought and culture of India. But in course of time during the reign of Aśoka the Great it reached the foreign land when missionaries were sent to thirteen countries for the propagation and dissemination of Buddhism on the instruction of Aśoka. Sri Lanka was the most blessed land to receive this light through Mahindra and Saṅghamitrā who were bequeathed to the Buddhist Order by Aśoka. Buddhism made its first debut in Sri Lanka and gave it a spiritually superior thought and culture. Happily Sri Lanka is now a Buddhist country. During the lifetime of the Buddha, Buddhism was confined to Kāśī, Kosala and Magadha but after his *mahāparinirvāṇa* it penetrated the territories extending from Gandhāra to China via Central Asia and to other countries from China. It reached Tibet a little late because the territory was inaccessible. It is interesting as well as gratifying to note that Buddhism gave a sublime culture and a spiritual wisdom to China and Tibet thereby effecting a total facelift. Before Buddhism reached these two countries there was total chaos and confusion. Buddhism gave basic lessons of culture and civilization to these countries. From these countries it was further propagated and disseminated to countries of East Asia and South-East Asia. In course of time it became the most popular religion of Burma, Thailand, Laos, Kampuchea, Indonesia, Vietnam, Korea, Japan, Mongolia and many other kingdoms of Himalayan regions.

The sublime thought and culture of Buddhism was so exalted and awe-inspiring that it was embraced by a vast population of Asian countries. The people found a refuge in the soothing and consolatory teaching of the Buddha which ensured equality and justice for one and all. Buddhism became more popular among the masses all over the world in general and Asian countries in particular because there was no caste or creed in this *dharma*. For the Buddha every one was equal. Peace and tolerance, sympathy and friendliness were the distinctive qualities of Buddhism which attracted the common mass inside and across the Asian continent. Buddhism offered a cultural bond in which almost all the Asian countries and their people got united during the course of the early centuries of the Christian era. Even now many Asian countries and their people where Buddhism is still a living faith revere both India and the Buddha and look upon our country as *jagadguru*.

In fact, the Buddhist thought and culture has contributed a lot in shaping the socio-religious life and civilization of the Asian people during the course of several centuries.

In the present research work we have discussed all the factors that influenced the socio-religious life of Asian people in general and Sri Lankan, Chinese and Tibetan people in particular. How the Buddhist thought and culture shaped the thought and culture of the Asian people is also researched in this dissertation.

We have studied the impact and influence of thought and culture of Buddhism on the socio-religious life, thought and culture of the Asian people. There are many affinities among the people of Asian countries, the most prominent among them being the religio-cultural affinity. Buddhism established a common cultural bond between most of the countries of Asia because it is a living faith and practised philosophy in those countries. It is the need of the time that when political hatred, belligerence, sectarian disputes, religious intolerance and territorial disputes are bringing the war-like situation among the fellow brothers of this planet, we should highlight and tell that originally we are all the followers of the same culture and the devotees of the same religion. It will minimize the hatred and promote the feeling of universal brotherhood.

The aim of the proposed research work is to highlight the religio-philosophical and socio-cultural background of Buddhist thought in which a strong lasting cultural relation was built-up between India and the other Buddhist countries of Asia. The role and contribution of Buddhist thought and culture had been very important and distinct in shaping the socio-religious life of Asian people for at least eight long centuries from the first century BCE. All the Buddhist countries of Asia owe a great cultural debt to Indian philosophy and more particularly to Buddhism and Buddhist paṇḍits who carried the teachings of the Buddha without caring for the terrible hardships of long and perilous journeys across the desert. Due to the intellectual and cultural intercourse, during the course of about eight centuries, Buddhistic scholars and missionaries and the pious devotees of Buddhism succeeded in transplanting Buddhist faith in the Asian countries. A sublime culture was accepted as the currency of civilization of large tracts of Asian continent and their inhabitants. The aim of this research work is to promote mutual religious and cultural understanding between the people of the different countries of Asia by reminding them of the old cultural relations.

A lot of printed material, both in form of books and as research articles, is available on this subject, but the research work that we have done is very interesting as well as fresh in the sense that their approach has been different. Most of the works are narrative or informative or in the form of chronicles. The clue for selecting this topic was taken from a number of standard works which include: Xinru Liu's *Silk and Religion*

(Oxford University Press, 1998), Edward Conge's *A Short History of Buddhism* (Boston, 1980), Jagat Pati Joshi's *Facets of Indian Civilization* (New Delhi, 1997), Samuel Johnson's *Indian and Oriented Religion* (New Delhi, 1983), P.N Chopra's *Contribution of Buddhism to World Civilization and Culture* (Delhi, 1988), B.N Puri's *Buddhism in Central Asia* (Delhi, 1975), P.V Bapat (ed.) *2500 Years of Buddhism* (Delhi, 1959), P.N Bose's *The Indian Teachers in China* (Madras, 1923), Lokesh Chandra's *India's Contribution to World Thought and Culture* (Madras, 1970), Sukumar Dutt's *Buddhist Monks and Monasteries in India* (Delhi 1988), Granet Marcel's *Chinese Civilization* (London, 1930), C.H Hamilton's *Buddhism in India, Ceylon, China and Japan* (Chicago, 1931), L.M Joshi's *Studies in the Buddhist Culture in India* (Delhi, 1967), K.S Latourette's *The Chinese : Their History and Culture* (New York, 1946), and H.Q.Q Wales's *The Indianization of China and South-East Asia* (London, 1967).

The present research work is spread over eight chapters and concludes with a select bibliography at the end. In the first chapter a brief introduction is given to the cultural geography of Buddhist Asia. In the second chapter sufficient light is thrown on the state of society and religion in pre-Buddhist Asian countries. The third chapter deals with Buddhism and cultural transformation of Asian people by devout royalty. Fourth, fifth and sixth chapters are devoted to study the impact of Buddhist thought and culture on Sri Lankan, Chinese and Tibetan people. Religio-cultural transformation of Korea, Japan and other South-East Asian countries forms the subject matter of the seventh chapter. The eighth chapter highlights the contribution of Buddhist thought and culture to the treasure of literature, art and architecture of Asian countries. In the conclusion, I have tried to establish that Buddhism is a universal religion meant for peace-loving and civilized mankind. It is not meant for any one caste, creed or race.

Contents

Key to Transliteration

VOWELS

अ *a*	आ *ā*	इ *i*	ई *ī*	उ *u*	ऊ *ū*
(but)	(palm)	(it)	(beet)	(put)	(pool)
ऋ *ṛ*	ए *e*	ऐ *ai*	ओ *o*	औ *au*	
(rhythm)	(play)	(air)	(toe)	(loud)	

CONSONANTS

Guttural	क *ka*	ख* *kha*	ग *ga*	घ *gha*	ङ *ṅa*
	(skate)	(blockhead)	(gate)	(ghost)	(sing)
Palatal	च *ca*	छ* *cha*	ज *ja*	झ *jha*	ञ *ña*
	(chunk)	(catch him)	(john)	(hedgehog)	(bunch)
Cerebral	ट *ṭa*	ठ* *ṭha*	ड *ḍa*	ढ* *ḍha*	ण* *ṇa*
	(start)	(anthill)	(dart)	(godhead)	(under)
Dental	त *ta*	थ *tha*	द *da*	ध* *dha*	न *na*
	(path)	(thunder)	(that)	(breathe)	(numb)
Labial	प *pa*	फ* *pha*	ब *ba*	भ *bha*	म *ma*
	(spin)	(philosophy)	(bin)	(abhor)	(much)
Semi-	य *ya*	र *ra*	ल *la*	व *va*	
vowels	(young)	(drama)	(luck)	(vile)	
Sibilants	श *śa*	ष *ṣa*	स *sa*	ह *ha*	
	(shove)	(bushel)	(so)	(hum)	
Others	क्ष *kṣa*	त्र *tra*	ज्ञ *jña*	ळ* ḷ	ॠ* *ṝ*
	(*kṣatriya*)	(*triśūla*)	(*jñānī*)	(*play*)	

अं (ं)*ṁ anusvāra* (nasalisation of preceding vowel) like *saṁskṛti*

अः *visarga* = *ḥ* (aspiration of preceding vowel) like (*prātaḥ*)

ऽ *Avagraha* consonant #'consonant (like:- *ime 'vasthitā*)

Anusvāra at the end of a line is presented by m (म्) and not ṁ

HINDI LETTERS (extras)

ँ = *ñ*	ं = ṅ	ड़ = *ṛa*	ढ़ = *ṛha*
(*candrabindu*)	(*anusvāra*)		

* No exact English equivalents for these letters.

Acknowledgement

IN tune with the illustrious Indian tradition of *cakṣurunmīlitaṁ yena tansmai śrī gurave namaḥ,* I record my deep sense of gratefulness from the core of my heart to my revered teacher Prof. Rakesh Kumar Mishra whose guidance and inspiration brought me to where I am. He guided me for this book quite painstakingly with meticulous care. In fact, I have no words to express my indebtedness to him. I am indebted to the great Buddhist scholars whose writings were of great help to me. It is not possible to mention all of them, but I am grateful to all those whose names figured in the bibliography. I have used their treasure-trove of knowledge, and therefore, I do not claim any originality. To be more humble, I must say that if there is something good in the book then the credit of it goes to these scholars only. I used the books from the Library of Dept. of Buddhist Studies, Delhi University. I sincerely acknowledge the help given by Dr H.P. Negi who introduced me to the library staff.

I express my thankfulness to my teachers — Dr B. Labh and Dr R.N. Singh of our department, who always extended their co-operation and encouraged me. I really value the affection that I received at their hands. I express my gratefulness, to Shri Kundan Lal Sharma, Librarian of the sectional library of our department and Shri Tarsem Singh, Assistant Librarian with the Dhanvantri Library. I could collect a lot of material for this research with the kind co-operation of these two noble souls. I cannot forget the co-operation and affection that I received from Shri Parshotam Lal, Junior Assistant of our department. I have also to praise Shri Vijay Arora and Joginder Singh of our department who stayed in the department even at late hours to assist me.

I remember with gratefulness and reverence, the affection and encouragement I received at the hands of my local guardians, Shri Romesh Chander Basotra and Smt Sudha Basotra. They cared so affectionately for my comfort and meals at Jammu during all these years. I reverentially express my personal gratitude to all my family members — my mother, my father (who unfortunately passed away when the work was in progress), my brothers Shri Surinder Heera, Shri Mohinder Heera, Shri Jatinder Heera, my sister Smt Khema Koul and brother-in-law Shri Bansi Lal Koul, my sister-in-law Smt Reenuka Heera and Dr Salone Heera my niece Karishma Koul, my nephews Rudransh Heera and Raghu Raj Heera.

Lastly, I am thankful to my close friends who kept my morale high, and always inspired me for the speedy completion of this work.

August 15, 2007 **Bhupender Heera**

1

Introduction to Cultural Geography of Buddhist Asia

AT the outset we shall try to clearly explain, "Cultural Geography" and "Buddhist Asia." The term geography consists of two combining forms — "geo" and "graphy" — meaning drawing, writing, recording, or description of the earth and the adjective "cultural" pertains to culture. The term "culture" covers so many human activities and it is scarcely possible for any writer, or even two writers, to cover all the various historical manifestation of people's cultural interests. Culture's lexical meaning is the quality in person or society that arises from a concern for what is regarded as excellent in arts, letters, manners, scholarly pursuits, etc. "Culture" also means development or improvement of the mind by education or training. It denotes or refers to the behaviours and beliefs characteristic of a particular social, ethnic, or religious group.

In respect of mankind, "culture" is virtually the cultivation of all that is excellent in habits, behaviours, manners, morals and human decency. Culture is the refinement of everything that is odd, embarrassing, primitive and wild in man. "Culture" also reflects righteousness and virtuousness marked by its historical and geographical uniqueness, e.g. Egyptian culture, Mesopotamian culture, Vedic culture, Buddhist culture, etc.

Thus "cultural geography" refers to the drawing and description of culture of a particular area in a particular epoch of time. Under "cultural geography" we study the culture that is popular and prevalent in a particular continent or country or region. With reference to Buddhism, the area, precisely the catchment area, is immensely vast because the awe-inspiring sublimity of Buddhism overshadowed a considerably vast tract of Asian continent, particularly the Greater India of the ancient times, the Central Asian countries and the countries of far-east including China, Korea and Japan. Buddhism stretched far and wide to reach as distant lands as Java and Sumatra. Like the *bodhi* tree, Buddhism cast its auspicious shadows on a cluster of countries surrounding Thailand and the isolated Malay archipelago.

By "Buddhist Asia," we mean that part of Asia where Buddhism originated, germinated, burgeoned, developed and ultimately spread to far-flung areas. The Buddha was really the "Light of Asia." Buddhism reached everywhere and its permanent religious settlements can be seen in high Leh-Ladakh. It also made its conspicuous impression in a vast tract of cold desert of Central Asia; it crossed the oceans and seas and reached Sri Lanka and Japan. It occupied the populous areas as well as sparse hinterlands. During the course of its expansion a line of demarcation of Buddhist Asia started from Kapilavastu. It proceeded through Lumbinī and reached Bodh-Gayā from where it once again came back to Sāranāth and from there this line of demarcation became zigzag and serpentine and it meandered through Śrāvastī, Rājagṛha, Nālandā, Pāvāpurī and then to Kuśinagara. The expansion of Buddhism and its sublime culture was confined to Kosala and Magadha during the lifetime of Buddha. It was the time when India was divided into sixteen *mahājanapadas*. Kosala and Magadha were among those.

In *Mahāvaṁsa* there is a lot of material on the cultural geography of Buddha's India. It is in no way lacking even in *Dīpavaṁsa*. We find frequent references of Rājagṛha, Kauśāmbī,

Vaiśālī, Ujjayinī, Puṣpapura, Kapilavastu, Kuśinārā, Girivajra, Jetavana, Venuvana, Mathurā, Uruvelā, Kāśī, Ṛṣipatana, Pāṭaliputra, Magadha, etc. Beside these we also find references about the Indian cities and sixteen *mahājanapadas* — Kāśī, Kosala, Aṅga, Magadha, Vajji, Malla, Cedi, Vatsa, Kuru, Pañcāla, Matsya, Sūrasena, Assaka, Avantī, etc.

Bimla Churn Law has made an interesting as well as a well researched study, *Geography of Early Buddhism*. Divided over six chapters and with an appendix at the end, the book deals with the following topics:

Sources — Buddhist Conception of India — Divisions of India.

Majjhimadeśa or Middle Country
Boundaries — towns, cities and countries — fourteen *mahājanapadas*, Kāśī, Kosala, Aṅga, Magadha, Vajji, Malla, Cedi, Vatsa, or Vaṁsa, Kuru, Pañcāla, Matsya, Sūrasena, Assaka and Avantī — janapadas, nigamas, nagaras and gāmas — rivers, lakes and tanks — mountains, hills and caves — parks, forests and jungles — caityas, arāmas and vihāras.

Uttarapatha or the Northern India
Boundaries — two *mahājanapadas*, Gandhāra and Kamboja — janapadas, nigamas, puras and gāmas — rivers, lakes and tanks — mountains, hills and precipices.

Dakkhinapatha or Deccan and the Far South
Boundaries — janapadas, nigamas, puras and gāmas — rivers and lakes — hills and caves — parks, forests and jungles.

Prācya or the Eastern Country
Boundaries — janapadas and puras. Ceylon, Burma and other foreign countries, countries, provinces, cities and villages — rivers, lakes and tanks — forests and mountains — caityas, ārāmas and vihāras.

A note on the Caitya in the Buddhist Literature Index

It would be a repetition if we write further on the cultural geography of Buddhist India in this short introductory chapter.

In a nutshell, the territorial map of Buddhist Asia starts from Kapilavastu. Its boundaries crawl from Kapilavastu and march ahead towards Magadha and then again proceed towards Mathurā and Kaśmīr — Gandhāra from where it branched off into two directions. One was carried ahead towards Bactrian and Greece by Menander who was converted to Buddhism around the beginning of the Christian era, and the other towards China through Central Asia by the Chinese missionaries. From China it proceeded further to Korea and then to Japan. The overhead march of this boundary was dragged to Tibet. The southern boundary started from Sri Lanka and it moved eastward slanting towards far south in the Malay and Indonesian archipelago. Burma, Thailand and other neighbouring countries in those ancient times were ruled by the Indian Hindu kings and Buddhism reached these countries due to the colonizing activities of the Hindu kings. Even Sri Lanka was being ruled by the Hindu king when Buddhism reached there.

With our present knowledge about Buddhism and its expansion in Asian countries, we can say with certainty that Buddhist Asia stretched its leg as under from Bactrian in the north-west to Borneo in the Malay archipelago and from Sri Lanka in the south to the international Silk Route in the north. Measured horizontally it spanned from Bactria to Japan (West-East expansion) and from Sri Lanka to Mongolia (South-North expansion).

After having located the lands and societies where Buddhism made an indelible impression, we are in a position to describe the cultural geography of Buddhist Asia. Here one thing must be made clear: that Buddhism of the Asian countries was an admixture of Buddhism and the local traditions and customs. During the course of its spread to China, Tibet, Korea and Japan it had to make many compromises and accommodated partially their native beliefs and traditions. Three forms of Buddhism — Hīnayāna, Mahāyāna and Tantrayāna — spread in these Asian countries. Sri Lanka, Burma and Thailand were the stronghold of Hīnayāna Buddhism, whereas Mahāyāna was deeply rooted in China. Tibet was the stronghold of Tāntric Buddhism. The Buddhist culture of Burma is different from that of Thailand and Sri Lanka. Though all these three countries are Hīnayānist there is some discernible difference between their way of life and also in their liturgy. The difference between their culture is due to their ancient beliefs and primal traditions. In every country where Buddhism made its impression, Buddhism got adulterated. This is why Chinese Buddhism is different from Japanese Buddhism and Ceylonese Buddhism is different from Tibetan Buddhism. There are many sectarian differences even in these different brands of Buddhism.

While writing on the impact of Buddhist thought and culture on socio-religious life of Sri Lankans, Chinese, Tibetans, Koreans, Japanese, Thais, etc. we shall indicate the brands of their culture and the school which they are wedded to. For the present it is enough to give a clear picture of the Buddhist Asia in the context of Buddhist culture.

2

State of Society and Religion in pre-Buddhist Asian Countries

IN the previous chapter we have demarcated the geographical territory of Buddhist Asia, the culture of which was mostly Buddhist. The Buddhist Asia emerged as a distinct religio-cultural geographical unit during the course of many centuries and this territorial boundary was marked by the land and sea routes through which the Buddhist missionaries carried the message of the Buddha to effect cultural transformation in those far-flung countries. Now we are going to discuss the state of society and religion in pre-Buddhist Asian countries.

Buddhism emerged as a distinct religion and culture only after the Buddha attained Enlightenment in the sixth century BCE. Many religions like Islam and Christianity were not in existence at that time. People over a large tract of Asian continent were practising some sort of primitive and tribal religions.

If we peep into the history of religions, we find that except Vedic religion and Jainism, all other religions are of comparatively late origin. Since India is the birth place of Buddhism, it would be worthwhile to take into account the socio-religious conditions of pre-Buddhist India first. As Buddhism developed and spread, it made a commendable and lasting impact on a vast tract of Asian continent. It was India where the Buddha lived and died, and again it was India which was the springboard for worldwide transmission of Buddhism. Its lofty ideals and endearing ethics and spirituality completely altered the thought and culture of a large chunk of population of the Indian, Central Asian and South-East Asian countries. It generates a curiosity in anyone's mind as to what was the state of society and religion before Buddhism came up and assumed the status of a universal faith, among all peace-loving and pious people. First, we shall have a look on the state of society of religion at the time of the Buddha in his own motherland.

State of Society and Religion in pre-Buddhist India

We know that before the advent of the Buddha, Vedic religion was the most dominant religion in India. This pre-Buddhist era was known as Vedic age. John Snelling[1] writes that at the centre of the religious life during the Vedic age lay the ritual of sacrifice. The world had been created by sacrifice and was maintained by sacrifice, it was thought. This was, however, completely controlled by the hereditary brāhmaṇa priesthood, who claimed that they alone were entitled by birth to perform sacrifice and jealously guarded the secrets of its rituals. The most elaborate sacrifice was the *Aśvamedha* or "Horse Sacrifice," which went on for about a year, involving a small army of specialist brāhmaṇas and the ritual slaughter of a large number of animals. It was an exceedingly costly affair. At the social centre of the new culture, on the other hand, there developed a caste system, which divided the population into various hierarchical groups: the brāhmaṇa priesthood (brāhmaṇa); the warriors and aristocrats (kṣatriya); the traders and other professionals (vaiśya); and the cultivators (śūdra). Later a sub-caste appeared: the Untouchables, who were

1. *The Buddhist Handbook,* pp. 14-15.

probably of aboriginal stock and who, strictly speaking, did not have any caste at all. Caste probably existed in the Indus Valley Civilization and rested on a racial basis — the Aryans merely adapted it to their own purposes, taking care to reserve the higher echelon for themselves. The caste system was a closed system; once born into a caste, there was no leaving it. Upward or downward mobility was unknown. Underpinning the whole thing was the notion of the *dharma*, a word with a range of meanings.

Besides the stigma of the caste system, the cult of sacrifice which developed out of the prayers in the Vedic Saṁhitās had a powerful hold on the minds of the early Aryans in India. People of that time in India were deeply involved in the elaborate rituals of the cult which was largely based on sacrificial performances. The *yajña*s were performed to attain absolute happiness. Inequality was also reigning as the society was caste-ridden. Caste was the determinant of one's position in society. Society of that time was dominated by śramaṇas and brāhmaṇas. The literature of the Buddhists and the Jains frequently refers to śramaṇas, brāhmaṇas, nigaṇṭhas and the ājīvakas. The *Brahmajala-Sūtta* of *Dīgha-Nikāya* tells us about six heretical thinkers at the time of Buddha. All of them were well known in the country as founders of religious schools with a large following. These six heretical thinkers were senior contemporaries of the Buddha. Of these six thinkers, Nigaṇṭha Nātaputta, who is no other than Mahāvīra the founder, or according to the Jain tradition the last prophet of the present world cycle, seems to have been slightly older than the Buddha. He preached ethical doctrines without apparently knowing that similar ideas had been held by an incomparably senior ascetic, Pārśva. Mahāvīra was the strong advocate of asceticism. The next important contemporary of Buddha was Makkhali Goṣāla. The doctrine advocated by Goṣāla is called *niyativāda* because he held that all creatures were helpless against destiny. Pūraṇa Kassapa, another contemporary of Buddha, held the doctrine of *akriyā* or non-action. He maintained that a man did not incur sin through actions which are popularly known as bad, e.g. killing, committing theft, taking another man's wife, or telling a lie. Even if a man killed all the creatures on earth and raised a heap of skulls, he incurred no sin. The doctrine that Kassapa preached resembles the doctrine of the Cārvākas in many respects.

Ajita Keśakambalin was another contemporary of Buddha. He did not believe in the utility of gifts, in sacrifice, the fruits of good and bad acts, the existence of heavenly world or persons possessing higher or supernatural powers. His views are also similar to those of the Cārvākas, and the doctrine may be styled *ucchedavāda*. Pakudha Kātyayāna another contemporary of the Buddha held that there are seven elements which are immutable, and do not in any way contribute to pleasure or pain. The body is ultimately dissolved into these seven eternal elements. The last among these heretical thinkers is Sañjaya Belaṭṭhiputta whose doctrine is known as *vikṣepavāda*, a doctrine which diverts the mind from right track. There were many more beliefs prevalent in the society.

Because of great diversions in the beliefs and speculations of the thinkers of that time, the society was fragmented and fractured into different groups and sects of misplaced ideologies. We have just seen how six heretical thinkers of Buddha's time were propagating their preposterous and rationally untenable views about ethics and metaphysics and above all about life. Society at their disposal could be compared like a blind man led by a blind. Of these six heretical thinkers, who had a powerful hold on the people of their time, some were sceptic and some were agnostic, some were materialist and some were epicurean and some were downright opportunist. It was ironical that these wandering ascetics,

Ājīvikas and Acelakas were commanding the society with their flawed reason and vision. The pretension and clout of brāhmaṇas was a threat to the society. People at large did not know which way to follow. Since there were different communities led by different heretical thinkers, the society was not organized into a holistic unit. When Buddha came, he set things right. He threw open the doors of organized religious life to women and men alike. Buddha brought women to the monasteries from the confines of households. He removed the distinction of poor and rich, high and low, caste, creed, etc., which was existing at that time in pre-Buddhist Indian society, by stressing on *karma* and making it determinant of all activities. Buddha changed the axis of human destiny from caste (*jāti*) to action (*karma*). In the beginning even Buddha was hesitant and also adamant not to allow women in his *saṅgha* but it was due to the persistent persuasion of Ananda that he agreed to allow the womenfolk to enter the *Saṅgha*. This hesitation of Buddha gives a faint idea of the position of women in his time.

State of Society and Religion in pre-Buddhist Ceylon

During Aśoka's reign the first Buddhist missionary which crossed the land and reached Ceylon consisted of his son and a daughter. It was after some time that this island and its people embraced the Buddhist faith. But what was the state of society and religion before Buddhism reached there? We would like to throw some light on this aspect and trace the origin of its inhabitants. Dr W.A. De Silva[2] in his article, "History of Buddhism in Ceylon" writes that early traditions of Ceylon trace the origin of its people to very remote and prehistoric times. As old chronicle thus puts it tersely, "from very early times this Laṅkā (Ceylon) was colonized by people from all parts of Jambūdvīpa (India) irrespective of race and

2. *Buddhistic Studies*, pp. 455-57.

country. First came Vararoja of *asura* dynasty from Vaṅga country, with people of the races, *asura, yakṣa, nāga* and *nara,* who freely mixed among themselves the people and land. The next invader was Rāvaṇa son of Visravan and grandson of Pulasttya, who founded the *rākṣasa* kingdom. Rāvaṇa was defeated by Rāma's forces and the country was handed over to Vibhīṣana, a brother of Rāvaṇa. The men of Laṅkā at that period were known as *rākṣasa* and *yakṣa*s. Their language was said to have been Andra. The last of their line was Jitindara who lived in Sirivattupura from where he governed the people. Next comes the Manurājavaṁsa when Prince Vijaya, son of King Sinhabāhu of Sinhapura, and his followers occupied the country and founded the Sinhalese dynasty. From this period we have more reliable accounts of the country than mere traditions, and the Sinhalese Chronicles start Prince Vijaya's period from the year 543 before the Christian era, the first year of the Buddhist era.

From about the beginning of the Buddhist era for the next 236 years to the time of the introduction of Buddhism the process of consolidation of the rule of the invading Sinhalese continued. They created a new form of government and a new civilization. The newcomers found the island inhabited by the *yakṣa* race whose mode of life, government and institutions differed from those of the invaders who belong to the advanced races inhabiting the Gangetic valley. The *yakṣa* like most primitive races lived in tribes in close vicinity to places where they were able to obtain a living either as hunters or primitive cultivators. The island was noted for pearls, precious stones and minerals for which the primitive inhabitants had hardly any use. Enterprising traders and adventurers from various parts of India were attracted to the land where they were able to exploit the natural wealth of the country. They did not form any permanent settlement of their own, nor was it to their advantage to engage in any conflict with the aboriginal inhabitants. It was during this period that Prince Vijaya from the newly formed Lāṭa country came with a band of adventurous youths bent on founding a new kingdom. He did not belong to the type of the traders who went to distant lands to trade and gather riches. Vijaya was a kṣatriya who sought adventure where he could obtain name and fame. He allied himself with an aboriginal princess named Kuveni and married her. With her influence, he soon became a master of the country. After his success he discarded the aboriginal princess and sought and obtained an alliance with the king of Madurā and obtained his daughter in marriage. From this date the opening of the country and settlement of the land were greatly assisted by a continuous and rapid arrival of settlers from the neighbouring continent. Prince Vijaya's success was communicated to his own country and as he had no children by his queen he wrote to his brother in Lāṭa to send out a successor from his own clan. Vijaya died after a rule of 38 years. In this year following his death his nephew Pānḍuvāsudeva arrived in the island with a large stream of followers and assumed the sovereignty. He was followed shortly by another large immigration, this time from the Śākya clan. A close look on the early introduction of Ceylon, before the history of Buddhism, reveals that there was a mixture of aboriginals, foreign settlers from neighbouring countries and celebrated personages from the Śākya clan. Needless to say, at that very early time Ceylon was colonized by people from all parts of Jambūdvīpa (India) irrespective of race and country.

Walpola Rahula[3] writes that in pre-Buddhist Ceylon there do not seem to have been kings in the proper sense of the word, and no central government which co-ordinated the different local or provincial government. It was not possible to maintain constant and regular contact between Anurādhapura

3. *History of Buddhism in Ceylon,* pp. 25-29.

and Mahāgāma or Kalyāṇī, as the means of communication were very limited. Therefore the chiefs of the different localities became automatically the rulers of those provinces. Little or no information is found about the details of this local government. But it is quite justifiable to say that there was a system of village committees or local bodies which managed the affairs of villages satisfactorily. Apart from this society, the pre-Buddhist Ceylon can be divided into two sections: religious and secular. There were very religious bodies and they enjoyed real patronage. The secular section of the society was divided, as usual, into four main groups: the kṣatriya or ruling class, the brāhmaṇas or learned priestly class, farmers and herdsmen who can be including in the vaiśya community and caṇḍālas or those of low caste who were employed in menial work. Mention is also made of various guilds the members of which belonged, most probably, to different sub-castes. The brāhmaṇas were wealthy and learned, and they formed the most influential and respected community in the villages. They are also teachers and were consulted by the people.

Pāṇḍukābhaya, evidently the greatest king of pre-Buddhist Ceylon, was the grandson of Dīrghāyu, one of the six Śākya princes who came from north India. It was through Pāṇḍukābhaya that Sinhalese kings traced their descent to the Śākya clan to which Buddha belonged. It must be pointed out here that Śākyas were the followers of Vedic religion and therefore the religion and customs brought by them to Ceylon must have been Brāhmanical.

In this connection the observation of V.C. Srivastava[4] which he made in his article "Hinduism in Ceylon" must be quoted verbatim. He writes that the coming of Vijaya in 543 BCE (or 483 BCE) from India to Ceylon marks another important

4. *India's Contribution to World Thought and Culture,* p. 414.

landmark in the history of India's contact with Ceylon. The *Mahāvaṁsa* contains references to this event. The Ajantā murals of India also bear witness to it. This may rightly be taken as the first planned settlement of the Indians in Ceylon. It appears that both the Dravidian and the Aryan streams are mingled in Vijaya's immigration to Ceylon as he is connected with two opposite regions — Orissa and Bengal in the east showing probably the Dravidian elements and Lāṭa (Kāṭhiāwaḍ) in the west disclosing probably the Aryan elements. Since there are evidences for the prevalence of the Hindu religion before the reign of Devanāmpiya-Tissa (247 BCE–207 BCE) it may be presumed that Vijaya's immigration coupled with a few sporadic colonization resulted in the introduction of the elements of Hindu culture in Ceylon such as the worship of Śiva, Viṣṇu, Skanda and Gaṇeśa.

About the state of religion in pre-Buddhist Ceylon, Dr W.A. De Silva[5] writes that the accounts given in the Ceylon Chronicles show that so far as religious beliefs were concerned the king and the people were very tolerant towards all faiths, and religion was recognized as one that did not divide the people, but each individual seems to have had perfect freedom as regards his beliefs. A difference of views was not marked by any antagonism, but on the other hand there is ample evidence to show that whatever the sect a person followed he too generally accepted the beliefs of other sects, as conducive to the maintenance of the social and economic conditions prevailing among them. The religion and code of life of the Hindus were the main factors on which the social and economic condition of the people were based. The different methods of expressions and worship were left to each individual's inclination. The main places of religious assemblies had no temples or elaborate buildings or rituals.

5. *Buddhistic Studies*, pp. 459-60.

In the city there were two places, one devoted to Vessavana under a ficus tree, being the guardian god of the city so far as the Sinhalese were concerned, and the other devoted to Vydhādeva the guardian god of the aboriginal population, symbolized by a *tala* (palm) tree. Where temples were concerned it is significant that they were built outside the city beyond the northern boundary and there were eight temples devoted to the worship of the various *deva*s recognized by the people. In addition there were certain places of worship that had been established for foreigners. The brāhmaṇas held their positions as teachers and they were entrusted with social ceremonies. There was a large number of important brāhamaṇa villages where they enjoyed independent social status and importance.

Walpola Rahula[6] in his *History of Buddhism in Ceylon* writes that before Buddhism came to Ceylon in the third century BCE there was evidently no national or state religion systematically organized in the island. Though Hiuen Tsang never visited Ceylon he writes that the kingdom of Ceylon formerly was addicted to immoral religious worship. This "immoral religious worship" was a brand of primitive animistic cults. There are references to supernatural being, *yakṣa*s and *yakṣiṇī*s in the Vijaya legend, but no mention is made of any form of worship or cult till we enter the period of Pāṇḍukābhaya in the fourth century BCE. From the account of Pāṇḍukābhaya's manifold activities in the Chronicles we can get some idea of the forms of worship that were prevalent at that time. Pāṇḍukābhaya seems to have followed the ancient customs of the kings of India and Ceylon and patronized with equal liberality and impartiality cults and religions in vogue in the day. But we are at a loss to discover what his own particular form of faith was. Perhaps he had no particular inclination towards any,

6. p. 34 ff.

and found one form of belief as good as another. The worship of the *yakṣas* seems to have been a popular and prevalent cult. Along with the *yakṣa* cult, there existed the ancestor worship or the veneration of the spirits of the dead in common with other primitive cultures. Pāṇḍukābhaya and the people of his day seem to have had the notion that faithful and devoted persons after their death were reborn as *yakṣas* and continued to watch over the interests of their former friends and patrons. Cittā and Kālavela were two such. In the same way Cittā, the faithful servant-maid of Pāṇḍukābhaya's family, was also reborn as *yakṣiṇī*. Pāṇḍukābhaya is reported to have lodged this *yakṣiṇī* at the south gate of the city out of gratitude to her for having been helpful to him in her previous birth. These instances show that there was a belief that the dead were sometimes reborn as *yakṣas* and *yakṣiṇīs* and that they came to the help of their dear ones in moments of need. This belief was current in ancient India before and even after Buddha. Mahinda is reported to have preached on the second day of his arrival in Ceylon the *Peṭavatthu* and the *Viamānavatthu* the Buddhist texts dealing with the spirits of the dead. This perhaps, indicates that Mahinda at the very beginning of his missionary activities here, thought of winning the hearts of the people by appealing to their sentiments through a sermon which they could easily understand and appreciate.

We are also told by Walapola Rahula[7] that, besides *yakṣa*-cult, references are found in the Chronicles indicating the existence in pre-Buddhist Ceylon of tree-worship. Tree-worship as a popular cult is mentioned in early Buddhist texts, and some trees were termed *cetiyas*. Even in lateral sculptures certain trees were included in the category of *cetiyas*. In the Indus Civilization of Mohenjo-Dāṛo and Haṛappā, tree-worship features prominently. It is believed that the bo-tree

7. *History of Buddhism in Ceylon*, p. 41.

was worshipped in Mohenjo-Dāṛo too. In pre-Buddhist Ceylon we have definite evidence of two trees which were considered sacred. One of them is the banyan tree, which even today is generally regarded as sacred and the abode of deities.

There were several Brāhmanical religious institutions in Anurādhapura in pre-Buddhist Ceylon. There were three well-known Nigaṇṭhas in Anurādhapura at the time of Pāṇḍukābhaya, namely Jotiya, Giri and Kumbhāṇḍa. Pāṇḍukābhaya built a house for the Nigaṇṭha Jotiya in the eastward direction. Śaivism also existed in Ceylon at that time. Thus the *Mahāvaṁsa* records that Pāṇḍukābhaya built a Śivika-Śālā. Phallic worship was also prevalent in ancient Ceylon. The *Mahāvaṁsa-Ṭīkā* says that Mahāsena (CE 334-62) destroyed Śivaliṅgas everywhere in the island, which shows that by the fourth century CE phallic worship was probably widespread. Parivājjakas and Ājīvikas, Pāsaṇḍas and Parivājjakas and many other ascetics, known as Sāmaṇas, seem to have been found in fair numbers in the island. The *Mahāvaṁsa* says that Pāṇḍukābhaya built a monastery for Parivrājakas and a house for Ājīvikas. Various Pāsaṇḍas and Sāmaṇas lived in the area where the Nigaṇṭhas, Giri and Jotiyas resided.

There were a number of cults and religious beliefs but there is no evidence that any of them was so systematically organized as to be a power of this island.

State of Society and Religion in pre-Buddhist China

The dream of Emperor Ming (CE 58-75) of the Han Dynasty has often been linked with the introduction of Buddhism into China. In the first century CE because of a prophetic dream in which a figure of 16 ft height and radiant like the sun appeared to the Emperor Ming Ti; agents were dispatched to the west. Somewhere in the wastes of Tokharistan they met two *bodhisattvas* who had with them a white horse, a picture of Śākyamuni Buddha and a copy of the *sūtra* in 42 Sections, a summary of basic Buddhist doctrines (with Mahāyāna interpolations) that still exists. The *bodhisattvas*, Kaśyapa Mataṅga and Dharmarakṣa, agreed to return to the Han capital, Lo-yang. There they set about translating the *sūtra* at a place called White Horse Temple (Pai-ma-ssu), which still exists though the present buildings are most recent. In factual terms, however what probably really happened was rather more prosaic. Around the turn of the common era, Buddhism simply began to filter into China from Central Asia. It was brought down the Silk Road by merchants, envoys, monks and other travellers and nurtured in the expatriate communities in Lo-yang and a few other northern cities. Down to the end of the Han period, during which China enjoyed a fairly stable centralization of government, its progress among the native Chinese themselves was probably fairly slow because a number of important factors stood in the way of its acceptance. There was the deep-seated xenophobia of the Chinese themselves. Self-consciously regarding themselves citizens of a great empire — the centre of the world, no less — with a long and glorious history, a sublime culture and noble tradition, what use then could they have for an alien cult? Buddhism was also in many ways inimical to the prevailing ideology, which derived from the sayings of the sage Confucius (551-479 BCE). This upheld the ideal of a stable, harmonious social order in which every human unit, from the Emperor or Empress down to the humblest peasant, played their part according to hallowed custom. Confucianism is very much a creed of this world and as such its devotees could only look with disfavour on any religion that seemed to encourage the abandonment of all worldly ties in favour of the pursuit of a remote and vague spiritual ideal. Also the fact that the Buddhist *Saṅgha* did not work but looked to other people to support them went totally against established Chinese values.

Gradually, however, the barriers began to break down and this process was probably aided by one particular factor: the presence in China of a homegrown mystical tradition called Taoism. This was traditionally said to derive from the teaching of the mythical Yellow Emperor, Huang Ti (2698-2597 BCE), but it was reformed and revived by the great sage Lao-tzu, author of the classic *Tao-te-Ching*. The Taoists were very un-Confucian in their dislike of the social world, which they thought was artificial and corrupt. They advocated a return to simplicity and harmony with nature, and their ideal was *wu wei*, a kind of uncontrived mode of being that flowed with all the effortless suppleness of water out of the darkness of the ultimate unknowable mystery and adapted itself to whatever it encountered. The Chinese seem to have found certain points of similarity between the teachings and practices of the Taoists and those of the Buddhists, and this opened up an avenue whereby Buddhism was able to penetrate their culture. In Arthur Waley's words, they could regard Buddhism as "a sort of foreign Taoism."[8]

A veritable account of the state of society just before the introduction of Buddhism in China is given by Buddha Prakash in his article, "Social Aspects of the Spread of Buddhism in China."[9] He writes that in the Han period power lay in the hands of the landlord class centring on great families. There were two categories of these families, those connected with the kings, queen and powerful eunuchs and those consisting of high officers and local magnate who rose through their own efforts. According to an estimate, under the Eastern Han, there were 61 families connected with kings, 344 families associated with disinherited princes, 89 families deriving from the households of queens and 79 families tracing their descent

8. *The Buddhist Handbook*, pp. 141-42.

9. *India's Contribution to World Thought and Culture*, pp. 333-35.

from eunuchs. These families owned large estates, worked them through serfs and dependents and ran the industries, connected with them, through slaves. They maintained sizeable armies, lived lavishly and luxuriously and were the centres of power, prestige and culture, but they also tyrannized the peasants, squeezed them out of their land and reduced them to misery and indigence. Faced with their competitions the landholding peasants found it difficult to make both ends meet. Their lot can be guessed from the budget of Li K'uei showing that a farming family of five persons, cultivating 10 mou ($16^2/_3$ acres) of land and producing 150 tan (1 tan = 100 catties) of corn, was short of 450 cash per year after paying the taxes and providing its bare necessities. Hence at the time of Emperor Huan (CE 147-68), the political theorist Ts'ui Shih wrote that "alive, they face a little time of land and labour — dead, they worry for lack of a decent burial. When the year is poor, they drift about and starve in ditches, they marry off their wives and sell their sons." Driven to desperation, the peasants left their fields, dabbled in crime, committed robbery, joined the armies of landlords or swelled the ranks of rebels forming the movements of the Red Eyebrows or Yellow Turbans. But the repression of the state was no less severe and to face it was frightfully difficult — one million people having been killed in the operation against the Yellow Turbans. Hence most of the masses gave way to despondency and defeatism and clamoured for doles and relief at the capital. At the time of Emperor An (CE 107-26) the number of people living on relief in Lo-yang was hundred times that of those earning their own bread. About the middle of the century, CE 153, during the reign of Emperor Huan, there were several hundred thousands of displaced families subsisting on doles. When Emperor Ho was on the throne, people of nearly all parts of the country needed relief, but, since its administration was very defective, the suffering of the masses knew no bounds. These disgruntled people, distracted masses and displaced persons could not seek any solace from Confucian principles, since the literati expounding them had joined hands with the great families and justified their oppressive acts. They turned to Taoism, but it proved to be a creed of negativist escapism holding out little promise of a positive redemption. Hence they became inclined towards Buddhism, which as we shall presently see, adapted itself to their requirement in a remarkable manner.

As regards the state of religion in pre-Buddhist China A.C. Banerjee[10] quoting many authorities on the subject writes that China, it is said, is the home of one of the earliest civilizations in the world. It has played a significant role in the history of its religious ideas and developments. The primitive Chinese, so as far as we know, believed in monotheism and not in henotheism. In other words, monotheism was the original religion of the Chinese. According to them, "there is one God supreme over all in heaven and earth, all other spirits being subordinate to Him." This monotheism was mainly based on One Great Being (Shun ti). But, in course of time, it was affected by the crude form of nature worships and superstitious divinations. Thus, "the religion of the old Chinese Empire, as it existed certainly from the twelfth century BCE and probably at a much earlier period, is best described as a purified and organized worship of spirits, with a predominant fetishist tendency, combined into a system before it was possible for a regular mythology to develop out of it. The sole object of worship are the spirits (Shan) which are divided into heavenly, earthy and human, and, as a rule, are still closely connected with the object of nature. Opinions, however, differ as to the nature of the earliest religion of the Chinese. Whatever Chinese religion

---

10. *Studies in Chinese Buddhism,* pp. 1-2.

might have been in its primitive stages, it is seen that towards the latter part of the Chou dynasty, it developed into a philosophic system out of this "vague generalization which had so long been a ccepted." This trend in the religious and philosophic thought was further developed and was also regarded as necessary for the well-being of man. During this period various schools of thought came into existence. Of them, two schools of thought came into prominence, one advocated by Confucius (551-479 BCE) and the other by Lao-tzu (570-490 BCE), the two contemporaneous sages of China. The ideas promulgated by Confucius were politico-religious while those of Lao-tzu were ascetico-mystical.

CONFUCIUS AND CONFUCIANISM

Before the advent of Buddhism in China, Confucianism was one of the great ideologies of China. Huston Smith[11] in his *The World's Religion* writes that if there is one name with which Chinese Culture has been associated it is Confucius — Kung Fu-tzu or Kung the Master. Chinese reverently speak of him as the First Teacher — not that there were no teachers before him, but because he stands first in rank. No one claims that he crafted Chinese culture singlehandedly, and he himself played down his originality by claiming to be no more than "a lover of the ancient." This designation, however, gives him less than his due; it stands as an example of the modesty and reticence he advocated. For though Confucius did not author Chinese culture, he was its supreme editor. Winnowing the past, underscoring here, playing down or discarding there, reordering and annotating throughout, he brought his culture to focus that he remained remarkably distinct for twenty-five centuries. Confucious was born around 551 BCE in the principality of Lu in what is now Shantung province. We know nothing for certain about his ancestors, but it is clear that his

11. p. 154.

early home life was modest. Confucius was both an ethical and political teacher and it was he who first codified his ethical and political ideas. He sought to guide his fellowmen by holding up to them the wisdom and virtue of the ancients. His teachings were purely ethical and political, confined to the daily life of man as a member of the state and of his family. He spoke little of God and he avoided talking about the supernatural. For this reason it is often said that he cannot be called a religious teacher, but only a moral philosopher, and Confucianism is rather a system of morality than religion. Incidentally we must also discuss the problem that Confucius faced. From the eight to the third centuries BCE China witnessed a collapse of the Chou Dynasty's ordering power. Rival baronies were left to their own devices, creating a precise parallel to conditions in Palestine in the period of the judges. "In those days there was no king in Israel; every man did what was right in his own eyes." In fact, pre-Buddhist China was another name for social anarchy. Confucianism was a politico-religious system. The political philosophy of Confucius was based on duties relating to filial piety. He maintained that universal brotherhood should be the aim of all corporate life in the family and social relations, as the emperor had duties towards the members of his family and neighbours. Thus the very essential in his system was filial piety which conveyed not only good behaviour of the children towards their parents but also loyalty to the state and authority. In short, Confucius insisted on the sanctity of the human relationship, viz. ruler and the ruled, parent and child, husband and wife, etc. which would make the social stability.

Confucius highlighted certain cardinal virtues which were as follows:

(a) The principle of benevolence

(b) Uprightness of mind

(c) Propriety of demeanour

(d) Knowledge of affairs

(e) Good faith

TAOISM

No civilization is monochrome. In China the classical tones of Confucianism have been balanced not only by the spiritual shades of Buddhism but also by the romantic hues of Taoism. Throwing light on Taoism, A.C. Banerjee[12] writes that Taoism is the old popular religion of China. It had its gods worshipped in temples. According to it the highest God was Yu-Huang or Yu Huang Shang Ti, who was deemed to be the Supreme God of all the universe. It had also belief in superstitions, astrology, fortune-telling, sacrifice and ancestor worship. As philosophy, it is opposed to Confucianism. It is ascetic, mystic and pantheistic. One of the chief features of Taoism was the means which it prescribed for the attainment of immortality, resembling Buddhism much in this respect. It had a voluminous literature agreeing roughly to the Buddhist *San Ts'ang* (*Tripiṭaka*). But the *Tao-te-Ching* was, however, the most revered and popular work.

In this connection the observations of H. Hackmann[13] are quite educative. He writes that Buddhism confronted an element in China which responded to it much more readily than Confucianism did, and indeed, blended with it to a very high degree. This was Taoism. This religion, indigenous to China — which is usually attributed to Lao-tzu, the elder contemporary to Confucius, sprang in reality from an earlier source, and had in the course of centuries become the vehicle in which an ancient nature and spirit worship was embodied; it was a chequered superstition void of a system, a kind of

12. *Studies in Chinese Buddhism,* p. 6.

13. *Buddhism as a Religion,* pp. 83-84.

philosophy of nature, formulated in a rude, fantastic way. The character of Taoism so far resembled Buddhism that it also possessed supernatural features, that it attributed great merit to the hermit or monastic life, and maintained the possibility of averting distress and danger by means of magic, and that it described the future life after death in vivid colouring. Buddhism and Taoism have approached very closely to one another by means of this common basis, but Taoism is perhaps rather the recipient than the donor. Competition, it is true, frequently set them at variance with one another, so that they were not always in friendly relationship. But in the main their ways lay parallel to one another, although they did not combine in the popular consciousness. It is related of the ruler of the kingdom of Ts'i, that he attempted by forcible means to unite the two religions into one. And a persecution of the sixth century fell upon both Buddhism and Taoism alike, in the kingdom of Chou, where they both appeared equally objectionable to the ruler. Again, there is a very popular book, *Hsi-yu-chi*, a narrative of the journeys and experiences of Yuan Chwang (the Buddhist traveller), written by a Taoist, and liberally interspersed with material drawn from the Taoist methodology, though the subject matter is derived from Buddhism.

It would be worthwhile to quote Kenneth K.S. Chen[14] for a proper understanding of Taoism. He writes: "the important names in Taoism are Lao-tzu and Chuang-tzu. They refer to persons as well as to texts. The person named Lao-tzu is of doubtful historicity, but the text by the same name also known as the *Tao-te-Ching* (The Way and its Power) and compiled by more than one person, is still extant and is one of the basic texts of Taoism. As for the man Chuang-tzu, there is no question that he lived c. 300 BCE, but whether or not the text

14. *Buddhism in China*, pp. 24-25.

Chuang-tzu was written entirely by him is another matter. The consensus is that more than one writer was involved. Taoism, as represented by these works, is a sort of nature mysticism. The Taoists discovered nature, expressed their joy and amazement over it, and sought to be identified with this nature, which they also called the Tao. Because they were preoccupied with this, Tao is the right way of action, moral, social and political. The Tao of the Taoist is metaphysical; it is the natural law of the universe. To him the Tao brings all things into existence and governs their every action. The guiding aim of the Taoist is to achieve union with this Tao through identification. Since the Tao is conceived to be eternal, everlasting, and unchanging, the individual achieving unity with it is also considered to have achieved eternity. To distinguish this aspect of Taoism from another development, this form is called philosophical Taoism.

After having said so much about Confucianism and Taoism, once again we shall remind that these two ideologies or systems were governing the socio-religious life of the people of China in pre-Buddhist times. This much about the state of society and religion in pre-Buddhist China.

State of Society and Religion in pre-Buddhist Asian Countries

By society we mean an organized group of persons associated together for religious, benevolent, cultural, scientific, political, patriotic or other purposes. If we talk of this type of society as a primitive society in pre-Buddhist Tibet, then decidedly Tibetan society was fractured into isolated tribal communities. In order to have a faint idea of society in pre-Buddhist Tibet, we must focus for a while on its territory and topography. Tibet has massive mountains on the south, west and north ranging in height from 6000 to 8000 m above sea level along the Himalaya and the Karakoram, and from 5000 to 7000 m along the Kun-lun range. It is almost inaccessible. There is no well-defined mountain barrier on the east, but the vast uninhabited wastes and a whole series of subsidiary mountain ranges keep the centre of Tibetan civilization cut off from the rest of the world. The general level of West and Central Tibet is from 4000 to 5000 m above sea level, and the whole country is traversed by subsidiary mountain ranges which rise to 6000 m or more. The Central part of the country lies on either side of the axis formed by the great river gTsang po (known in India as the Brahmaputra), which arises near Ti se (mount Kailāsa) and the lake Ma pham (Mānasarovar) and flows eastward along the whole southern length of the country and then south-westwards through Assam in India to join the Bay of Bengal. Its source lies close to those of two other major rivers, the Indus and the Sutlej, which flow in the opposite direction, from the north-east flow the mighty rivers, the Salween, the Mekong, and the Kinsha Kiang (known in China as the Yang-tse), from the north to the south, with high mountain ranges keeping them apart.[15]

David L. Snellgrove and Hugh E. Richardson[16] in their, *A Cultural History of Tibet* write about the geography of Tibet and tell us that about three-sevenths of Tibet constituting its northern part is a virtually uninhabited wilderness of mountain spur and ranges, interspersed with black barren plains and numerous pools and lakes of brackish water. It is an area of intense cold and bitter winds and short spell of heat. Here live wild yaks (*drong*), asses (*rkyang*), and antelopes (*gstod*), as also the wolves that prey upon them. Rarely do hunters visit these regions, but the area was traversed by several adventurous foreign travellers in the late nineteenth and early twentieth centuries. Another two-seventh

15. R.A. Stein, *Tibetan Civilization*, p. 20.
16. pp. 9-21.

of the country, again high and cold, is a rolling plateau of lofty ranges of snowcapped mountains and great lakes. The region is inhabited by nomadic groups of men and their large herds of yaks, sheep and goats. The rest of the country comprises the extensive valleys of the gTsang po and the Salween, the Mekong and the Kinsha Kiang. As these areas contain the only favourable agricultural lands in the whole country, it is here that much of the sparse population of Tibet (estimated at three-and-a-half to four million) is concentrated. They contain many scattered villages and a few towns peopled by traders, officials and the landed gentry. They also have a number of temples, monasteries and nunneries of different religious orders. This threefold division of Tibet into valley lands, pasture lands, and wastes does not include the extreme western areas which drain into the upper waters of the Indus and the Sutlej; and a few low lying fertile valleys bordering Nepal. If one forgets the political frontiers, Tibetan culture extends to the regions of Ladakh and Lahaul and Spiti which are now under Indian administration, to Dolpo and Mustang which form part of Western Nepal, and to Sikkim and Bhutan. Sikkim is now a part of the Indian Union; Bhutan is an independent country. The two basic ways of life in Tibet are the agricultural and the nomadic. The two are in fact complementary to each other. The products of herdsmen such as meat, butter, cheese and wool are exchanged for grain. In the intermediate areas there are those who practise both agriculture and animal husbandry. Almost all Tibetans, like herdsmen everywhere else, keep animals of some kind or other. Nomads who live nearest to the farm lands are familiar with the ways and habits of settled communities. The majority of the people live in the southern valleys and pastured lands. With their simple basic requirements the Tibetans have achieved higher standards of living than elsewhere in Asia, but severe conditions of travel have isolated them from the surrounding cultures.

Robert E. Ekval[17] in his *Religious Observances in Tibet* tells us something more about Tibet and writes that Tibet is a vast land with a population sparsely spread over the high plateau. There is very little human activity except in the valleys. It is more than 1500 miles from the borders of China on the east to the borders of Kashmir on the west. From the north to the south the width varies from 600 to 800 miles. This distance would appear to be all the greater if viewed in the light of the topography of Tibet and the primitive means of travel its people employ. Much of the country is high terrain where only sturdy people can go. High mountain passes, deep gorges, unbridged rivers and great plains which are either waterless deserts or vast bogs are common features of the country. The difficulty of negotiating long distances in the harsh conditions of the country causes the people to live in small isolated communities. Individuals too are particularly alone on the mountains as they go about their concerns. The common Tibetan is much on his own. He knows solitude; for he and his fellows are spread so thinly across the bleak, austere landscape.

R.A. Stein[18] in his *Tibetan Civilization* writes that the ethnic make-up of Tibet consists of different racial types living side by side. The predominant strain is Mongoloid. Some travellers have noted the prevalence of what they describe as the Red Indian type, notably in Kongpo and among the Hor nomads. Some others have noted European, Hellenic or Caucasian elements, especially in north-east Tibet. A dwarfish type occurs in Chala, a district of Kham. Of course, all these are but impressions, but the fact remains that different types obtain in Tibet. However, the anthropologists distinguish just two types — one distinctly Mongoloid, and of slight build, spread

17. p. 6.
18. p. 20.

throughout Tibet and the other of taller build typical of Kham. Blue-eyed blond types have also been observed in the north-east. The explanation for the presence of different ethnic groups seems to be that different populations have occupied various parts of Tibet in the course of history. They remain there still.

W. Woodvile Rockhill[19] tells us that the Chinese sources link the origin of the Tibetan people to the nomadic, non-Chinese Chiang tribes who herded sheep and cattle in East Central Asia up to the farthest north-western border of China many centuries before the Christian era. According to them this is clear from the extensive nature of Tibetan farming with its ever-present element of animal husbandry, from the readiness of the Tibetans to travel long distances, from their seemingly inborn ability to handle and look after horses, yaks and other air and open spaces coupled with their sturdy individualism. The most important part of this legacy was the presence of a large number of nomads, depending entirely on their flock of sheep and goats and their herds of yaks. These nomads were forever on the move, and, whenever they encamped, they lived in tents. They scarcely ever saw four walls in the whole of their lives except for those of small remote monasteries. Till recently they were divided into small clans which were constantly at war with one another. The Chinese considered them as an assemblage of ferocious, barbarous tribes. Each year these nomads took "a little oath" to affirm their loyalty to their chiefs (*brtsan po*, "noble") and sacrificed sheep, dogs and monkeys. Every three years they took "the great oath" and sacrificed men, horses, oxen and donkeys.

Snellgrove and Richardson[20] tell us that literary sources suggest a continuous movement of rival clans of Tibetan-

---

19. *Land of the Lamas*, no. 13, p. 206.
20. *Cultural History of Tibet*, no. 3, p. 22.

speaking people from the general complex of tribes in the far north-eastern part of the country towards the more fertile valleys of Central and South Tibet, where they adopted a partly agricultural way of life and settled down about the beginning of the Christian era. Each of these clans presumably consisted of a chief with his family and hereditary retainers and bondsmen. When they settled down, the chief's family became a kind of aristocracy. A world of rival chiefs then came into existence, with their fortified strongholds in the valleys of the central and eastern tributaries of the gTsang po. To the north of them were areas inhabited by nomadic people who now and then displaced those who had become settled. This went on till the sixth century CE. Central Tibet then took the offensive, and the infiltrations from the north-east ceased except for occasional marriage alliances. At a particular stage of these developments some local chiefs accepted as their overlord the powerful chief who ruled the Yar lung Valley, building him up into a king strong enough to force his neighbours to take notice of his pre-eminence.

H.V. Guenther in his Foreword to Eva. M. Dargyay's book *The Rise of Esoteric Buddhism in Tibet* writes that by its geography Tibet was exposed to different influences, if by this term we understand a recasting of ideas rather than a mere super-imposition. To the west it was a country of vague definition, known as Shang-shung (Zhang-zhung). Its capital to the west of Mount Kailāsa was until recently a favourite place of pilgrimage for Hindus. The country seems to have had contacts with the neighbouring Indian regions of Kullu and Jalandhar bypasses which are still used today. But it also seems to have had close contacts with Kashmir, noted as a great Buddhist Country, attracting visitors from as far as China, especially from the fifth to the eighth centuries. According to Tibetan tradition Shang-shung is the home of the Bon religion which shows both Buddhist and even Iranian influences and which must be credited to have paved the way for the ready acceptance of new ideas. But before Tibet proper emerged as an Asian power and established formal contacts with its neighbours, Nepal and India in the south and China to the east, its main cultural link has been with the Ch'iang tribes on China's north-western borders, who lived within the reach of the trade routes that linked China with India, Iran and ultimately, Byzantium and along which all kinds of cultural ideas and artistic motifs found their way into Tibet.

Now something about the religion of pre-Buddhist Tibet. Bon, the earliest religion of Tibet, was, according to early writings, founded by Gshen-rab or "Gshen-rab-mi-bo or Gshan-rab, the main." There are many sects among the followers of Bon (Bon-pos) in Tibet. Of them two are mostly well known — the Bon-chhal-nag (Black Bon), the original Bon and the Bon-chhal-kar with Bon-terma (White Bon and treasured Bon), the transformed Bon. According to some non-Bon-po historian, when Gshen-rab was only twelve years old, he was taken away by the demon and was with them for long twelve years. But when he came back he could tell the whereabouts of the spirits as also which kind of offering would be beneficial to the people. He pointed out to the people the way of performing such rituals which gradually developed into a ritualistic system, and people respected him as a great teacher. It is to be seen that rituals were chiefly concerned with the way of making offerings to the worldly gods (mostly local spirits), taming the evil spirits, subduing the enemies (by black magic, etc.), curing illness, predicating and displaying minor miracles and the like. They did not refer to any kind of philosophy or religion. Such was the actual state of Bon of Gshen-rab, which is commonly known as Bon-Chhal-nag (Black Bon).[21]

---

21. *Aspects of Buddhist Culture from Tibetan Sources,* p. 4.

The followers of the Bon religion (Bon-pos) agree that Gshen-rab was born in Ol-mo-lung-ring valley of Zhang-zhung country. Zhang-zhung is identified with Guge, one of the three districts of Nga-ri province of Tibet. It lies on the other side of the Indo-Tibetan border. Some Buddhist Tibetan historians, however, maintain that Gshen-rab was born in Central Tibet at a place called Am-shod-on — it still lacks identification. Gshen-rab who was born as the son of King Thod-kar and Queen Yo-chhi-rgyal-zhed of Guge was married to Hos-za-rgyal-med. He had sons and daughters. He could control the spirits under his power and exhibit miracles. He had the foreknowledge and he could also prophesy. He preached in his own way the ritual of the gods which subsequently became the Bon of Gshen-rab.

Throwing light on what is Bon, A.C. Banerjee[22] referring to various authorities on the subject writes that the Tibetan historical sources provide us with materials which prove the existence of another religion, known as Bon, a kind of Shamanism, prior to the advent of Buddhism. The meaning of the word "Bon" still remains unknown. This is also corroborated by Waddell. In dictionaries is not found the meaning of the word Bon; simply a vague account of this religion is given. In his *A Tibetan English Dictionary,* S.C. Das writes that "Bon is the ancient religion of Tibet which was fetishism, demon worship and propitiation by means of incantation. The word Chos which ordinarily means religion is used as antithesis to Bon. Bon signifies the kind of Shamanism which was followed by the Tibetans before the introduction of Buddhism and in certain parts still extant." Jaschke holds the view that Bon is the name of the early religion of Tibet, concerning which very imperfect accounts are existing; so much is certain that sorcery was the principal

22. Ibid., pp. 1-2.

feature of it. When Buddhism became the religion of the state, the former was considered heretical and condemnable and Lha-cos and Bon-cos, or shorter Cos and Bon, were placed in opposition, as with Christianity and Paganism; at the present time, both of them seem to exist peacefully side by side, and the primitive religion has not only numerous adherents and converts in (Central Tibet), but manifold traces of it may be found still in the creed of the Tibetans today. H. Hoffmann writes that "origin of the word 'Bon' to describe it is lost in the past, and it is not readily definable, but in all probability once referred to the conjuring of the gods by magic formulas." Rockhill observes that "Mr Brian Hodgson connects it with the primitive Turanian superstitions and the doctrines of Caivism, but, he adds, in the Himalayas even the Bon-po priests themselves can tell nothing of the origin of their belief." He further observes that the word Bon-po is unquestionably derived from *puṇya* one of the names of the *svastika*s or worshippers of the mystic cross *svastika,* which in Tibetan is called *gyang drung*. It would not be irrelevant to point out in this context that the word "Bon" signifies seed, usually found in the scriptures with the word *sa* (ground) which shows some affinity with the word *vija,* the Sanskrit word frequently employed in the Indian Tantrism in a symbolic sense of the cult.

Writing about the religion of pre-Buddhist Tibet H. Hoffmann[23] says that the Tibetans of those days were apparently completely subject to the powerful and formidable nature of their natural surroundings. Their completely nature-rooted and nature-dominated religious ideas revolved reverently and submissively around the powers and forces of their wild highland landscapes whose divinities were reflected in the idea of numerous good and evil spirits the

---

23. *The Religion of Tibet,* p. 17.

Tibetans thought to see all around them. Almost all these many and varied spirits are still alive today in the belief of ordinary Tibetan people. They are recognized by Lamaism and accepted into its Pantheon, whereas the old God of Heaven has for a long time been a typical Deus Otisus, rarely referred to, seldom revered and almost entirely forgotten. Valuable material on the age-old ideas of living spirits which are still current amongst the Tibetans today, mainly in the districts of the Western Tibet, has been collected by A.H. Francke; and particularly by Ribbach in his excellent book *Drogpa Namgyal.*

After discussing elaborately the state of society and religion in Tibet, we conclude by pointing out that till the introduction of Buddhism in Tibet in the seventh century CE it was steeped in "barbaric darkness."

India has played a unique role in the socio-religious and cultural life of the whole of Asia. She has been responsible for weaving a variegated fabric to clothe the Asian countries with a garment which is distinguished for each region. Yet bearing an indelible imprint of Indian culture this process called "colonization" by some was in essence a spontaneous and peaceful process of sharing her spiritual and material attainment with her near and distant neighbours. The observations of Bernard Groslier[24] in his *Indo-China* about Indian expansion into Indo-China is worth quoting: "It was one of the most important civilizing movements of ancient times, worthy to compare with the Hellenization of the Mediterranean world. And India can be justly proud to have spread the light of her understanding over such distant lands, which without her might have remained in darkness." Among the many countries that came under the spell of Indian influence was Campa or that part of the present day, war-torn Vietnam which is known as Annam. The ancient name of this region is

24. p. 47.

Campa[25] and occurs in many Sanskrit inscriptions of that country as Campadesh. Campa first felt the impact of Indian culture as early as the second century CE. It is common knowledge that the prosperous trade with the Far-East which began about this time attracted a large number of enterprising Indian merchants and princes to migrate to these regions and establish themselves as pioneers in the field. Before long they identified themselves with these developing countries and soon came to the forefront as political and economic stabilizers of the region. *Periplus*[26] mentions trade routes from these harbours on the eastern coast near Masulipatam across the Bay of Bengal to the eastern Peninsula.

About the state of society and religion in pre-Buddhist Laos, Vietnam, Cambodia and Burma, J.S. Nigam[27] in his article, "India and Laos" writes that Laos was founded in CE 1353. On the north it is bounded by Burma and China, by Thailand in the west, Vietnam on the east and Cambodia on the south. Buddhism is the predominant religion. The Khmers conquered the savage mountain tribes who were anciently living in Laos, Cambodia and Cochin-China and forced them to take shelter in the hills and forests. The Mons who inhabited the lower valleys of the Irawadi and Salween in Burma, however, along with the Khmers, extended further south and dominated over the Lavas. Archaeological evidence in Laos is found from prehistoric times down to the Iron Age. Chinese records speak of land-route trade between India and China, through Eastern Bengal, Manipur and Assam as early as the second century BCE. The Hindus colonized and established their kingdom not only in Burma but also in the upper valleys of Chindwin, the

25. R.C. Majumdar's *Ancient Indian Colonies in the Far East*, Book III, pp. 11, 15 and 29 (Greater Indian Society Lahore, 1927).

26. Schoff, *The Periplus of the Erythraen Sea*, p. 46.

27. *India's Contribution to World Thought and Culture*, p. 483.

Irawadi, the Salween, the Mekong and the Red River. There is evidence that Hindu kingdom also existed in Laos. Huen-tien is mentioned in the Chinese records of the third century CE, and even in later Chinese texts, as the king of Fu-nan. This Huen-tien is variously known, and one of his forms represents the Indian name "Kauṇdivyā." Huen-tien had married the female sovereign of Fu-nan and became king of that land. It is generally believed that he was a Hindu from India and had established a Hindu kingdom in Cambodia and Cochin-China by about the first century CE. After the death of Pan-Pan the last ruler of his lineage in about CE 200, a general Fan-che-man was elected to kingship. He conquered several other neighbouring regions which included Siam and Laos. The Hindu Mon dynasty ruled over Siam and Laos in circa sixth century CE.

Regarding the state of society and religion in Japan and Korea, we shall briefly discuss this issue in the seventh chapter of this book. Since the scope of our research is specially confined to Sri Lanka, China and Tibet, we shall give a full stop to our discussion about other Asian countries of Far-East and South-East. However, we have briefly discussed about the state of society and religion wherever it seemed necessary and indispensable.

3

Buddhism and Cultural Transformation of Asian People by Devout Royalty

BUDDHISM has the fortune and glory of gifting an all-embracing universal religion of compassion and wisdom to a large number of countries of Asia. This supremely sublime and altruistic religion gave rise to a puritan culture. This unique culture got carpeted over a vast tract of Central Asian and South-East Asian countries including its motherland during the course of many centuries under royal patronage, missionary zeal of devout Buddhist mercantile community and monk scholars. Deeply influenced by philosophy, art, architecture, religious literature and liturgy of the Buddhists, the people of many Asian countries embraced this peace-loving faith. Poets, philosophers, sculptors and painters also played a great role in the cultural transformation of the Asian people by their sublime poetry, lively paintings pertaining to Buddha's life, marvellous *stūpas*, *caityas* and architectural structures.

The Buddha : A Peripatetic Propagator of His Own Religion

The sublime thought and refined culture of Buddhism started leaving its evangelical imprint on the life, thought and culture of the Asian people soon after the Buddha attained enlightenment at Bodh-Gayā beneath the *bodhi* tree. We must be cautious enough to distinguish between Siddhārtha and the Buddha. It was the Buddha whose wisdom became the light of Asia. Magadha was the first place on the earth where wisdom dawned upon the Buddha and it was from here that the exalted teachings of the Compassionate Buddha spread across its native boundaries. Soon after getting enlightenment the Buddha felt the urgent necessity of disseminating the wisdom that dawned upon him for the weal of mankind. Leaving nothing to chance or for posterity, the Buddha engaged himself quite seriously in propagating the ethico-spiritual wisdom among the masses. He was neither a classroom teacher nor a pulpiteer; instead he was a mobile but dedicated and missionary sermoniser. While in solitude he used to practise meditation for long hours. Whatever he gained as knowledge and whatever he attained as wisdom he never kept it secret or hidden or hoarded like a greedy merchant. The Buddha was very clear that wisdom and truth are to be shared by one and all. This pious and altruist intention of the Buddha motivated him to go from place to place and from door to door to exhort the people who are trapped in curse, ignorance, infatuation, avarice, frustation and despondency. The divine and spiritually radiant countenance of the Buddha attracted the masses. The Buddha preached his *Dharma* not for a select scholarly elite or for the influential royalty but for the common mass and that too in their *lingua franca* because the Buddha was seriously and deeply concerned about *bahujana hitāya, bahujana sukhāya*. After the attainment of Enlightenment at the age of 35 till his death at the age of 80, in a span of 45 years, the Buddha personally kept on sauntering sometimes lonely and sometimes flanked by *Bhikṣu Saṅgha* teaching his sermons and impressing upon the people the importance of virtuous life and the benefits of meditation.

If we look at the activities of the Buddha in his daily life, we find that he never sat in a place idly and was always busy in preaching and moralizing. The divine and the spiritual person of the Buddha itself was like a vast canvas of a highly refined human culture and philosophy, impregnable, practical and behavioural ethics. On these grounds we can sanely conclude that the Buddha was the first harbinger and propagator of that sublime faith and exalted ideology which was professed by none other than himself.

During the lifetime of the Buddha, the spread of his teachings extended not much beyond the kingdoms of Magadha and Kosala. During the succeeding centuries its influence slowly and gradually widened. For about 45 years the Buddha spread his thought and religion amongst his people, wandering from place to place. With ever-increasing care he elaborated his system of thoughts by means of discussion with foes and friends alike. He won adherents. Soon he was surrounded by an inner circle of disciples faithfully devoted to him, and whom he taught and trained. He gained respect besides from a large number of outsiders, even if they did not accept his deeper instructions, and could not live up to his highest requirements. Although opposition was not altogether lacking, the impression gathered was mainly that of success and of rapid spread of his doctrine. The Buddha also converted his own family, his father, his former wife, his son and his relatives. The extent of the country traversed by Gautama in his itinerary work far exceeded the paternal domain. He travelled in the eastern part of north India where the old kingdoms of Magadha and Kosala were situated in a region the centre of which is the city of Benares. These tours, on which he was accompanied by his disciples, were interrupted every year for several months by the rainy season. Then they sought shelter at a place where the gifts and care of adherents made a longer stay possible. Thus four-and-a-half decades had passed. The Buddha had become an old man while still engaged in his labours. He saw the result of a remarkable life-work surrounding him — a great community, obedient to the rule of salvation, framed by him.

We are told in legends that the Buddha was too hesitant to divulge the truth when it dawned upon him for the first time. But Brahmā appeared and persuaded him to preach for the weal of suffering mankind. The Buddha acceded to his request. The Buddha really took a vow to preach in order to mitigate the suffering of mankind. The Buddha gifted to mankind a threefold spiritual culture and an Eightfold Noble Path. He was not a dogmatist. Truly speaking, he was an analyst, *vibhajyavādī*. He gave us a philosophy of life which was based on ethics and spirituality. He eschewed all the theoretical considerations as vain and stressed upon people to lead a life of rectitude and purity. He showed us *viśuddhi-mārga* (The Path of Purification). On the basis of his personal realisation, he preached us the essencelessness of all worldly possessions and mental evils. He taught us both *sevā* and *sādhanā* but he gave preference to *sevā*. *Śīla* (virtuous conduct) was the cornerstone of his ethics and culture. Here *śīla* means *daśaśīla* — five for the laity (*upāsaka*) and five more for the monks. Everyway the Buddha gave us a unique *ācāra-śāstra*. He also made it clear that we should not hanker after or fight for petty worldly possessions. He gave the message of peace, tolerance, sympathy, friendliness and, above all, compassion.

The Buddha's life and conduct itself was a torch in the wilderness of ignorance and infatuation. His entire life and all his activities preach us the lesson of an exalted detachment. In his exhortations he warned us against any kind of temptation. He also advised us to desist from three kinds of violence — physical, mental and vocal. In himself the Buddha was the embodiment of *saddharma*. There was a unique, rather divine, glow and spiritual radiance on his face. In every posture his person and face reflected a spiritual message and ethical gospel. Wherever the Buddha went on missionary trip he spread his message. Many kings and traders also became his disciples and they all came forward to follow and disseminate his teachings. Thus, we can say that the Buddha himself was an unmatching propagator of his own religion which he called *saddharma.*

Buddhism became very popular among the kings and the traders too. Probably the cause of its popularity was that it does not demand that anyone accept its teachings on trust. The practitioner is instead invited to try them out to experiment with them. If he finds they work in practice, then by all means he can take them on board. But there is no compulsion; and if he happens to find the truth elsewhere or otherwise, all well and good. The essential freedom from dogmas is the uniqueness of Buddhist thought. It became popular among the masses of his time because it was a casteless, creedless and cultless religion.

We have already said that Buddhism was confined particularly to *mahājanapada*s of Magadha and Kosala during his lifetime but was disseminated and propagated under royal patronage in subsequent centuries.

Role and Contribution of Aśoka in Propagation of Saddharma and Cultural Transformation of Asian People

Buddhism has tremendous civilizing influence in Asia. Its indelible ethico-spiritual and religio-philosophical impact is left on a vast tract of land comprising India of ancient times, Tibet, entire Central Asia, China, Korea, Japan and several other South-East Asian countries including the Indonesian archipelago. Religion, philosophy, culture, art and literature of these countries eloquently speak volumes about a perpetual Buddhist influence. Buddhism, through its thought and culture, has influenced the culture of most countries of Asia since its first propagation in the Island of Ceylon by Mahindra and Saṅghamitrā — son and daughter respectively of Aśoka the Great — in the third century BCE. It must be pointed out here that in the Council which was convened in Aśokārama of Pāṭaliputra (in the seventeenth year after Aśoka's coronation), it was decided to send the Buddhist missionaries under the leadership of celebrated monks on the advice of Moggaliputta Tissa, who was the spiritual teacher of Aśoka the Great, is said to have presided over the Council held by Aśoka and expelled 80,000 heretics from the *Saṅgha*. In the Ceylonese Chronicles, as well as in Buddhaghoṣa's *Sāmantapāsādika*, the credit for sending out the missionaries is given to Moggaliputta Tissa himself. The *Dīpavaṁsa* (chapter VIII) mentions the missionaries by their names and records somewhat briefly their achievements, and the whole chapter XII of the *Mahāvaṁsa*, headed by the "Conversion of Different Countries," describes in verse 1-52 how the missionaries named in the earlier Chronicles converted people to Buddhism by thousands, preached in Mahiṣamaṇḍala (Mysore), Vanavāsī (North Kanara), Aparāntaka (western border province of the empire) and Maharaṭṭha (Maharashtra), and adds that they bestowed ordination of thousands. Buddhaghoṣa bases his account in the *Sāmantapāsādika* on the *Dīpāvaṁsa* Chronicle. From these Ceylonese sources, we get the names of the missionaries and the countries to which they were deputed.

1.	Majjhāntika	to Kashmir and Gandhāra.
2.	Yona Dhammarakkhita	to Appārantaka (a monk of Greek origin).
3.	Majjhima	to Himalayan region.
4.	Mahārakkhita	to the country of the Yonas (Perhaps to the Bactrian kingdom to the north-west).
5.	Mahā-dhammarakkhita	to Maharashtra.
6.	Rakkhita	to Vanavāsī (North Kanara).
7.	Mahādeva	to Mahiṣamaṇḍala (Mysore).
8.	Sona and Uttara	to Suvarṇabhūmi (Burma).
9.	Mahinda and Moggaliputta's own disciples, Itthiya, Uttiya, Sambala and Bhaddasāla	to Ceylon.

The missionary caravan of Buddhism which proceeded for dissemination of Buddhism and for cultural transformation across Asian countries under the leadership of Aśoka the Great was subsequently joined by important royal personages of different dynasties and different countries for many centuries. The Ceylon Chronicles refer to these Buddhist missions to nine different countries. This information is confirmed and further supplemented by Aśoka's thirteenth rock edict wherein it is stated that he tried to spread the *Dhamma* not only in his territory or among the peoples of the border lands but also in kingdoms far off, such as those of Antiochus (Antiyoka) II, king of Syria, and the kingdoms of four other kings, still farther off, i.e. Ptolemy (Turameya) of Egypt; Antigonas (Antakini) of Macedonia; Alexandra (Aliasundara) of Epirus, an ancient district of northern Greece, and Magas of Cyrenia, in North Africa. He also mentioned the names of Yavanas, Kambojas, Pāṇḍyas, Coḷas, Āndhras, Pulindas, Ceylon, etc.

Aśoka thus became a zealous follower of the Buddha and took upon himself the task of making known to the people the teachings of the Lord. In the Bhabru Edict, seven passages occur and most of these have been identified with certain passages in Pāli literature. He wanted all people — monks as well as laymen — to have these read out to them. He thought that by inculcating the teachings of the Buddha, men and women would become better people. He paid reverence to the Buddha, the *Dhamma,* his Law, and the *Saṅgha,* his Order for Buddhist monks.

Archaeology has confirmed the historicity of Tissa's mission. In a *stūpa* (no. 2) at Sāñcī were found two relic-caskets, probably deposited there in the second or the first century BCE on which some of the names of the missionaries are inscribed — Majjhima (the missionary to the Himalayan region) and two of his associates, Kassapagota and Dundubhissara, out of the four mentioned in the *Sāmantapāsādika* as having been associated with him on the mission, viz. Kassapagota, Alkadeva, Dundubhissara and Sahadeva. We have no further trace of these missionaries and no subsequent record of their achievements except in respect of those who worked in Ceylon. There is no doubt that these missions met with a measure of success.[1]

The Council convened by Aśoka at Pāṭaliputra played a great role in the cultural transformation of a number of Asian

1. *Buddhist Monks and Monasteries of India*, pp. 114-15.

countries. K.L. Hazra[2] endorses this fact when he writes that the session of the Third Buddhist Council and the sending of the religious missions to nine different countries by Moggaliputta Tissa after this Council were the most important events in the history of Buddhism. This was for the first time in the history that Buddhist monks went to foreign countries to propagate the teachings of the Buddha. India and the countries, belonging to the region now known as South and South-East Asia, were familiar with each other from the time of the Buddha. Several Jātakas refer to the sea voyages of merchants from India to this region. So from very ancient times trade relations were established between these two regions and it is very probable that through traders Buddhism was also introduced there. The Third Buddhist Council was an important landmark in the history of Buddhism. It produced important results in Ceylon, Burma and other places of South-East Asia. The Theravāda form of Buddhism was introduced into Ceylon and South-East Asia by Buddhist monks sent by King Aśoka in the second half of the third century BCE. In course of time after its introduction Ceylon became the headquarters of Theravāda Buddhism and from there it flourished in South-East Asia. After its disappearance from India, Ceylon as an important centre took the leading part for the spread of this form of Buddhism. A.L. Basham[3] remarks that with the support of Aśoka, Buddhism greatly expanded, spreading throughout India and to Ceylon. There is some doubt as to how far the doctrine had developed at this time, but at least a rudimentary canon existed, though perhaps not yet committed to writing.

2. *History of Theravāda Buddhism in South-East Asian Countries*, p. 40.
3. *The Wonder That Was India*, p. 265.

The propagation of the Buddhism, says Nalinaksha Dutt,[4] in Gandhāra and Kashmir has an independent history of its own. Both the Pāli and Sanskrit traditions state that Madhyāntika (Majjhāntika) was responsible for the propagation of the religion in these two countries. Madhyāntika was a disciple of Ānanda and so he was a contemporary of Sambhūta Sanavasi and senior to Upagupta. Madhyāntika preached Sarvāstivāda Buddhism in Kashmir. This is corroborated by the testimony of Hiuen Tsang, who tells us that Aśoka not only sent Buddhist monks to Kashmir but also built monasteries at that place. He writes that during Aśoka's reign there was in Magadha "a subtle investigator of *nāma-rūpa* (mind and matter), who put extraordinary thought in a treatise which taught heresy." An attempt was made to drown these monks into the Ganges, but they saved themselves by fleeing to Kashmir where they settled on hills and in the valleys. On hearing this, Aśoka felt remorse and requested them to return, and on their refusal, built for them 500 monasteries and "gave up all Kashmir for the benefit of the Buddhist Church." The fact underlying this story is that the "investigators of mind and matter" were none other than the *Sarvāstivādins*, whose principal tenet is that *nāma* and *rūpa* are real and are divisible into 64 elements, which exist for ever (*sarvam asti*), and it is for this view that they had the appellation of Sarvāstivāda. Then the statement that they resorted to the hills and valleys of Kashmir corroborates the flight of the *Sarvāstivādin* monks to the north in Kashmir. The statement that Aśoka became repentant later on and that he wanted the monks who fled to Kashmir to return to Magadha may be an indirect reference to the fact recorded in the *Divyāvadāna* and *Aśokāvadāna* that Aśoka made an attempt toward the end of his life to reconcile the monks of different

4. *Buddhist Sects in India*, pp. 129-30.

schools of Buddhist thought by convening a Council to which he particularly invited the monks living at Tamasavana in Kashmir. The Ceylonese Chronicles maintained a discreet silence over this incident, and this is not unusual in view of the sectarian spirit permeating the Chronicles.

Buddhism continued to flourish in northern India after the reign of Aśoka. But it is said in the Buddhist texts that it had suffered a set-back in north-east India during the reign of Puṣyamitra, the founder of the Śuṅga dynasty, who after assassinating Bṛhadratha, the last king of the Maurya empire, ascended the throne and ruled for 36 years (c. 187-151 BCE). According to the Buddhist tradition, Puṣyamitra destroyed monasteries and killed many monks on his journey to Sialkot in Punjab. Here he announced a prize of one hundred gold coins on the head of each Buddhist monk. Buddhism flourished in north-western India in the region of Indo-Greek rulers. Of the Greek rulers of India, Menander alone occupied an important place in the Buddhist world for his love toward Buddhism and his scholastic approach. He has been identified with King Milinda of the *Milindapañha*, "Questions of Milinda," a Buddhist book composed in the form of questions and answers between King Milinda and Nāgasena, the famous Buddhist monk. It is said that King Menander after his meeting with Nāgasena took Buddhism as his religion and helped to spread Buddhism in his kingdom. He joined the *Saṅgha* as a monk and became an *arhat*.[5]

In this context it would be worthwhile to settle the controversy about the Indo-Greek King Menander, being a Buddhist (convert). The evidence which may be given to prove him a Buddhist is that the coins of Menander bear the Buddhist wheel. The Śinkoṭ inscription proves unmistakably that the

5. *History of Theravāda Buddhism in South-East Asia*, pp. 40-41.

Greek King helped in the propagation of Buddhism in the region between the Hindukush and Sindh. Kṣemendra, in his *Avadāna Kalpalatā*, has described him as Milindra.

Bharat Singh Upadhyaya[6] writes that after Aśoka, the torch of the Buddhism was kept burning by the efforts of Milinda (Menander), Kaniṣka, Harṣa and the rulers of the Pāla dynasty (CE 750-1150). Menander, the Indo-Greek king, was a great patron and supporter of Buddhism. During the two centuries that followed the decline of the power of the imperial Mauryas, the Greek invaders held suzerainty over north-western India and Afghanistan. Some thirty rulers flourished during this period, of whom only King Menander has left a permanent impression on the Indian mind. This is evidently due to his association with the *Dhamma*. True essence of Buddhism was explained to him so convincingly by Buddhist monk Nāgasena that all the doubts and misgivings which were hitherto cherished about Buddhism by him were removed. Out of sheer reverence for Nāgasena and his profound wisdom, Menander embraced Buddhism and got constructed Milind-Vihāra and donated it to the *Saṅgha*. He also made large donations to the *Bhikṣu Saṅgha*.

After Milinda there comes another name in Indian history which is equally illustrious among the rulers of India and in Buddhist tradition. This is the name of Kaniṣka who completed the work of Aśoka and helped in the triumphant spread of the Buddha-Dharma throughout Asia. Kaniṣka belonged to the Kuṣāṇa (Kuei-Shuang) branch of the Yueh-chi tribe which originally inhabits parts of Chinese Turkestan (modern Sinkiang). The first Kuṣāṇa chief who occupied territories in India was Kaḍphises I (*Kujul-Kasa*) who was a Buddhist. Some of his coins which have been found in the Kharoṣṭhī script at

6. *2500 Years of Buddhism* (ed.), p. 175.

the excavations at Taxila bear the inscription, *Kujul-kasasa Kusāṇa-Yavugasa Dharma-Thidasa,* i.e of *Kujul Kasa,* the Kuṣāṇa Chief, who is steadfast in the *dharma*. That by the word *Dharma* is meant here the Buddhist religion is made clear by some other coins which have the word *sacca dharma-thiṭa* (steadfast in the true *dharma*) instead of *dharma thiṭa*. It was in the line of such an illustrious forefather that Kaniṣka comes to rule India in the last quarter of the first century CE.

Eulogizing the contributions of Kaniṣka towards the cause of Buddhism, Bharat Singh Upadhyaya[7] writes that Kaniṣka's reign (CE 78-101) also marked a turning point in the history of Buddhism and Buddhist literature. It witnessed the rise of Mahāyāna Buddhism and the magnificent literary activity started by Pārśva, Aśvaghoṣa, Vasumitra and others. It was in this age that Pāli gave place to Sanskrit. In the field of art, the celebrated Gāndhāra sculptures developed and figures of the Buddha and *bodhisattvas* began to appear. It was during Kaniṣka's reign and largely through his efforts that Buddhism was successfully introduced into Central and Eastern Asia. There was ceaseless missionary activity throughout his vast empire which extended from Madhyadeśa in India to Central Asia. A truly integrated Asian culture came into existence at this time, based as it was on the highest purposes of life for which Buddhism stood.

In many respects Kaniṣka was like Aśoka the Great. He was also an enthusiastic propagator and promoter of Buddhism. After the bloodshed of Kashgar, Yarkand and Khoṭan, Kaniṣka was moved and as an atonement he took refuge in the teachings of the Buddha. He greatly repented over his victory. For the compilations of doctrines of Buddhism and writing commentaries on them from the Sthaviravāda

7. Ibid., p. 176.

point of view, he convened a Council. Here 500 monks took part in this Council and they compiled commentaries known as *Vibhāsā-Śāstra* on the three *Piṭaka*s of the Buddhist canon. These great commentaries are still preserved in Chinese. These treatises were copied on copperplates and after enclosing them in stone boxes were safely deposited in a *stūpa* which Kaniṣka had specially erected for this purpose. Kaniṣka also donated the kingdom of Kashmir to the Buddhist *Saṅgha*. On the testimony of Kalhana — the author of *Rājataraṅgiṇī* — it is said that Kaniṣka founded many monasteries and *caitya*s. He also founded a city named Kaniṣkapur which has been identified with modern Kaniṣpur in Kashmir. He erected a great tope which was named after him. To the west of the tope he built a large monastery named Kaniṣka Mahāvihāra. Both these structures were erected at Puruṣapur (Modern Peshawar). The Chinese pilgrims have greatly lauded the architectural beauty of this important relic tower. Alberuni also testifies to it.

The Buddhist philosophy and religion which was being contemplated and practised inside the Buddhist monasteries by the monastic community — both monks and nuns — germinated in the form of an altruistic ethico-spiritual culture. The Buddha must not have advised the erection of *stūpa*s and *caitya*s but in order to pay their homage his followers raised such holy structures because for them they were reminiscent of the Buddha. More so the erection of such structures and the construction of monasteries was virtually a great *dāna* to the Buddhist *saṅgha*. In course of time these holy structures came to be identified as the objects of veneration. Inspired by such religious structures, kings and the wealthy devout Buddhists started constructing such holy structures and shrines. The laity started thronging these places of veneration. Not only in India but anywhere Buddhism went, such holy structures and shrines were constructed. This was the beginning of the *stūpa* worship. Perhaps the beginnings of the *stūpa*s were in the late Mauryan period, but the decorative slabs on them were the work of later times when this part of northern India was under Śuṅga rule. Worship at these *stūpa*s was undoubtedly held on a grand ceremonial scale and it were the Buddhists who were most zealous of *stūpa* worship and *stūpa* decoration. Their sculptures have been studied minutely by competent scholars in its immensely varied themes and breathtaking profusion. This *stūpa* art is also interesting and significant from a different point of view — as the first tangible expression of Buddhist culture that has grown up since Aśoka's reign among common people in northern India. Its accents are different from the culture of the monasteries; it is to all appearance neither monk-moulded nor monk-directed; it is just a reflection of the popular mind under the impact and influence of Buddhist faith. This first efflorescence of a Buddhist culture among the people is in stone, not in texts. Monks only had the ability to compose text; laymen could write their faith only in pictures and symbols on stone. This lithic expression of lay Buddhist culture in northern India during the closing decades of the centuries before Christ is revelatory of its free and spontaneous folk character.

How the religious structure like *stūpa* and *caitya*s became helpful in the propagation of the faith is an interesting story. Those who were able to understand the complicated philosophy of the Buddhist canons were able to comprehend the story and catholicity of this altruistic faith through the paintings and Jātaka stories sketched on frescoes and engraved on the slabs of the *stūpas*. The *stūpa* art and frescoes helped a lot in the propagation of Buddhist faith and culture in most of the Asian countries. The observations of Sukumar Dutt[8] are

8. *Buddhist Monks and Monasteries of India*, p. 121.

worth quoting in this context. He writes, "The *stūpa* decorators evidently knew the main legends of the Lord, a number of Jātaka stories, the sacred symbols and their significance. But their work is untouched by the influence of monkish learning; it gives no hint of the special interpretation and doctrinal matters developed in the monks' Abhidhamma philosophy." Evidently their faith was intimate with life, forming one complex — the sacred unshifted from the profane, and the ideal element of Buddhism promiscuously bent with folk cults, folk superstitions and concepts alien from canonical teachings. It was a faith that had stirred their hearts, activised their imagination and evoked the emotion of *bhakti* — an emotion that lies near the surface of untutored folk mind. Their concept of Him who gave this faith to the world was not the canonical concept of a teacher (*sattha*) or even of a superman (*mahāpuruṣa*), but of one who transcended all earthly relations and could not therefore be represented in art by a human figure, however idealized. To the *stūpa,* which since the days of Aśoka had become the grand visible emblem of the faith, they flocked to avow and articulate their faith in the Three Refuges (*tri-saraṇa*), and the *stūpa* stood to them not, as the canon contemplated it, as a memorial monument to the Lord, but as a symbol of Divine Presence.

With this slight digression now let us come to the real issue. We have already said that cultural transformation of the Asian people was brought about by the Buddhist thought and culture under the royal patronage of Aśoka, Menander, Kaniṣka, Gupta kings, Harṣa and the Pāla rulers. These rulers established Buddhist monastic universities like Nālandā, Vikramaśilā, Valabhi, etc. Buddhist philosophy and culture were disseminated and propagated through these centres of higher learning, particularly Nālandā, where many students studied Buddhist Śāstras and after completing their education returned to their countries with bundles of Buddhist manuscripts and translated them in their own languages. After the destruction of two great monastic universities of Nālandā and Vikramaśilā many of the learned scholars flew to Tibet, Nepal and China. Hiuen Tsang, during his first sojourn at Nālandā stayed for fifteen months, perfecting his knowledge of Buddhist philosophy and of Sanskrit. The reputation of Hiuen Tsang was so great in India that many rulers wanted to see and to honour him. One of these was Bhaskara Kumāra, king of Kāmarūpa (Assam), whom Hiuen Tsang visited. Afterwards both Kumāra and the Chinese cleric travelled together to call on Harṣa, emperor of India. The emperor, having heard of the arrival of the famous Chinese monk, hurried over to pay his respect, which he did first by bowing to the ground and kissing Hiuen Tsang's feet. Harṣa then convened a grand assembly, over which the pilgrim presided, to dissipate the blindness of Hīnayāna and to shatter the period of the brāhmaṇas, as Harṣa put it. For 18 days the contestants debated, but in the end Hiuen Tsang emerged triumphant over all. He took with him to his country 657 items packed in 520 cases. Of these he only translated 73 items. He died in CE 664.

In the seventh century, Harṣa — a great Hindu king — contributed a lot to the cause of Buddhism. We have just mentioned that it was during his reign that Hiuen Tsang visited India. His reign was an important period in the political, social and religious history of northern India. He unified the whole northern India into one empire. He patronized Buddhism and popularized Buddhistic learning at the monastic university of Nālandā.

The reign of the kings of Pāla dynasty was a great epoch in the history of Buddhism in India. The Pāla king ruled in eastern India from about the second half of the eighth century CE and gave a new life to Buddhism. The founder of the dynasty was Gopāla who was a Buddhist. The next king was Dharma-pāla (CE 770-810) who was a zealous patron of Buddhism and played a great role for the establishment of Buddhism. He established the Vikramaśilā monastery at Patharghata near Bhagalpur. It became an important centre of Buddhist learning and culture. The great Buddhist *vihāra* at Somapuri in the Rajashahi district of present-day Bangladesh was also constructed by him. Devapāla, the worthy son of Dharmapāla, ascended the throne of the Pāla dynasty after his father. The reigns of Dharmapāla and Devapāla constitute the most brilliant chapter in the history of Bengal. Never before or since, till the advent of the British, did Bengal play such an important role in Indian politics. Devapāla reigned for about 40 years (CE 810-50). Under him the Pāla empire reached the height of its glory. His empire extended from the Himalayas to Vindhya mountains and from the eastern to the western seas. He too, like his father, occupied an important place in the history of Buddhism for his important contribution to the spread of Buddhism in India as well as in the Buddhist countries of South-East Asia. About this time the Śailendra dynasty of the kingdom of Śrīvijaya in Sumatra was ruling over an extensive empire in South-East Asia. Balaputradeva, a king of this dynasty, was a devout follower of the Buddha. He dispatched a mission to Devapāla, asking for a grant of five villages for the upkeep of the monastery, built by him at Nālandā. Devapāla granted his request. The Śailendra rulers were followers of Mahāyāna Buddhism. Under the patronage of Pālas Mahāyāna Buddhism flourished in Bengal and Magadha in Bihar. It was a Mahāyāna tinged with Tantrayāna. At that time Hīnayāna Buddhism disappeared from the land of its birth and made its home in Ceylon. Tāntric Buddhism, which was originated from the Mahāyāna school of Yogācāra, and which played a great role in the history of Buddhism in India during this period, flourished in Bengal from about the middle of the seventh century CE and Nālandā became the important centre of this form of Buddhism. Several schools, viz. Vajrayāna, Kālacakrayāna, Mantrayāna and Sahajayāna came into existence. The Śailendra dynasty established its close contact with Bengal and Magadha and most probably this dynasty received its Mahāyāna Buddhism from these regions. Thus under the patronage of the Pāla rulers there was a revival of missionary zeal and the Buddhist monks of Bengal and Magadha visited many Buddhist centres of South-East Asia and helped to spread Mahāyāna Buddhism there.

A.L. Basham[9] writes that the Pāla kings are chiefly notable for their patronage of Buddhism, which, in a rather corrupt form, flourished in their dominions during the three centuries of their rule. It was from the Pāla empire that Buddhism was introduced into Tibet, where, combined with many native beliefs, it survives to the present day.

While highlighting the contributions of Pāla kings towards the promotion and propagation of Buddhist thought and culture and the cultural transformation of the society through Buddhism, it is imperative that we should describe something about the contributions of the Nālandā University which was founded during the Gupta Age sometimes in the beginning of fifth century CE by Śakrāditya. There is a great controversy over this date. Nālandā as a *mahāvihāra* was a little over a century old when Hiuen Tsang visited it. Chinese monk scholars were attracted by its fame. The academic life and activities that prevailed here at the peak of its fame in the seventh century are known to us almost exclusively from

9. *The Wonder That Was India*, pp. 71-73.

Chinese sources. Tibetans also had started on a cultural intercourse with India and came to know of the Nālandā Mahāvihāra as India's premier Buddhist seat of learning. It is almost definite that Nālandā in seventh century CE was regarded as a seat and seminary of higher learning. Tibetans had started coming to Nālandā at the time Hiuen Tsang was a resident there. Srong-btsang sgam-po (born in CE 617), the Tibetan king, had sent to Nālandā a scholar who had been in his own country a minister to him. He was Thon-mi Sambhota. Commissioned by the king who, under the influence of his Chinese Buddhist wife, had a leaning to Buddhism, Thon-mi Sambhota left Tibet to study the religion at its sources in India. He returned after a course of study at Nālandā to report on what he had learnt. The king was converted and Buddhism was for the first time declared the state religion of Tibet. Thon-mi Sambhota is credited with having remodelled the Tibetan language on the principles of Sanskrit grammar. It is not known who came from Tibet in the footsteps of this pioneer, but they evidently carried home reports of what they saw at India's premier monastic university. Nālandā became in the eyes of later generations of Tibetans the name and symbol for a monastic establishment that concerned itself with study of learning and philosophy. In 1351, a monastery named Nālandā was founded in Tibet and maintained a "school of philosophy." This great monastery was a place filled with monks of different sects, where preaching and study continued without inter-ruption. It was a self-refuge for preachers who wandered about the country. The Tibetan monastery, it appears, was modelled on Nālandā's liberal traditions of culture. So it proudly bore Nālandā's name.

Sukumar Dutt[10] draws our attention to a very important fact that Nālandā was perhaps the longest-lived of the

10. *Buddhist Monks and Monasteries of India*, pp. 344-45.

*mahāvihāra*s of India. Its history falls into two main divisions — the first, one of growth, development and fruition from the sixth century to the ninth, when it was dominated by the liberal cultural traditions inherited from the Gupta age; the second, one of gradual decline and final dissolution from the ninth century to the thirteenth — a period during which the Tāntric developments of Buddhism became most pronounced in eastern India under the Pālas and laid their killing influence on Nālandā's culture. We may label the first as the "Gupta Period" of Nālandā and second as the "Pāla Period." There is also a prehistory of over a century when Nālandā was in the making by Gupta kings from Śakrāditya to Vajra. The "Gupta period" of Nālandā closed with the rise of the Pāla dynasty. Its founder Gopala is said in the Tibetan legend to have founded a *mahāvihāra* of grand proportions in the newly-built city of Odantapuri, only about six miles from Nālandā. Its name was known to the Arabs as Adwand-Bihar, its modern name is Bihar-Sharif. At the time of its foundation by Gopāla, Nālandā was still functioning and was perhaps not in decline. The Pāla kings were Buddhist and it may be supposed that Gopāla and his descendants were keen on developing the Odantapuri monastery as a parallel, if not as a rival seat of Buddhist learning. In course of time, other seats of learning, for which Nālandā was the most obvious and ready-to-hand example, were established by other kings of the dynasty. The Pāla establishment must have drawn away a number of learned monks from Nālandā when all of them, including Nālandā itself, came under the aegis of the Pālas. There is evidence in the Tibetan legends that there used to be migration of scholars from one place to another. Nālandā's pride of place must have been largely impaired by these adventitious circumstances. Also, from the eighth century onward, Buddhism was shrinking in northern India; it was only in the eastern areas over which the Buddhist Pāla kings ruled that its waning influence lingered and the kings sought to consolidate it by the establishment of new monastic centres. Its once widespread fame in the country that had extended in the seventh century beyond its border into the Far-East and Tibet dwindled to a regional or local reputation. What is more important and significant is that during the "Pāla period" of its history Buddhism itself was already in a phase wherein it was heavily adulterated by the Tāntric cult and its magic spells and practices. During this period of Tāntric predominance at Nālandā, this centre of liberal learning seems to have fallen from its standard of liberal scholarship to become more and more a centre of studies in Tāntric doctrines and Tāntric magic rites. The end of Nālandā, after a lifetime of seven centuries is shrouded in mystery. Odantapuri Mahāvihāra was sacked and razed to the ground around 1198.

One thing that needs to be mentioned here is that Nālandā of the Pāla period is scarcely represented in Chinese records which assemble so fascinating a picture of it in its earlier, more glorious epoch. In fact, there are few instances after the turn of the eighth century of Chinese monks coming to India for study and learning. Perhaps the movement which had started the exodus of Chinese monk-scholars to India was then at its ebb. But from Nālandā and other centres Indian monks did not cease to migrate to China. They introduced into the country the prevailing Tāntric Buddhism of India of the period. Sino-Indian intercourse was definitely petering out on the Chinese side by the middle of the eighth century. Tibet now took the place of China in cultural intercourse with India. The comings and goings between Tibet and eastern India of Tibetan Lamas and Indian Paṇḍits, through the windswept winding la's (passes) of the eastern Himalayas, never came to a stop till the last days of the Pālas.

We know of the contributions of Guru Padmasambhava (a saint scholar of Kashmir) and two eminent scholars of Nālandā — Śāntirakṣita and his pupil Kamalaśīla — who instituted the lamaist system in Tibet and established the first Buddhist monastery, of which Śāntirakṣita was named the first abbot. The contribution of the Dīpaṅkara Śrījñāna was no less in cultural transformation of Tibet. The great Tāntric saint and scholar Naropa was *dvārapāla* of Vikramaśilā. Tibetan lamas were held in great esteem at Vikramśīlā. After the destruction of Vikramashila University towards the close of the twelfth century, Guru Śākya Śrībhadra flew to Tibet to avoid the Muslim marauders. Two other Indian monk scholars of Jagaddala university — Vibhuticandra and Dānaśīla — who were the students of Śākya Śrībhadra also flew to Nepal and Tibet from the Muslim terror.

Thus we see how the royal patronage, the monastic universities, affluent mercantile community and the learned monk scholars from India, Tibet, China and Korea contributed in the cultural transformation of their land and people. In this gigantic exercise, the eager and devout laymen also played a great role. To adopt and embrace an alien faith by the masses of those primitive times was really a wonder and this wonder was the creation of the sublimity of Buddhist thought and culture.

How did Buddhism leave an evangelical influence on the socio-religious life and thought of Asian people in general, and on the people of Sri Lanka, China and Tibet in particular? In subsequent chapters we shall discuss these issues in detail.

4

Impact of Buddhist Thought and Culture on Sri Lankan People

IN the second chapter of this volume we have discussed in detail about the state of society and religion in pre-Buddhist Sri Lanka (also called Ceylon until recently). Due to its proximity with India and also due to the missionary enthusiasm and commitment of the Mauryan king Aśoka the Great, Buddhism was introduced in Sri Lanka by the first royal missionary. Sri Lanka was the first overseas island country where Buddhism reached, and it is interesting as well as glorifying that its thought and culture altogether changed the way of life of the Sri Lankan people. Rightly speaking, the ethico-spiritual philosophy of Buddhism and its highly refined altruistic culture brought about a total change, first in the thought and culture of Sri Lankan and then in their way of life.

It is desirable here to tell very briefly about culture. "Culture" denotes a quality in the person or society that arises from a concern for what is regarded as excellent in arts, letters, manners, scholarly pursuits, etc. "Culture" also refers to the sum total of the ways of living built by a group of human beings and transmitted from one generation to another. Culture involves the development or improvement of mind by education and training. Thought means a judgement, option or belief. Thought also means the act or process of thinking. It is synonymous with meditation or contemplation. In this chapter we shall see how the Buddhist thought and culture influenced and altered the thought and culture of Sri Lankans.

Buddhism could make its headway in Sri Lanka, or in any other foreign country, squarely due to the co-operation and patronage of royalty, merchants and scholars. Missionary enthusiasm played the greatest role in the insemination of this alien but sublime and all-embracing faith in this isolated island. The plantation of a sapling of the *bodhi* tree was symbolically the first advent of Buddhism in Sri Lanka. It was in and around this *bodhi* tree that Sri Lankans thronged to receive and embrace a religion which preached compassion, wisdom and universal brotherhood. With the introduction of Buddhism, Sri Lanka saw its total face lift. Religious structures, monuments, monasteries and shrines were built and the first light of Saddharma fell on Anurādhapura which in course of time became a great monastic centre of Buddhist learning where a vast commentarial literature was produced in the form of *aṭṭakathā*s. Due to the impact of Buddhism a large number of *stūpas*, *caitya*s, *vihāra*s and monastic institutions came in existence and the people saw in these structures a compassionate Buddha. For the masses all these religious structures were the *Dharmakāya* of the Buddha. These religious structures were virtually the memorial marks of the Buddha. The philosophy of Buddha was translated into practice both by the monk community and the laity alike. Sri Lankans are proud that they followed the original Buddhism, i.e. Theravāda form of Buddhism. The process of urbanization was also accelerated with the introduction of Buddhism. In every walk of life — arts, letters, manners, scholarship — Buddhist thought and culture made its indelible imprint on the life of Sri Lankans.

In order to project a panoramic view of the life of the Sri Lankan people, we must peep into the history of the introduction of Buddhism in Sri Lanka. The tremendous zeal and commitment of Sri Lankans in accepting this alien faith is quite interesting. While Buddhism entered Tibet for the first time, it had to face the aggressive hostility of the Tibetans who were wedded to Bon faith but this was not the case in Sri Lanka. Sri Lankans were very receptive.

Mahinda and Introduction of Buddhism in Sri Lanka

The Ceylonese Chronicles — *Dīpavaṁsa* and *Mahāvaṁsa* — attribute the introduction of Buddhism to Ceylon to Aśoka's son Mahinda who came to the island about the middle of third century BCE. Walapola Rahula[1] writes in his *History of Buddhism in Ceylon* that although this may be regarded as the official introduction of Buddhism to Ceylon, it is not reasonable to believe that information about the Buddha and his teachings and the news of the great activities of the mighty Buddhist Emperor of India had not reached the Island earlier. We have seen that from the time of Vijaya (483-445 BCE) there had been constant intercourse between the two countries.

There may be dispute about the introduction of Buddhism in Ceylon among the scholars but we can reasonably say that as an organized institution Buddhism was decidedly introduced in Sri Lanka by Mahinda. Mahinda came to Ceylon with four other *theras*. His purpose in bringing them was evidently to confer the *Upāsapāda* on anyone who desired to get it. In this party which consisted of seven, there were two who were too close in relations. Sumana Samanera, the son of Mahinda's sister Saṅghamitrā and Baṇḍuka Upāsaka, the son of his mother's sister's daughter. Their inclusion in the party signified, perhaps, a particular intimacy with and friendliness towards Ceylon. When Mahinda reached Ceylon Devanāmpiya-Tissa (247-207 BCE) was ruling the island. Mahinda came to Ceylon when he was a young man

1. p. 48.

of thirty-two. His arrival in this island can be regarded as the beginning of the Sinhalese culture. He brought here not only a new religion but also a whole civilization then at the heights of its glory. He introduced art and architecture into the island along with *saṅghārāma*s and *cetiya*s. The bringing of the *bodhi* branch and relics of the Buddha along with his *pātra* (alms bowl) further strengthened the great cultural link between India and Ceylon. The relics of the Buddha were regarded as representing the Buddha himself and their enshrinement. Enshrinement was as good as Buddha's residence in Laṅkā. At the time of planting of *bodhi* branch which was an occasion of great historical importance, representatives from all parts of the island were present. Subsequently the saplings of this *bodhi* were planted in Anurādhapura and its vicinity and in Jambukilapattana and in the village of Tivikka Brāhmaṇa in the north, in Kajaragāma (Kataragāma) in the south and in Candangāma. Later, some 32 saplings were distributed all over the island.

The *pātra-dhātū* (the alms bowl of the Buddha) was kept within the king's house and it became a national "palladium" of the Sinhalese, just as happened later to the Tooth Relic. As the brotherhood of the *bhikkhu*s increased in number Devanāmpiya-Tissa had to establish several monasteries besides the *mahāvihāra* and *cetiya-pabbata*. The *Mahāvaṁsa* records that the place where those who entered the Order of monks from noble families lived became Issarasamanaka (place of noble monks), and the place where those who entered the order from the vaiśya caste lived become Vessagiri (mountain of the vaiśyas). Devanāmpiya-Tissa also built a public refectory called Mahāpāli in Anurādhapura for the use of the Saṅgha. He is also said to have built a *vihāra* in Jambukilapattana in Nāgadīpa, and the well known Tissa Mahāvihāra.

During his first conversation with Devanāmpiya-Tissa, Mahinda, in order to gauge the king's intelligence and capacity to understand, put to him some questions. The test, which can be regarded as the first intelligent test recorded in history and, though simple and easy at first glance required a clear and acute mind to answer it. Mahinda was convinced that Devanāmpiya-Tissa was intelligent enough to understand the teaching of the Buddha and proceeded at once to preach the *Cūlahatthipadopama-sutta* to him. The selection of this *sutta* by Mahinda for his first sermon was very appropriate. The *sutta* gives a clear idea of the Buddha *Dhamma* and *Saṅgha* and describes how one is converted to Buddhism and becomes a *bhikku*. It also describes in detail the simple and holy life of a *bhikku*, the sublime qualities he practises and possesses, the things from which he abstains, the various stages of development in his life and his attainment of Arahatship which is the final fruit in Buddhism. The *sutta* contains also almost all the principle teachings of Buddhism, such as the Four Noble Truths. Apart from a general knowledge of Buddhism it was necessary for Mahinda to convey to his host, who knew nothing about Buddhist practices, an idea of the *Saṅgha* and its mode of life, so that the king might learn how to treat his new guests. At the end of the sermon Devanāmpiya-Tissa and his retinue expressed their willingness to embrace the new faith.

Mahinda is reported to have preached on the second day of his arrival in Ceylon the *Peṭavatthu* and the *Vimānavatthu*, two Buddhist texts dealing with the spirits of the dead. This perhaps indicates that Mahinda, at the very beginning of his missionary activities thought of winning the hearts of the people by appealing to their sentiments through a sermon which they could easily understand and appreciate. Incidentally, it must be told that Mahinda came to Ceylon when he was thirty-two and he died at the ripe age of eighty at Ceitya Pabbata while spending *vassa* retreat there during the eighth year of King Utteya (200 BCE), Devanāmpiya-Tissa's younger brother and successor to the throne. *Cetiyas* enshrining his relics were built at Anurādhapura, Ceitya Pabbata and several other places in Sri Lanka. Saṅghamitrā died in the following year at the Hatthathak nunnery at Anurādhapura. Buddhaghoṣa says that Mahinda brought to the island of the Sinhalese, commentaries of the *Tripiṭaka* and put them in Sinhalese for the benefit for the people of the Island. He thus made Sinhalese a literary language and inaugurated its literature. It is probable that he introduced Aśokan alphabets as well. Saṅghamitrā's influence over the women of Sri Lanka in moulding their life and character was equally great.

Eulogizing the role and contributions of Mahinda and Devanāmpiya-Tissa in the propagation of Buddhist faith on this island Walpola Rahula[2] writes that the remarkable success of Mahinda's mission and the unusually rapid spread of Buddhism in the island were due to many reasons. Mahinda's arrival was the consummation of a series of social, cultural and diplomatic relations between India and Ceylon. Devanāmpiya-Tissa was eager to earn the friendship of Aśoka. After the king of Ceylon and the important ministers who were his relatives had accepted Buddhism, the rest was plain sailing. Although there were a number of various religious groups scattered about the country, there was none systematically organized or powerful enough to oppose the new faith. On the other hand, Buddhism offered to the people of Ceylon a new order of life which was far superior to that which they had known and followed so far. The example of the simple, saintly life of the monks who devoted their time for the good of the many was an inspiration to the king as well as to the peasant. The code of morality that the new religion taught was certainly conducive to a happy and peaceful home life.

2. *History of Buddhism in Ceylon*, p. 60.

Now it is clear that during the forty-eight years that Mahinda worked in Ceylon, Buddhism was firmly established in the island and spread to most parts of the country. The following centuries saw a very rapid progress of the new faith among the people. According to the *Mahāvaṁsa* many hundreds of *vihāras*, great and small, were established during the period. Devanāmpiya-Tissa's four brothers who ruled in succession after him at Anurādhapura did their best to spread the religion by opening new centres and providing maintenance for *bhikkhus*. Kakavanna Tissa and other rulers of Rohana, the southern principality, built a large number of *vihāras*. Among these all Tissamaharama, Cittalapabbata (the famous centres of meditation) and Kirivehera at Kataragāma should be mentioned. Tissa of Kalyāni (modern Kalaniya) played his part in propagating Buddhism in the western principality. Kakavanna's younger son, Tissa, was in charge of Dighavapi in the eastern province of the Island.

Incidentally, it must be mentioned here that the honorific term "Devanāmpiya" was conferred by Aśoka as an imperial honour upon the king of Ceylon whose name was only Tissa. No king in Ceylon before Devanāmpiya seems to have used this prefix.[3] Mahinda's father Aśoka advised Devanāmpiya-Tissa, through the envoys, to hold a proper coronation ceremony and sent him the articles used at a king's coronation in India. As regards the overseas kingdom's relations with his empire, he touched upon his state-policy of *Dhamma-Vijaya* (conquest through *Dhamma*), telling the envoys that it was "the *Dhamma* of the *Sākyaputta*" that he had adopted and his relations therefore with other states would be regulated by that state policy. His message to the Ceylonese king was : "I have taken refuge in the Buddha, the *Dhamma* and the *Saṅgha*. I have declared myself a lay disciple in the religion of the *Sākyaputta* (vide Minor Rock Edict, No. 1; A.C. Sen's *Aśoka's*

3. *Buddhism in East Asia*, by Sukumar Dutt, p. 25.

Edicts pp. 52-53). Seek then, even though the best of men, refuge in these three best of gems (*Triratna* — Buddha, *Dhamma* and *Saṅgha*), converting thy mind will believing heart." The suggestion was that the desired entente cordiale could be established through adoption by Ceylon of the "religion of the *Sākyaputta*." The king, dropping the humble title of Gāmaṇi, adopted the dignified Maurya title of Devanāmpiya; he had a regular coronation, and embraced the religion recommended by the Indian emperor. The title Devanāmpiya was kept up by the kings of Ceylon till the middle of the sixth century CE. The conversion of the Ceylonese to Buddhism went on with vigour under Mahinda's guidance.

When Mahinda reached Sri Lanka for the first time, he was accorded a rousing welcome by the king at Anurādhapura. Next morning Mahinda addressed the royal household. He selected for the occasion a subject which would appeal to an audience mainly consisting of the ladies of the king's house. He related to them stories from the *Peṭavatthu* and *Vimānavatthu*, two Pāli texts which deal with the dead in the *Peta*-world and in the *Deva-loka* (Heavenly world) according to their past *karma*. This must have appealed to the audience already possessing faith in the spirit of the dead, and would make Buddhism agreeable and acceptable to them. Mahinda ended his sermon by expounding the Four Noble Truth of Buddhism according to the *Saccasaṁyuta*. Here he had occasion to show them how dreadful was *saṁsāra*, the cycle of the births and deaths they were endlessly subjected to. At Anurādhapura, Mahinda kept on sermonizing for many days before the masses. Mahinda stayed in Anurādhapura for 26 days. He delivered a number of sermons to convince the people of the values of the new faith. During this period things moved rapidly and great changes took place. Most of these sermons dealt with the transitoriness of life, the dreadful nature of *saṁsāra* and ways to attain *nibbāna*. His sermons also included the *Dhammacakkappavattana-sutta* which deals with the fundamental teachings of the Buddha. On the twenty-seventh day Mahinda left Anurādhapura and went to Missaka-Pabbata to spend *vassa-vās*. The same day the king's nephew Mahā-Arittha, the minister, with fifty-five others joined the Order of the *Saṅgha*. In all there were sixty-two monks at the Missaka-Pabbata for the first *vassa* season. Meanwhile, the sub-queen Anūlā and her companions also joined the Order on Mahinda's suggestion. Devanāmpiya-Tissa dispatched an embassy to the court of Emperor Aśoka to fetch Theri Saṅghamittā, and Anūlā and her companions awaited her arrival in *upāsikā-vihāra* built for them on one side of the city. On the suggestion of Mahinda, Devanāmpiya-Tissa ordered the construction of a *cetiya* to enshrine the relics of the Buddha. Sumana Sāmanera, the grandson of Aśoka obtained the right collarbone, and a large quantity of other bone relics together with the alms-bowl of the Buddha. These relics were kept at Missaka-Pabbata for the time being, and henceforth the mountain was named as Ceitya-pabbata. The collarbone of the Buddha was enshrined in the Thuparam Dagaba which thus became the first *cetiya* to be built in Ceylon. Anūlā and her companions were initiated by Saṅghamittā and they stayed in Hatthathaka Vihāra.

It was largely due to the magnanimity and patronage of Devanāmpiya-Tissa and the formidable missionary zeal of Mahinda that Buddhism was firmly established in the soil of Sri Lanka. The king by embracing Buddhism showed the example to the public, and inspired by the king the people of Sri Lanka embraced the faith with great fervour and enthusiasm. Devanāmpiya-Tissa offered the *Mahāmeghavana* to the *Saṅgha*. This gift was the expression of the inner religious devotion of the kings to the Buddhist *Saṅgha*. After the *Mahāmeghavana* was offered to the *Saṅgha*, Mahinda at once set about to plan the headquarters of Buddhism which in later times became the famous Mahāvihāra, the great centre of

Buddhist culture and learning in the Island, the stronghold of the Theravāda. There is very good reason to believe that what later came to be called the holy city of Anurādhapura was originally planned and laid out by Mahinda. There was no one at the time in Ceylon better educated, cultured and refined, more widely travelled and better informed than Mahinda himself. He had lived in large cities, like Pāṭaliputra, the magnificent capital of the Magadhan Empire; he had seen great monasteries like Aśokārama built by his father and Cetiyagiri (modern Sāñcī) in Vidiśā built by his mother. There was no one therefore who could plan an *arama*, a monastery, better.

Mahinda's sole concern was that the religion of the Buddha should secure a firm hold in the island and continue to develop for the benefit of the people. If this achievement could be called a conquest, it was only a moral, spiritual, and cultural conquest of the highest order conceivable, and not a political or economic acquisition.

Missionary Activities of Sri Lankan Royalty

Devanāmpiya-Tissa ruled in Ceylon for 40 years. It was in the first year of his reign that Buddhism was introduced. Both Mahinda and Saṅghamittā survived Devanāmpiya-Tissa. They spent nearly 48 years in the island. They passed away in the reign of King Uttiya (207-197 BCE), brother and successor of Devanāmpiya-Tissa. The hierarchy of the disciples was continued in pupilary succession. Thera Arittha succeeded Mahinda Thera. He was in turn succeeded by Isidatta, Kālasumana, Dhiganāma and Dhigasumana. Twenty years after the death of Uttiya, the Tamilians of south India seized Anurādhapura. During their domination, the progress of Buddhism was restarted. It was again Duṭṭa-Gāmiṇī (101-77 BCE) who restored the last glories of Sinhalese and their religion. The Tamil King Elara (145-101 BCE) was defeated in a battle by Duṭṭa-Gāmiṇī and the sovereignty of the Sinhalese rulers was again established. Buddhism gained momentum during his reign. Even the two Tamils, Sena and Guttika (177-155 BCE) who ruled at Anurādhapura about 30 years before Elara seem to have been Buddhists. Duṭṭa-Gāmiṇī erected many religious edifices, such as the Mahathapa (Ruvanvalisaya), Maricavatti (Mirisavitiya) and the nine-storeyed Lohapasada which was the Uposatha house of the Mahāvihāra. He made Buddhism the pride of his people and according to the *Mahāvaṁsa* very large numbers of people came from foreign countries to see the dedication festival of the Mahattupa. The prototype of the modern *Vesāk* festival is the first referred to during this period. Duṭṭa-Gāmiṇī is said to have held 24 *Vesākha-Pūjās*. Another great patron of Buddhism was Vaṭṭagāmiṇī-Abhaya (29-17 BCE) who defeated the Tamils and reoccupied Anurādhapura after a supreme struggle. It must be mentioned here that a brāhmaṇa named Tissa (or Tīya) in Rohaṇa declared war on Vaṭṭagāmiṇī (43 BCE). Meanwhile, seven Tamils from south India landed at Mahatittha (Mannar) with strong forces and marched towards Anurādhapura. The country from the south to the north was devastated by war. From 43 BCE for 14 years five Tamils ruled in succession at Anurādhapura. King Vaṭṭagāmiṇī lay in hiding in remote places during the period. Vaṭṭagāmiṇī demolished the Giri monastery of the *Nigaṇṭhas* (Jains) and built the Great Abhayagiri-Vihāra prefixing his name to it. Soon after the establishment of the Abhayagiri-Vihāra there were dissensions in the *Saṅgha*.

The following period of about three centuries was attended by unusual vicissitudes of history. Gothabhaya (CE 309-22) was a strong king, and did a great deal to improve the material conditions of Buddhism by providing in abundance for the requisites for *bhikkhus*, repairing old monasteries, building new ones, and holding popular festivals such as the *Vesākha-Pūjā*. The difference between Anurādhapura Mahāvihāra and Abhayagiri Mahāvihāra continued for a long time and the monks and the kings always tried to settle the disputes. The political situation in Ceylon from about the middle of the fifth century CE until the third quarter of the eleventh century CE was not favourable towards the progress of Buddhism.

During the course of the eighth century or even much before that, to be precise, from the time of introduction of Buddhism in Ceylon, a bewildering vast commentarial literature was created in the monasteries of Sri Lanka and it was here that for the first time the *Tripiṭaka*s were compiled into black and white. Going to Sri Lanka was an academic pilgrimage, and two great commentators Buddhadatta and Buddhaghoṣa went there and did a commendable job. *Vissudhimagga* was written on the motivation of the monk scholars of Anurādhapura Mahāvihāra.

Once Buddhism became the faith of Sri Lanka, it exercised its ethico-spiritual influence on the religious, social and political life of Sri Lankans. But the clash between Tamilians and native Sinhalese is still going on. It is a great irony that even among the Buddhist fraternity of Sri Lanka there was a lot of sectarian disagreement and difference between the followers of Anurādhapura and Abhayagiri Mahāvihāras. Edward Conze[4] in his *A Short History of Buddhism* writes that in CE 1160 a Council at Anurādhapura terminated the dissensions between the Mahāvihāra and its rivals by the suppression of the latter. Soon after CE 1200 there was a collapse, not so much of Buddhism, as of the social system which supported it. Invasions from India weakened the central power, which could no longer enforce the irrigation works, and soon Muslim pirates and even Chinese eunuchs ruled over large stretches of the land. The economic basis of the *Saṅgha* in this way became extremely precarious. Later on, beginning in the sixteenth century the Portuguese persecuted Buddhism, claimed to have destroyed

4. pp. 103-04.

the Sacred Tooth, and forced many Ceylonese to become Roman Catholics; then followed the Dutch and finally the English (until 1948). The long centuries of European rule did great harm to the Buddhist cause. The *Saṅgha* often died out completely, and monks had to be repeatedly imported from Burma and Siam, in the seventeenth, eighteenth, and nineteenth centuries. The revival began about 1880, first stimulated by the Theosophical Society, and then carried out under the impulse of awakening nationalism. Since that time Ceylonese Buddhists have become increasingly active and have done a great deal of valuable scholarly work, though generally within the limit of a rather narrow orthodoxy. In 1950 they took the lead in trying to bring all Buddhist countries together, and set up the World Fellowship of Buddhists.

In this context the observations of John Snelling[5] are that the revival of Buddhism got fully under way in Sri Lanka towards the end of the nineteenth century. Venerable Sri Sumangala and Venerable Dharmananda established two Buddhist monastic colleges, the Vidyodaya and the Vidyolankara Pirivenas (monastic colleges) in 1873 and 1875 respectively. Here traditional education in Buddhism, Pāli, Sanskrit and Sinhalese history and related subjects could be obtained. At about the same time a brilliant young monk named Ven. Mohottivatte Gunananda challenged the Christians to an open religious debate. The Christians took up the challenge, most notably at Pandura in 1873, when they bandied arguments rather unsuccessfully with Ven. Gunananda in public for about a week. Reports of these debates got into the foreign newspapers and so attracted the attention of the distinguished pioneer theosophist, Colonel Henery Steel Olcott, in the U.S.A. He came to Sri Lanka with the leader of the Theosophical Society, Madame H.P. Blavatsky, and both

5. *The Buddhist Handbook*, pp. 124-25.

of them "took Pansl" (i.e. the Five Percepts) at Galle in 1880. Thereafter the Theosophists worked alongside native Buddhist idealists like Ven. Sri Sumangala and Anāgārika Dharmapāla (David Hewavitarne, 1864–1933), to regenerate Sinhalese Buddhism. The movement was very successful. In 1887, after 12 years of effort, there were 46 schools on the island providing Buddhist education whereas formerly there had been only Christian schools. By 1903 there were 174 Buddhist training schools. During the twentieth century numerous Europeans had received ordination and/or Buddhist training in Sri Lanka, notably the German-born *bhikkhu*, Ven. Nyanaponika, and the British-born *bhikku* Ven. Nanamuli. The island hermitage at Dodandawa (Galle district) has been a notable centre for training European *bhikkhus*. Meanwhile the Buddhist Publication Society, founded by Ven. Nyanaponika, has done much useful Buddhist literary propaganda work in the English language. Its headquarters are in Kandy. Mention must be made of the noble efforts made by the Sri Lankans themselves to help bring knowledge of Buddhism to the West. A Sri Lankan Buddhist *vihāra* was established in London in 1926 by Anāgārika Dharmapāla, and though closed in 1940, was reopened in 1954 by Ven. Narada Mahāthera, who also performed valuable *Dhammadita* (or Buddhist missionary) work elsewhere, notably in Indonesia and Vietnam. Many important *bhikkhu* teachers have resided at the London *vihāra*. Meanwhile, Dr G.P. Malalasekera, the professional diplomat and scholar, was also a notable ambassador for Buddhism in the West. He became the first Editor-in-Chief of the Sri Lankan Government-sponsored *Encylopaedia of Buddhism* (1966). Buddhist monks have enjoyed a high measure of social influence, even of political power, right from the early days of Buddhism upon the island. They have also been rich and powerful landowners. Since national independence was won in 1947, the role of the monk as a political animal has been a matter of keen controversy.

K.L. Hazra[6] in his *History of Theravāda Buddhism in South-East Asia* throws a flood of light on the development of rival sects of Buddhism and Buddhist traditions of Anurādhapura Mahāvihāra and Abhayagiri-Vihāra, and writes that the Mahāvihāra, the seat of Theravāda Buddhism and the citadel of orthodoxy, played an important role in the history of Buddhism in Ceylon. Its conflict with the Abhayagiri-Vihāra (built by Vaṭṭagāmiṇī-Abhaya 29-17 BCE) and other rival sects of Buddhism form the main theme of the religious history of Ceylon. Almost all the kings patronized either the Abhayagiri-Vihāra or the Anurādhapura Mahāvihāra. Although the Ceylon Chronicles and other religious texts often refer to the rise of new sects opposed to the Theravāda, and in spite of the patronage offered to the Abhayagiri-Vihāra by a few rulers and occasional disagreements between the Mahāvihāra (at Anurādhapura) and the State regarding religious matters, the Mahāvihāra and its tradition remained pre-eminent throughout the religious history of Ceylon. In the third century CE, Voharika Tissa, by suppressing the Vetulyavāda, purified the religion. The suppression of the Vetulyavāda by King Gothabhaya took place in the first half of the fourth century CE. Saṅghamittā, a Mahāyāna Buddhist monk, arrived in Ceylon during this time and was patronized by Mahāsena (CE 334-362) after his accession. Due to Mahāsena's hostile attitude toward the Mahāvihāra many monks belonging to this sect fled to Rohana in southern Ceylon and to the Malay hills. Many buildings including the Lohapasada of the Mahāvihāra were demolished by the ruler, but Meghavanna Abhaya, a minister of the Mahāsena, restored the Mahāvihāra. The Jetavanarama (Jetavana-Vihāra) was

6. p. 50 ff.

constructed by the King Mahāsena within the precincts of the Mahāvihāra in spite of the protests by the latter *vihāra*, and it was dedicated to Tissa, a friend of the king who dwelt in the *Dakkhinarāma*. But the Chief Minister (Mahamacco) in spite of the king's opposition disrobed Tissa. This shows that Mahāsena towards the end of his reign was quite helpless to do anything against the followers of Mahāvihāra. The Chinese traveller Fa-Hien, who visited Ceylon, in the reign of Buddhism, at the beginning of the fifth century CE, stayed at the Abhayagiri-Vihāra. He states that there were 5000 monks at the Abhayagiri-Vihāra and 3000 monks at the Mahāvihāra. The Chinese traveller's account indicates that the Abhayagiri-Vihāra was flourishing at this time. But it is doubtful whether the Mahāvihāra had lost its popularity to the extent indicated by the Chinese traveller. It was about this time, in the reign of Mahānāma (CE 409-31), that Buddhaghoṣa, the great commentator, on hearing of the fame and scholastic activities of the monks of the Mahāvihāra, came to Anurādhapura and stayed at the Mahāvihāra and translated the Sinhala commentaries on the *Tripiṭaka* into the Pāli language. At the beginning of the sixth century CE, a further purification of the Buddhist *Saṅgha* took place during the reign of Moggallāna I. His son, Kumāra Dhātusena (CE 513-22) also purified the Buddhist *Saṅgha*. Towards the end of the sixth century CE, the followers of the Vetulyavāda were defeated by Jotipalathera in a public controversy. The *Nikāyasaṅgrahava* states that after the defeat of this sect in a public controversy, the Vetulyavāda had lost its popularity and the monks of the two *Nikāya*s the Abhayagiri-Vihāra and Jetavana-Vihāra dismissed pride and lived in submission to the Mahāvihāra. This indicates the importance of the Mahāvihāra in the sixth century CE. From the Chinese records and several Sanskrit inscriptions belonging to this period we learn that there was frequent religious intercourse between Ceylon and India and many Ceylonese monks visited the Buddhist shrines at Bodh-Gayā. The Chinese text, *Hing-Tchoan* of Wang Hiuen ts'e refers to the erection of a monastery at Bodh-Gayā by a ruler of Ceylon for the accommodation of monks from Ceylon. Two Sanskrit inscriptions, belonging to the sixth century CE found at Bodh-Gayā, mention the erection of a Buddhist monastery and the presentation of the statue of the Buddha to the Bodh-Gayā monastery by Mahānāma, a Ceylonese monk of the sixth century CE. Another inscription, belonging to the sixth or seventh century CE found at Bodh-Gayā refers to Prakhyātakīrtti, a Sinhalese monk, who erected a dwelling place at Bodh-Gayā. He is said to have belonged to the royal family of Ceylon. In the seventh century CE the king of Kaliṅga visited Ceylon and became a monk under Jotipālathera. He was followed by his wife and minister who entered the *Saṅgha*. A recital of the *Tripiṭaka* was held under the patronage of Dall Moggallāna III (CE 611-617), and an impetus was given to Buddhist literary activity.

King Silameghavanna (CE 619-628), in order to ensure the unity among the monks in the *Saṅgha* invited the monks of the Mahāvihāra and other fraternities (very probably monks of the Abhayagiri-Vihāra and Jetavanarama) and asked them to observe the *uposatha* ceremony in one place. He thought that the religion would progress if the monks of the different fraternities worked together, but he was refused. The Mahāvihāra monks did not agree to hold the *uposatha* ceremony with the others and the king was powerless to do anything against the monks of the Mahāvihāra. Dathopatissa II (CE 659-67) wanted to erect a *vihāra* for the Abhayagiri-Vihāra. But the monks of the Mahāvihāra protested against the king's idea. But the latter carried out his plan. The monks of the Mahāvihāra applied the *Pattanikkujjanakamma* "turning down of the alms bowl" on King Dathopatissa II. It would seem that the monks of Mahāvihāra were powerful enough to openly criticize the acts of the king. These facts clearly signify the important position occupied by the Mahāvihāra in the seventh century CE. During this period all the three *Nikāya*s of Ceylon flourished under royal patronage. Maintenance of villages was sanctioned by the king of the dwellers of the three *Nikāya*s. Aggabodhi VII (CE 766-822) purified the Buddhist *Saṅgha* and patronized the three *Nikāya*s.

Impact of Buddhism on Sri Lanka

In the beginning Buddhism could be firmly established in Sri Lanka due to royal patronage. The initiatives taken by the Mauryan Emperor Aśoka the Great and Sri Lankan Emperor Devanāmpiya-Tissa paved way for the transformation of Sri Lanka into a Buddhist land and Sri Lankans into Buddhist society. Sri Lankan people at large were in the grip of superstitions and were reigned by primitive beliefs of ancestors and tree-worship. Besides there was a plethora of local tribal traditions at the time of introduction of Buddhism in Sri Lanka. Its people were mostly uneducated and dogmatic. This isolated island was a small tract of land and every part of it was accessible. Rightly speaking they all were living in a dark age. Buddhism brought a new hope and a new light for them. It was very easy to propagate the Buddhist faith, its thought and culture, its rituals and practices, among the masses in a monarchical form of government. We know that the order and wishes of the king were not less than divine dictates. The untiring and missionary enthusiasm and activism of Mahinda and Saṅghamittā added a lot to ensure that people are largely attracted towards this philanthrophic religion. The efforts of royalty and the indefatigable missionary zeal of the royal converts in the propagation of Buddhist teachings and Buddhist way of life brought about incredibly great results. Many religious, foundation monasteries, *vihāras*, *stūpas*, shrines and religious parks came up with the introduction of

Buddhism. Many rituals, ceremonies and festivals related to Buddhism were also brought with the harbingers of the Enlightenment of Buddhist thought and culture from India to Sri Lanka. It was all done and arranged by the kings. In order to attract the masses towards the exalted and altruistic teachings of the Buddha and ways of his life, public sermons were organized. We have already told that Sri Lankan Buddhist kings right from Devanāmpiya-Tissa to those in the subsequent centuries of the Christian era did their best and doled heavy benefactions for erecting *vihāra*s, monasteries and *stūpa*s. It is natural that the profound teachings of the Buddha were quite impenetrable to the ordinary people, and therefore, just to start with they introduced the *bodhi* tree, *stūpa*s and the relic worship. For the enlightened and intellectuals Buddha-*vacana*s were first committed to writing in the reign of Vaṭṭagāmiṇī and thereafter a concerted effort was made to write elaborate and exhaustive commentaries (*aṭṭakathā*s) in the two celebrated monasteries of Anurādhapura and Abhayagiri. Thus, side by side, the thought and culture of Buddhism penetrated and permeated into the religious and social life of Sri Lankans. Though there were sectarian differences among the Buddhists belonging to Anurādhapura and Abhayagiri Vihāras, as we have already said, they were settled in a Council held at Anurādhapura in CE 1160. Most of Sri Lankan population professed Buddhism to be their faith regardless of the sect which they were wedded to. We have already said how enthusiastically and devotionally the royalty of Sri Lanka embraced and propagated Buddhist thought and culture during their reigns. The adoption of Buddhism by the Sri Lankan royalty as their religion accelerated the pace of construction of *vihāra*s and *stūpa*s on the whole tract of Sri Lankan island. Due to this kind of royal patronage Buddhist thought and culture made its conspicuous presence in every part of Sri Lanka. On imitation of Jetavana, Velūvana and

Aśokārama many religious parks and Saṅghāramas were constructed thoughout the length and breadth of the island.

It needs to be reiterated that extensive propagation and large-scale religio-cultural transformation of Buddhism in Sri Lanka could be made incredibly successful due to the royal patronage. The impact of the Buddhism on the royalty was so deep-rooted that the kings could inculcate in the minds of their subjects the sublimity and universality of such an altruistic everywhere-pacifying Buddhist thought and culture.

Once again it must be mentioned that Mahinda during his long years of ministration and sermonizing had produced a large number of enlightened and pious Buddhist propagators in Sri Lanka who further proved themselves — both by their action and dedication — to be the true torch-bearers of the *Dharma* and the *Saṅgha*. Saṅghamittā had also left a glorious and large legacy of the devout nuns who kept the flame of *Dharma* kindled from generation to generation. While all this was going on, Sri Lankans were too vigilant and caring in recording the history of the *Dharma* to which they were wedded. *Dīpavaṁsa* and *Mahāvaṁsa* are eloquent testimony of the historical sense that the Buddhist fraternity of Sri Lankans had. Sri Lankans were very receptive to the thought and culture and Buddhism was equally accommodating. Buddhism imbibed some of the local traditions of the pre-Buddhist Sri Lankan society. It was always submissive and assimilative.

In this context the observations of Kitsiri Malalgoda[7] are worth quoting. Quoting many authorities of the subject, he remarks that Buddhism was introduced in Ceylon during a period when the connection between Buddhism and political authority was already developed to a high degree under Aśoka in India. This feature had a marked impact on the kind of Buddhist institutions that eventually developed in the Island.

7. *Buddhism in Sinhalese Society, 1750–1900,* p. 12 ff.

From the very beginning (the first to be won over to Buddhism was the king himself), Buddhism came to be very closely associated with the institution of kingship in Ceylon. Indeed, it has been plausibly argued that the reign of the Tissa (250-210 BCE), who was Aśoka's contemporary in Ceylon, established a landmark not merely in the religious but also in the political history of the island. For it witnessed the formal establishment of the institution of the kingship, with all its ritualistic paraphernalia as well as the monarchical form of government in place of the more popular forms of government that had prevailed since the time of the early Aryan settlements. An *abhiṣeka* (consecration) ceremony — a necessary rite of passage in the Indian tradition whereby a prince is acknowledged as sovereign — was held in Ceylon with Aśoka's help and Tissa, as well as a number of his successors, assumed that Mauryan royal title *Devanāmpiya*, meaning "beloved of the Gods." These political contacts with India preceded the subsequent religious contacts and paved the way for the acceptance and establishment of the doctrines preached by Aśoka's missionaries. And if the idea and institution of kingship helped to unite the country at a political level, the introduction of Buddhism helped to consolidate this unity at an ideological level. Inferences based on historical and archaeological research have ascertained with considerable success aspects of religious beliefs and practices that prevailed in pre-Buddhist Ceylon. Such beliefs and practices, deriving their elements from a multitude of sources, served the religious needs of the masses who lived in relatively isolated communities. But this primordial and parochial character of religion and society necessarily hindered ideological unification at wider levels, and thus created a gap which became all the more conspicuous when unification was gradually attained at the political level. It was precisely this gap that was filled by the establishment of Buddhism. With this event, over and above the pre-Buddhist "little tradition" was introduced a Buddhist "great tradition" a tradition which came to embody the "central value system" or the official ideology of the kingdom. The new symbol and institutions, places and objects of worship that cohered around the centre of the "great community" inspired veneration at the wider social level. The *bodhi* tree and the *cetiya* (in which the corporeal relics of the Buddha were enshrined) became symbols of political unity. Gorgeous ceremonies giving expression to mass religiosity were held in connection with these sacred objects and the Chronicles as well many other contemporary records are replete with references to them. One of them which rose to pre-eminence was the festival connected with the Tooth Relic, which was brought to Ceylon and received with much honour and festivity during the reign of Siri-Meghavanna (CE 301-28). It was kept in a shrine within the royal precincts and proclamations were issued that a grand festival should be celebrated in its honour when the Relic was temporarily removed from the palace to the Abhayagiri monastery each year. Fa-Hien, who visited Ceylon a few year after the arrival of the Tooth Relic, witnessed this annual festival and has left a graphic account of it. The Tooth Relic eventually became the palladium of the Sinhalese kings and therefore was taken from one city to another when the capital was shifted during the course of Ceylon history. Thus Parākramabāhu I (CE 1153-83) held a grand festival in its honour when it was finally brought to Polonnaruva after a long series of adventures in Rohana, where rival claimants to the throne fought among themselves to take possession of this symbol of sovereignty. The *Dalada Sirita* (History of the Tooth Relic), a fourteenth-century prose work, described in detail the procedure in which this work was written. All those accounts clearly point to immense religio-political significance of festivals of this sort. The patronage extended, and the conspicuous role played by the king himself, symbolized the fundamental unity of the sacred values that held society together. These intermittent rituals bringing the peripheral masses repeatedly in contact with the sacred values of the centre generated that group feeling, the transcendental social factor *sui generis* that Durkheim so vividly portrayed. "There can be no society," wrote Durkheim, "which does not feel the need of upholding and reaffirming at regular intervals the collective sentiments and the collective ideas which make its unity and its personality." Now this moral remaking cannot be achieved except by the means of reunions, assemblies and meetings where the individuals, being closely united to one another, reaffirm in common sentiments; hence come ceremonies.

The pre-Buddhist Ceylon society was divided into caste and classes in the same way as in India; but in Buddhist Ceylon the scheme was under some modification through Buddhist influence. There was the king as the absolute ruler over the whole state; his ministers, generals and other officers who were drawn from the nobility. Brāhmaṇas were mentioned occasionally in the Buddhist Ceylon. But they were not able to form themselves into a consolidated group as a Sinhalese caste with vested rights and interests. In a Buddhist society they had no religious rites and ceremonies to perform, and their place was occupied by *bhikkhus* as teachers and advisers of the community. If brāhmaṇas were absorbed in the Sinhalese Buddhist community, they lost their individuality automatically, and we hear no more of them as brāhmaṇas. The impact of Buddhist thought and culture on Sri Lankan people was so great that they adopted Buddhist names as their own names in Sri Lanka, like Buddhadāsa, Saṅgha-Tissa, Saṅghadatta, Moggallāna, Kassapa and Mahinda. King Buddhadāsa is said to have given to his sons the names of the great disciples of the Buddha. The adoption of Buddhist name seems to have become a vogue somewhat later, for no

Buddhist names appear among the early Buddhist kings. It is interesting in this connection to observe the influence exercised by different Buddhist relics on personal names. The branch of the *bodhi* tree at Anurādhapura and the Buddha's Tooth, both brought from India, were the two most important Buddhist relics. The Tooth Relic was of greater importance and was always in the royal possession. Many were the kings who compounded the word *dātha* (tooth) with their names, like Dātha-Pabhuti, Dathopatissa and Hatha-Dātha. The name of the daughter of Aggabodhi I was simply Dātha. In the same manner, the word *bodhi* was also added tc persons name like Saṅgha bodhi and Agga bodhi. There was a Thera called Bodhi-mato-Mahātissa. One of the two daughters of Kassapa I was simply called Bodhi. In the eleventh century there was a general named Kesadhātu-Kassapa. Some added to their name the word *dhātu* without any specification, as in the case of Dhātu-Sena. It may be that there was a belief that the name of a relic added on to a personal name brought blessing and happiness to the person who bore it. In ancient Buddhist Sri Lanka the *Uposatha* (*poyā*) day was a public holiday. We learn from the Badulla Pillar inscription that all business stopped on *poyā* days. Agga bodhi VIII (CE 801-812) had prohibited fish, meat and liquor from being brought into the city on *poyā* days. The *poyā* day was meant for observances like *ata-sīla* (*atthaṅga-sīla*) and religious activities. There were four such days in a month: full moon and new moon and two quarter-moon days. All these four were public holidays. Incidentally, it must be mentioned here that the Tooth Relic was, from the very beginning, associated with the Abhayagiri. Therefore, its exposition and its annual festival were held in Abhayagiri-Vihāra. There was a particular building for Tooth Relic. The left eye-tooth of the Buddha (Vamadatha-*dhātu*) was brought to Sri Lanka by Mahāsena's son Siri Meghavanna (CE 371). It was the most precious of all Buddhist relics ever brought to

Ceylon. Meghavana has the honour of inaugurating a new festival in honour of Mahinda. It was due to the impact of the Buddha's teachings and the light of his thought and culture that several kings and commoners offered themselves, their children and relatives as "slaves" to monasteries and redeemed them again. All this was done to acquire double-fold merit in one act, first by offering them as slaves and then by donating money to monasteries to liberate them from slavery. "The offering of the kingdom" by several kings to the *śāsana* was in the same category. The monks were wise and they always returned the "offer" to the king himself with advice to administer the government justly and righteously. Religion was often no deterrent to kings. When their political power was endangered they forgot religion and killed one another, even plundered monasteries as long as they were intent on seizing the throne. But immediately after ascending the throne they became devoted and religious, and began to perform "meritorious" activities, mainly to evade the evil consequences of their path. Dāthopatissavana seized the valuable objects in the three fraternities and in the relic chambers, carried away the golden images, broke the umbrella of the *cetiya* at the Thuparama and took away the golden ornaments and precious jewels. Later he repented and to atone for his evil deeds he built the Sakavattha-Vihāra, endowing it with revenues. Among the rulers of Sri Lanka Agga bodhi IV (CE 658-674) was very pious and religious. Dathopatissa II (CE 650-658) was in the habit of observing *uposadha* and listening to the *Dhamma*.

The most outstanding feature of the religion of the laity in Sri Lanka was their tremendous devotion to the *Saṅgha*. This was due to two reasons: first, the monk was the most trusted teacher and guide and the friend of the people. He intervened at all critical moments and settled their disputes — even in state affairs. In all matters, great and small, people went to him for advice, guidance and consolation with the greatest trust. Secondly, the monk was even more helpful to them in the next world. Generally, men and women were more anxious about the security and welfare of their next world than this one. It was the monk, and no one else who could help them there. The vast majority of people had neither the earnestness nor the peace of mind necessary for practising the higher teachings of the Buddha. Nor did they have the intelligence to understand its significance. But they had the greatest respect and attachment to the religion. They could give their life in its name, even if they did not know what it really meant. So they expected monks, who were the guardians of their life and conscience, here and hereafter, to practise the religion for them. They could take part in that noble work and acquire some merit vicariously by supporting and protecting a devout *Saṅgha*, just as King Duṭṭa-Gāmaṇī supported and honoured the preachers in order to acquire some merit of the *Dhamadāna*, because he himself was not able to preach. For the ordinary layman, the monastery was the place where Buddhism was preserved. Buddhist monk scholars in Ceylon used to go on pilgrimage to places of worship not only in the island but also in India. But monks of austere practices, like *Pamsukulika*s and *Pindapātika*s, usually went alone. There were several well-known places of pilgrimage in Ceylon. The Mahābodhi and the Mahācetiya (Ruvanvalisaya) at Anurādhapura were very popular. Nāgadīpa (in modern Jaffna Peninsula) was equally popular. Tissamaha-Vihāra in the south and Kalyani cetiya in the west were two other well-known places. Sometimes Samāntakuta (*Śrī-pada*) is also mentioned. On their way to these famous places, pilgrims did not fail to worship at other religious places they happened to pass. Pilgrimages to celebrated places of worship were a common feature for the life of *bhikkhu*s. This was encouraged by the Buddha himself. The benefits of a pilgrimage at that time were manifold. It was primarily a *cetiya-*

cārikā in the ancient tradition, according to the advice of Buddha himself. Travelling through the countries, seeing new things and meeting new people was a healthy change from monotonous life of the monastery. Travelling with a learned teacher was always profitable for the *bhikkhus* who could discuss important points with him all along the way. It was like a peripatetic school. A pilgrimage also helped monks to get rid of their attachment to their own monasteries. Besides it helped in the propagation of Buddhist faith. As education was in the hands of monks it was but natural that it should be primarily religious. No one who was not well versed in religion was considered cultured. A sound knowledge of Buddhism including the *Vinaya* and the *Abhidhamma* was of primary importance for a cultured person, whether *bhikkhu* or layman. The high officials of the government were usually well versed in Buddhism. A general knowledge of Buddhism was considered essential to create good citizens. The aim of education was the development of moral and spiritual character. Mere learning devoid of this purpose was considered worthless. While every monastery in the country serves the purpose of a free school, there were centres of learning holding the position of universities for higher studies and specialized knowledge. Chief among them was the Mahāvihāra at Anurādhapura. But there were a few other centres, even more reputed then the Mahāvihāra for certain specialized knowledge. Rohana had several such places. Although learning was chiefly in the hands of the monks there were among the laity, too, both men and women who were highly learned and cultured. Some of them were so learned that the monks themselves seemed to have agreed to accept them as authority.

The Buddhist thought and culture left an indelible imprint not only on the life, thought and culture of Sri Lankans but also on their psyche. Despite political upheavals and invasion of Tamilians Buddhism helped in uniting the entire island and its people in the bond of universal fraternity.

The spiritual glow and sheen of Buddhism has lost its virginity of the days of Mahinda when it was in its purest form. But even today Sri Lanka has given us great scholars of Buddhism and there are many great centres of Buddhist learning. Buddhist thought and culture has penetrated deep into Sri Lankans' way of life. The vast majority of the lay people of Sri Lanka were not in the position to understand or practise the essential teachings of the Buddha. But they had the highest regard and deepest devotion to their faith, and they too required a way of giving expression to their religious sentiments.

The development of spiritual character was too subtle for them far beyond the grasp. They needed something more tangible and visible that appealed to their senses, and rituals, ceremonies and festivals supplied this urgently felt need.

Ceremonies and Festivals of Sri Lanka

In ancient Ceylon a very popular and great festival was held to celebrate the preaching of the *Āriyavaṁsa-Sutta*. It would appear that during several centuries before and after the fifth century CE, the *Āriyavaṁsa* was not only a popular sermon, but also an important institution held in high esteem, for the perpetuation of which grants were made by kings and ministers and rich people at the time. Even today the *Āriyavaṁsa* festival is not altogether forgotten in Ceylon. Recently at a newly discovered cave-temple near Gurulabadda in Pasdun Korale in Ceylon, the *Āriyavaṁsa-Sutta* was preached today at Dimbulagala during *vassa* season.

The *Vesāk* festival which is held in the month of *Vesāk* (May) to celebrate the birth of the Buddha was a traditional custom of the state. *Vesāk* seems to be one of the most ancient Buddhist festivals, celebrated even in India from the early days. The first reference in the *Mahāvaṁsa* to the *Vesāk* festival in Ceylon is during the time of Duṭṭa-Gāmaṇī (101-77 BCE) who is said to have celebrated 24 *Vesāk* festivals. It is quite likely, however that the festival was in existence in Ceylon much earlier. Duṭṭa-Gāmaṇī was the hero of the ancient Buddhist Ceylon, and perhaps he revived the festival and celebrated it on a grandeur scale than before. After him many kings are reported to have celebrated the festival regularly. Bhatiya (CE 38-67), conducted 28 *Vesāk* festivals while Vasabha (CE 127-71) celebrated 44 festivals. These two kings organized regular annual celebrations.

Vohara-Tissa (CE 269-291), Gothabhaya (CE 309-322), Jettha-Tissa (CE 323-333), Dalla-Moggallāna (CE 611-617), Sena II (CE 851-885), are all mentioned as kings who organized great *Vesāk* festivals. The last mentioned king is particularly said to have celebrated the *Vesāk* festival with the poor people, giving them food and drink, and clothes as they desired.

Another great festival namely, *Giribhanda Pūjā* seems to have been originated by Mahādathika Mahānaya (CE 67-79). Having completed the building of the Mahathupa at Mihintale, a task of great difficulty, the king organized this grand festival which was like a carnival to celebrate the historic occasion. We also hear of another ceremony, namely Gangārohaṇa inaugurated by Buddhadāsa's son Upatissa I in the early fifth century CE when the island was afflicted by famine and diseases. Pirit (Pāli *Paritta*) which means "protection," was a ceremony held for various purposes like exorcizing evil spirits and dispelling disease as well as blessing an auspicious occasion like occupying a new house. The Tooth Relic festival was another important festival of Sri Lanka. Mahāsena's son Siri-Meghavanna (during whose reign the Tooth Relic was brought to Ceylon) has the honour of inaugurating a new festival in honour of Mahinda. He had a life-size image of Mahinda made of gold and on the seventh day of the month of *Vap*

(Pubbakattika, October-November) took it to Ambatthala at Mihintale where they had met Devanāmpiya-Tissa. A great alms-giving was organized in honour of the occasion. From Mihintale to Anurādhapura the road was beautifully decorated. On the ninth day of the month, in a mammoth procession led by the king himself, the image was taken to Sotthiyakara, a *vihāra* built by Siri Meghavanna himself, near the eastern gate of the city. For three days the image remained there. Meanwhile the city was beautifully decorated. On the twelfth day of the month, the image was taken in procession through the city to the Mala Vihāra, and it was exhibited for three months in the courtyard of the Mahā-Bodhī. Ultimately, the image was placed in a specially built house in the south-east direction, near the royal palace. The king had also built in that house images of Itthiya and other companions of Mahinda. Endowments were made for the maintenance of the place and the performance of the festival — a decree was made that it should be held annually by all succeeding kings. *Abhiṣeka* was another ceremony popular among Sri Lankans. *Dīpa Pūjā,* the offering of lamps, was a very popular festival.

The impact of Buddhism on the life of Sri Lankans was considerably great. B. Sangharakshita[8] rightly remarks that the achievement of Ceylon, considering that it is a tiny island with a little more than five million Buddhist inhabitants, has indeed been remarkable. It gave birth to two great international Buddhist organizations, the Maha-Bodhi Society and the World Fellowship of Buddhists. With the possible exception of Japan, Ceylon, out of her scanty resources, has sent abroad far more *dharmadūtas*, or messengers of the *dharma*, than any other Buddhist land. Her contribution to culture has been no less significant and far-reaching. Scholars like Coomaraswamy,

8. *2500 years of Buddhism*, p. 400.

Malalasekera and Buddhadatta, painters like Manusri Thera and George Keyt, and writers and poets like Sri Nissanka, Dhanapala and Tambimuttu are known and respected far beyond the confines of their native land. Within the country itself, the indigenous arts and crafts, customs and traditions are being revived.

It is impossible to overrate the influence exercised by Buddhism in Ceylon. Practically her whole culture and civilization were derived from it. Pāli became the literary language of Ceylon and still holds that position. Ceylonese literature was an offshoot of Indian literature, and the art of Ceylon — architecture, sculpture and painting — was derived from India. The Ceylonese alphabet also came from India. On the other hand, the Buddhist world owes a great debt to Ceylon.

The Pāli canon has been preserved in its entirety in this island and Ceylonese Buddhism had great influence upon Burma, Cambodia, Siam and Laos, the only other countries where Theravāda Buddhism flourishes today. Ceylon was not however merely a passive recipient; it contributed to the development of Buddhism through its commentaries.

5

Impact of Buddhist Thought and Culture on Chinese People

WE have already discussed in chapter 2 of this volume about the state of society and religion in pre-Buddhist China. One thing that requires special mention here is that Chinese culture and civilization are among the most ancient and advanced civilizations of the world. In pre-Buddhist times, China was not in that barbaric age in which Tibet was languishing and stifling. Buddhism must have been a very unique and extraordinarily exalted faith because it could deeply penetrate the life and minds of the Chinese people. Adoption of an alien faith and giving preference to it over one's own faith is clearly indicative of the fact that there was something excellent in it which suited the Chinese people. It appears that the Chinese of those ancient times very honestly realized for themselves that Buddhism would guide and bind them more closely as a united society. This must have been the reason behind pushing their own thought and culture to the rear seat. Shigeo Kamata[1] in his article "Cultural Relation Between India, China and Japan" draws our attention to a very interesting issue when he says that India and China are two heterogeneous culture-spheres isolated from each other by the Himalayan ranges. How do we explain, then, the spread of a culture to the other

1. *India's Contribution to World Thought and Culture* (ed.), p. 315.

despite such completely differing cultural elements? It might be attributable to the fact that Buddhism by nature was not a religion intended for any nation, but it possessed a universal character above the narrow concept of race or frontiers of a country so that it could be adhered to by any one; however, one must also remember the fact that there were China's own peculiar cultural traits that made the reception of Buddhism possible. Especially important was the existence of Taoism which played an important role in the reception and understanding of Buddhism. Buddhism which was founded in India, was introduced to China by Buddhist missionaries through the deserts of Central Asia. With its introduction into Chinese society, it gradually strengthened its influences, and under the Sui and T'ang Dynasties assumed the form of a sinicized religious sect. Thus with the Sui-T'ang empires at its centre, a new sphere of Buddhist culture emerged in East Asia, covering Korea, Japan, Pohai, Vietnam and other countries surrounding China. The greatest factor in the spread of Buddhism throughout China was the production of the Chinese translation of Buddhist scriptures by Indian monks who came to China and by Chinese monks who went from China to India. That such an immense amount of translation work should have been accomplished in a relatively short space of time is something worthy of admiration in the cultural annals of the world.

The harbingers and missionary carriers of Buddhist thought and culture who transported and transmitted this ethico-spiritual culture and sublime thought to China had to pass through a very hostile terrain and exceedingly inhospitable climate. The route through which Buddhist thought and culture was transmitted to China from India and the countries of Central Asia is commonly known as the Silk Route.

Buddhist Cultural Impact on Chinese Life and the Silk Route

Before we focus our attention on the impact of Buddhist thought and culture on the life of Chinese people, it is imperative that we dwell on the geography of the Silk Route and the countries through which it passed. The early history of the regions through which this caravan route passed is equally important for the proper study of cultural transmission of Buddhist faith from India particularly Kashmir via Central Asia to China. Then only we would be in a position to understand the greatness of Buddhism as a world religion. It was, in fact, a universal religion without any geographical territory; it was a religion of the man, by a man and for the man. Its universal acceptability testifies to the fact that it knew no boundaries. It never differentiated between countries and races. Truly speaking, it was a religion and faith of the humans. This was the reason why its propagators never cared about the hostility and aggressiveness of the climate as well as the hazards of a risky journey through extremely dangerous and unpredictable routes. Buddhism reached China after wading through a very monstrous and challenging journey.

Oliver Wild in his write-up "The Silk Route" has thrown much light on the geography of this route. He writes that the region separating China from Europe and Western Asia is not the most hospitable in the world. Much of it is taken up by the Taklamakan desert, one of the most hostile environments on our planet. There is very little vegetation, and almost no rainfall; sandstorms are very common, and have claimed the lives of countless people. The locals have a very great respect for the "Land of Death," few travellers in the past have had anything good to say about it. It covers a vast area, through which few roads pass; caravans have skirted its edges, from one isolated oasis to the other. The climate is harsh; in the summer the daytime temperatures are in the 40s with temperature greater than 50° C measured frequently in the sub-sealevel basin of Trufan. In winter the temperature dips below –20° C. Temperatures soar in the sun, but drop very rapidly at dusk. Sandstorms here are very common and particularly dangerous due to the strength of the winds and the nature of the surface. Unlike the Gobi desert, where there are a relatively large number of oases, and water can be found not too far below the surface, the Taklamakan has much sparser resources. The land surrounding the Taklamakan is equally hostile. To the north-east lies the Gobi desert, almost as harsh in climate as the Taklamakan itself; on the remaining three sides lie some of the highest mountains in the world. To the south are the Himalaya, Karakoram and Kun-lun ranges, which provide an effective barrier separating Central Asia from the Indian subcontinent. Only a few icy passes cross these ranges, and they are some of the most difficult in the world; they are mostly over 5000 metres in altitude, and are dangerously narrow, with precipitous drop into deep ravines. To the north and west lie the Tianshan and Pamir ranges; though greener and less high, the passes crossing these have still provided more than enough problems for the travellers of the past. Approaching the area from the east, the least difficult entry is along the "Gansu Corridor," a relatively fertile strip running along the base of the Qilian mountains, separating the great Mongolian plateau and the Gobi from the Tibetan High Plateau. Coming from the west or south, the only way in is over the passes. On the eastern and western sides of the continent, the civilizations of China and the West developed. The western end of the trade route appears to have developed earlier than the eastern end, principally because of the development of the empires in the west, and the easier terrain of Persia and Syria. The Iranian empire of Persia was in control of the Middle East, extending as far as the Indian kingdoms to the east. Trade between these two neighbours were already starting to influence the cultures of these regions. This region was taken over by Alexander the Great of Macedonia, who finally conquered the Iranian empire, and colonized the area in about 330 BCE superimposing the culture of the Greeks. Although he only ruled the area until 325 BCE the effect of the Greek invasion was quite considerable. The Greek language was brought to the area, and Greek mythology was introduced. The aesthetics of Greek sculpture were merged with the ideas developed from the Indian kingdoms, and a separate local school of art emerged. By the third century BCE, the area had already become a crossroads of Asia, where Persian, Indian and Greek ideas met. It is believed that the residents of the Hunza valley in the Karakoram are the direct descendents of the army of Alexander; this valley is now followed by the Karakoram Highway, on its way from Pakistan over to Kashgar, and indicates how close to the Taklamakan Alexander may have gone. This "crossroads" region, covering the area to the south of the Hindu Kush and Karakoram ranges, now Pakistan and Afghanistan, was overrun by a number of different peoples. After the Greeks, the tribes from Palymra, in Syria and then Parthia, to the east of the Mediterranean, took over the region — these peoples were less sophisticated than the Greeks, and adopted the Greek language and coin system in this region, introducing their own influences in the field of sculpture and art. Close on the heels of the Parthians came the Yuezhi people from the northern border of the Taklamakan. They had been driven from their traditional homeland by the Xiongnu tribe (who later became the Hūṇas and transferred their attention towards Europe), and settled in northern India. Their descendents became the Kuṣāṇa people, and in the first century CE they moved into this crossroads area, bringing their adopted Buddhist religion with them. Like the other tribes before them, they adopted much of the Greek system that existed in the region. The product of this marriage of cultures was the Gāndhāra culture, based in what is now the Peshawar region of north-west Pakistan. This fused Greek and Buddhist art into a unique form; many of the sculptures of Buddhist deities bearing strong resemblances to the Greek mythological figure Heracles. The Kuṣāṇa people were the first to show Buddha in human form, as before this time artists had preferred symbols such as footprints, *stūpa* or tree of Enlightenment, either out of a sense of sacrilege or simply to avoid persecution.

The Kuṣāṇas dominated the areas of Hindu Kush into Kabul, Gandhāra, northern Pakistan and north-western Pakistan and north-western India. They controlled the trade between India, China, Parthia and the Roman Empire. This provided an ideal medium for the further spread of Buddhism from the second century BCE to the second century CE. Buddhism gradually developed in north-western India and the great Kuṣāṇa ruler, Kaniṣka was converted to Buddhism. Under his influence, Gandhāra, a Buddhist settlement, flourished and created a distinctive Graeco-Buddhist art form, which affected the arts in Central Asia and eastward in the first four centuries of our era.

Oliver Wild, writing about this route, remarks that the most significant commodity carried along this route was not silk, but religion. Buddhism came to China from India this way, along the northern branch of the route. The first influence came as the passes over the Karakoram were first explored. The Eastern Han emperor Ming-ti is thought to have sent a representative to India to discover more about this strange faith, and further missions returned bearing scriptures, and bringing with them Indian priests. With this came influences from the Indian subcontinent, including Buddhist art work, examples of which have been found in several early second century tombs in present-day Sichuan province. This was considerably influenced by the Himalayan massif, an effective barrier between China and India, and hence Buddhism in China is effectively derived from the Gāndhāra culture by the bend in the Indus river, rather than directly from India. Buddhism reached the pastures of Tibet at a rather later period, not developing fully until the seventh century. Along the way it developed under many different influences, before reaching Central China. This is displayed very clearly in the artwork, where many of the cave paintings show people with different ethnic backgrounds, rather than the expected Central and East Asian peoples. The greatest flux of Buddhism into China occurred during the northern Wei dynasty, in the fourth and fifth centuries CE. This was at a time when China was divided into several different kingdoms, and the northern Wei dynasty had its capital in Datong in present-day Shanxi province. The ruler encouraged the development of Buddhism, and more missions were sent toward India. The new religion spread slowly eastward, through the oases surrounding the Taklamakan, encouraged by an increasing number of merchants, missionaries and pilgrims. Many of the local people, the Huihe included, adopted Buddhism as their own religion. Fa-Hien, a pilgrim from China, records the religious life in the kingdoms of Khotan and Kashgar in CE 399 in great detail. He describes the large number of monasteries that had been built, and a large Buddhist festival that was held while he was there. Some devotees were sufficiently inspired by the new ideas that they headed off in search of the source, towards Gandhāra and India; others started to build monasteries, grottos and *stūpa*s. The development of the grotto is particularly interesting; the edges of Taklamakan hide some of the best examples in the world. The hills surrounding the desert are mostly of sandstone, with many streams, rivers and carving cliffs that can be relatively easily dug into; there was also no shortage of funds for the work, particularly from wealthy merchants. Gifts and donations of this kind were seen as an act of merit, which might enable the donor to escape rebirth into this world. In many of the murals, the donors themselves are depicted, often in pious attitudes. This explains why the Mogao grottos contain some of the best examples of Buddhist artwork; Tun-Huang is the starting point for the most difficult section of the Taklamakan crossing.

Throwing more light on Tun-Huang on the caravan route Sukumar Dutt[2] writes that since Han times (early Christian centuries) the Chinese had made several advances into Mid-Asia, mostly by fits and starts and from stage to stage. Remains of ancient Chinese times (military roads from a base of operation) have been found in Mid-Asia demarcating the limit of each advance. By the eighth century CE, a large number of mid-Asian states passed under Chinese suzerainty, and Ambams (local Chinese governors) were posted at their capitals. The most strategic approach by the Chinese to mid-Asia was through the border town of Tun-Huang outside the Great wall. Around 102 BCE, a Chinese general Li Kuang-li had proceeded on a punitive expedition along the Tarim river to Ferangana with a huge army. Small states in the basin of the river fell to Chinese power and came under Chinese suzerainty. The outward route-march of Kuang-li's army was through Tun-Huang, then a small agricultural-military settlement. This ancient Han expedition blasted the way for advance from China into the Tarim basin; the route remained serviceable down to the close of the eighth century, when China lost her suzerainty over the Tarim states. But this one-time highway of military advance became afterwards a way of more peaceful approach, facilitating intercourse between foreign monks and Chinese and trade communications between Mid-Asia and China. One of the landmarks of Tun-Huang was a range of hills to the south-west with a narrow

2. *Buddhism in East Asia*, pp. 122-23.

stream running through the foothills and smothered quickly in desert sands. Some grottos of these hills were preferred by monks for solitary meditation and perhaps for this reason the hill range became a centre of attraction to Chinese Buddhists. It was some time during the Changan period (fourth-fifth centuries) that the idea was conceived by imperial authorities at Changan to convert the hill range with its caves into a Buddhist centre. About five hundred caves were taken in hand and as many as three hundred of them were decorated with sculpture and mural paintings. They were then known to the Chinese as "Chi'an-fo-tung," i.e. caves of a thousand Buddhas. Monks coming from Mid-Asia into China used to break journey here and sojourn for some time for rest and refreshment. The incoming monks were provided with quarters for their stay before going into the interior. The place was kept by the Chinese Buddhists.

The transmission of Buddhist thought and culture to China was largely through this Silk Route and this is the reason why we are dwelling on the history and geography of this famous trade route which was frequented by the merchants. It is not certain when Buddhism reached China, but when the Silk Route opened in the second century BCE, missionaries and pilgrims began to travel between China, Central Asia and India. The record described that Chang Ch'ien, on his return from Ta-hsia (Ferghana) in the second century BCE, heard of a country named Tien-chu (India) and their Buddhist teachings. This is probably the first time a Chinese heard about Buddhism. A century later, a Buddhist community is recorded at the court of a Han prince. However the most famous story is of the Han emperor Ming-ti's dream about Buddha. In CE 68, Ming-ti sent his official Cai Yin to Central Asia to learn more about Buddhism after a vision of a golden figure appeared to him in a dream. The next morning he asked his ministers what the dream meant and was told that he had seen the Buddha —

the God of the West. Cai Yin returned after three years in India and brought back with him not only the images of the Buddha and Buddhist scriptures but also two Buddhist monks named She-mo-teng and Chu-fa-lan to preach in China.

This was the first time that China had Buddhist monks and their ways of worship. A few years later, a Buddhist community was established in Lo-yang, the capital, itself. From then on, the Buddhist community grew continuously. They introduced the sacred books, texts and most importantly the examples of Buddhist art, never before seen in China. In CE 148, a Parthian missionary, An Shih-Kao arrived in China. He set up a Buddhist temple at Lo-yang and began the long work of the translation of the Buddhist scriptures into the Chinese language. The work of scripture translation continued until the eighth century when access to Central Asia and India by land was cut off by the Arabs. In CE 166, Han Emperor Huan formally announced Buddhism by having Taoist and Buddhist ceremonies performed in the palace. The unrest situation in China at the end of the Han dynasty was such that people were in a receptive mood for the coming of a new religion.

Sea Route and the Transmission of Buddhism to China

Buddhism reached China through two other routes. It is therefore, desirable to discuss these routes which are eloquent witness to the missionary activities of the cultural harbingers of Buddhism from either side, i.e. from India to China and vice versa. D.P. Singhal[3] throwing light on this subject says that long before the north-western routes were opened in about the second century BCE, and long before the development of these Indianized states, there were two other routes from India to China. One of these began at Pāṭaliputra (modern Patna), passed through Assam and upper Burma near Bhamo and proceeded over the mountains and across the river valleys

3. *Buddhism in East Asia*, pp. 42-43.

to Yunnanfu (Kunming), the main city of the southern province of China. The other route lay through Nepal and Tibet. We have no contemporary description of this route, but there is definite evidence of its use. These routes were difficult and dangerous, because they lay through inaccessible, turbulent, and barren lands offering scanty food and security. The route across Tibet was developed much later, in the middle of the seventh century, when Tibet had accepted Buddhism and established political relation with China. During the second half of the seventh century, a large number of Chinese monks came to India by this route. In addition to land routes there was an important sea link between India and China through South-East Asia. During the course of the first few centuries of the Christian era, a number of Indianized states had been founded all over South-East Asia. Both cultures met in this region, and Indianized states served as an intermediary stage for the further transmission of Indian culture and Buddhism to China. Ancient Greek geographers knew that South-East Asia and China (Thinae) was accessible by sea. Ptolemy mentions an important but unidentified Chinese port on the Tonkinese coast. Ports on the western coast of India were Bharukaccha (Broach); Surparaka (Sopara); Kalyana; on the Bay of Bengal at the mouth of the Kaverī, Kaveripattam (Puhar); and at the mouth of the Ganges, Tāmralipti (Tamluk). At least two of these ports on the Bay of Bengal — Kaveripattam and Tāmralipti — were known to the Greek sailors as Khaberos and Tamalitis. At first Indian ships sailed to Tonkin (Kia-che) which was the principal port of China, Tonking being a Chinese protectorate. Later all foreign ships were required to sail to Canton in China proper. Canton became a prosperous port and from the seventh century onward was the most important landing place for Buddhist missionaries arriving from India and South-East Asia. Reading the accounts of Chinese travellers, it is impossible not to be impressed by their intrepid spirit. The perils of the desert, the danger of the "moving sands," and the loneliness of the journey were so complete that travellers often lost their lives. There were not even a bird or animal to be seen. Travellers often lost their way and the sands were littered with the bones of those who had perished. The rigours of the journey were relieved only by the hospitality offered by the few Buddhist principalities and towns. The route continued through the difficult crests and gorges of the sand-eroded Karakoram and Kohibaba into north Afghanistan or into Ladakh on the Tibetan border. South of Kapisa, then a small state to the north of the modern city of Kabul, India commenced with the kingdom of Gandhāra, lying alongside the stretch of the Kabul river between the Kumar and Indus. The sea was only slightly less dangerous. Navigation at the time was crude and without any scientific aids except the mariner's compass. The timber ships — tall floundering vessels of three tiers — were apt to spring leaks and there was constant danger from typhoons between China and the Indonesian Islands. Fa-Hien vividly describes how he escaped a watery grave. It took him fourteen days to reach Ceylon from Tāmralipti and yet another ninety days from Ceylon to Java. On his journey from Java to Canton, his ship lost its course in a storm, and it took eighty-two days of anxious drifting to reach Shantung. Merchants and monks travelled together; although the traders faced the same hard climatic and physical conditions as did the pilgrims, they were better organized. The pilgrims too, were probably weaker physically because of fasts and other self-imposed restrictions. They often depended on the goodwill of the kings through whose kingdoms they passed for protection, and frequently these kings, who had only recently embraced Buddhism, would coerce the monks to stay behind. But their single-minded devotion to their pilgrimages and their irrepressible urge to acquire learning sustained the pilgrims, although tests of physical endurance did not end with the journey. Living in strange and distant lands was no less trying. While some scholars and pilgrims adapted easily to the ways of the new land, where they either stayed for several years or settled permanently, others longed to return to their homes.

Buddhist thought and culture was transported and transmitted to China through these routes by the enthusiastic missionary torch-bearers of a most refined and spiritually exalted culture and civilization of Buddhism. We must not miss the fact that India, and particularly Kashmir, at that time had a very extensive spiritual and cultural history and in most of the countries of Central Asia the paṇḍits of this blessed land were arousing the entire populace from their dogmatic slumber and cultural hibernation. The Central Asian countries, particularly those on the Silk Route, were inhabited by the people who were mostly practising primitive religions. It was only due to the cultural activities of the Indian paṇḍits that these countries could see the dawn of an excellent civilization. Many paṇḍits and scholars reached China to inseminate the seeds of a spiritual culture, and they were Bactrians, Parthians, Khotanese, Kuchanese, Tokharians, etc. These propagators and paṇḍits of Buddhism who took the message of the Buddha to China were either Indians or the direct disciples of the Indian paṇḍits, most of whom hailed from Kashmir.

It is necessary to have a cursory look on the missionary contributions of these cultural ambassadors in brief. The India of that time was culturally extended to the entire Central Asian tract and this was the reason why Buddhism could be firmly established very easily in these remote and geographically inaccessible and climatically hostile lands.

Missionary Cultural Torch-Bearers of Buddhism from Central Asia

Before Buddhist thought and culture made its debut on Chinese soil it had already left its deep and incorrigible impression on the thought and culture of several Central Asian countries. This was all done under royal patronage. It is quite interesting to note that in the transmission of Buddhist thought and culture to the Central Asian countries as well as to China, the paṇḍits of Kashmir played a great role. They undertook the perilous and risky journey through extreme cold and geographically treacheous terrains of Taklamakan and Gobi deserts, the entire route from India to China. Its people embraced the Buddhist faith and they also became the missionary propagandists, who in course of time, disseminated this sublime faith to China wherefrom its further journey to Far-East continued till the entire Central and Far-East Asia became a land dotted with Buddhist monuments and shrines. The most celebrated monument of that time which is still existing is in the form of caves at Tun-Huang.

What impact the Buddhist thought and culture left on the people of South Asian countries as well as China can be simply gauged from the fact that even the missionaries of many Central Asian countries came to China for the propagation and dissemination of Buddhist faith. The contribution of India in making China a land of Buddhist faith was enormously great and no less was the contribution of Kucheans, Khotanese, Yeuch-Chis, Parthians, Tokharin and Sogdian monk scholars. The first inflow of Buddhist culture to China was from Tokharistan. It was in the second year BCE that the Chinese ambassador Tsing-Kiang received a Buddhist text as present to the Chinese court. The role of the Yeuch-chi in popularizing Buddhism in China is not disputed. Tokharistan seems to have played a constant and steady role in propagating Buddhism in China. The famous scholar Ghosaka, born in Tokharistan, played a prominent part at the fourth Buddhist Council in Purushpur. He was the author of the commentary on the *Abhidharma-Vibhāṣā* which was compiled there. A monk of rare learning named Lokasema of Tukhara origin went to Lo-yang in CE 147 and translated there some of the most important texts of Buddhist canon into Chinese. He worked at translations till CE 186. There are twelve translations ascribed to him. Towards the end of the same century (CE 190-220), one of his young disciples, Che-kien, also of Tukhara origin was working in North China, but had to leave on account of political trouble and settled down at Nanking where he worked till the middle of third century CE. He translated over a hundred Buddhist texts. Yet another Buddhist monk named Dharmarakṣa (Chinese name Fa-hu) was born of a Tukhara family. He had settled down in Tun-Huang towards the middle of third century CE. The Chinese literature distinguishes Tokharian monks by prefixing the word Che (from Yueh-che) to their names. Parthian scholars also contributed a lot towards the propagation of Buddhist faith by their translation of the Buddhist texts into Chinese. The names of Parthian Buddhist monks in Chinese are distinguished by the prefix An (Ngan) from the old Chinese name of Parthia An-She (Arsak), a name given to the country in the period of the Arsacidan dynasty. The Chinese historian mentions a Parthian prince Ngan-She-Kao (same as An-Sheh-Kao) or Lokottama who appeared in the western frontier country of China with a burden of Buddhist texts after the fall of Arsacidan dynasty in CE 148. He worked at translations till CE 170. He personally translated into Chinese more than a hundred Buddhist texts of which 55 are recorded by Nanjio.

The Sogdians, originally from their centre at Samarkhand to the north of Tokharestan, were famous traders who had their colonies in different parts of Central Asia and had come into association with Buddhism and Buddhist culture. The Sogdian monks also contributed towards the transmission of Buddhist culture and religious thought in China. Their names are distinguished by the prefix Kang, as the ancient name of Sogdian in China was Kang-kir. Some of those monks had collaborated with Ngan-She-Kao. An illustrious Sogdian monk who worked in South China in the third century was Seng-Hui. His ancestors had at first settled down in India. His father was a merchant who had to stay in Tonkin (Kiao-Che) where Seng-hin was born. After his father's death, this young boy left the world and became a monk. He soon proceeded to Nanking where he built a monastery and founded a Buddhist school. He was the first to introduce Buddhism in Southern China. At the beginning of the third century, the Sogdian monks again figured as translators and this process continued throughout, largely due to the efforts of those whose ancestors had imigrated from Western Turkestan. The contribution of Buddhist monks and savants from different nationalities towards the dissemination of Buddhism and translation of canonical Buddhist texts was very great. The spread of Buddhism in Central Asia was no doubt stimulated by the formulation of Kuṣāṇa Empire, which at its zenith seems to have overshadowed the Graeco-Bactrian. The first ruler Kujula Kadphises styles himself on his coins as "steadfast in true law" (*Saccadharma-thitasa = Satyadharma sthitasya*) and the figure of Buddha is depicted on his coins. The Buddha figures prominently on the coins of the great Kuṣāṇa ruler, Kaniṣka. His name is also associated with a *vihāra* or monastery set up for the Sarvāstivādins in an inscription dated in the year 1 from Shah ji ki Dheri near Peshawar.[4]

B.N. Puri[5] writes that while Western Turkestan, Bactria and Parthia as also Afghanistan and Kashmir contributed a lot towards the spreading and development of Buddhism during the first few centuries of the Christian era the area now forming part of Chinese Turkestan — Kashgar, Yarkand, Khotan and various sites of Kroraina — was equally humming

4. *Buddhism in Central Asia.*
5. *Buddhism in Central Asia*, pp. 104-05.

with Buddhist activities. The States on the northern route comprising Kucha and Turfan seem to have been under the spell of a separate wave of Buddhism.

After having said so much about the missionary traffic of Buddhist propagators and their cultural routes, now it is an occasion to give an idea as to how Buddhism made its debut on Chinese soil under royal patronage around the beginning of Christian era. The history of introduction of Buddhism in China is quite interestingly overlaid with some legendary and mythical details.

Cultural History of Debut of Buddhism on Chinese Soil

There are many legends and myths connected with every event of Buddha's life and Buddhism. The same holds good even in case of its expansion and dissemination. How and when Buddhism reached China first is a question that is still disputed. P.C. Bagchi[6] in his book *India and China* throws some light on this issue; he writes that the story of the first contact between India and China is mixed up with legend. We are told that Buddhist missionaries from India made their first appearance in the Chinese capital as early as under the Ts'in dynasty. But this story has no historical confirmation and has been discarded as a pious legend forged in later times when Buddhism had been well established in China. We are informed by a quasi-historical account that a golden statue of the Buddha was taken by a Chinese general in 121 BCE from the Hun country where he had led a military expedition. It is not probable however that Buddhism had reached the Chinese capital before the end of the first century BCE. It is known on undisputed authority that in the second year BCE, Buddhist texts and image were first presented to the Chinese court by the Yueh-che rulers. Buddhist missionaries however did not

6. P.C. Bagchi, *India and China*, p. 42.

arrive in China before the year CE 65. The story of the arrival of the first Buddhist missionaries is again mixed up with a legend. It is said that the Emperor Ming of the Han dynasty saw a golden man in a dream. On learning from his courtiers that it was the Buddha, he sent in CE 65 ambassadors to the west to invite Buddhist missionaries to China. The ambassadors brought with them two Buddhist monks, both of whom were Indians, named Dharmarakṣa and Kaśyapa Mataṅga. The two missionaries had with them a white horse laden with sacred texts and relics. The first Buddhist monastery built for them in the capital at the Imperial order came to be known as Poma-sse (the White Horse Monastery) in memory of the horse. The two monks are said to have lived in China for the rest of their lives, translating Buddhist texts into Chinese and preaching Buddhism among the people. A number of translations is attributed to them. Only one of them has come down to us. It is entitled *The Sūtra of the Forty-two Sections,* a catechism of the Buddhist religion such as would be useful for the first preachers of the law. It contains explanations of terms relating to the Buddhist order and gives the rules of initiation, ordination, etc. to guide the conduct of monks. This is the story of the first official relation between China and India by the Central Asian route. South China however seems to have come into contact with India a little earlier and in an independent way.

The issue of introduction of Buddhism in China is discussed more elaborately and critically by K.S. Ch'en[7] in his book *Buddhism in China.* He writes that one legend concerning the introduction of Buddhism into China says that Confucius knew about the existence of Buddha. The source for this statement is the Lieh-tzu, which is generally regarded by Chinese scholars as a forgery of the third century CE or later.

7. pp. 27 ff.

Another account tells us that the religion was already known in 317 BCE, when a foreign magician carrying a staff and begging bowl visited the court of Prince Chao of Yen and created a *stūpa* 3 ft. high on his finger tips. Quite apart from any reference to the magic feat, this story is groundless and unreliable, for at the date mentioned Buddhism had not yet left the confines of India. There are a number of Buddhist works that attempt to connect the introduction of the religion with the evangelical activities of King Aśoka during the third century BCE. Among the 84,000 *stūpa*s erected by Aśoka, some were said to have been discovered in China, and relic bones of the Buddha were said to have been unearthed from one of them. Likewise, it is thought that the foreign monk Shih-Li-fang, who reportedly arrived carrying Buddhist *sūtra*s into China during the reign of Ch'in Shih-huang (221-210 BCE), was one of the missionaries dispatched by Aśoka. These attempts by the Chinese Buddhists to find some connections with Aśoka are understandable, but there is nothing in the Aśokan inscription nor in the Ceylonese Chronicles to indicate the slightest hint of Aśoka having propagated the religion in China. Other accounts would place the introduction during the reign of Emperor Wu (140-87 BCE); when a lake was being dug during his reign, some black ash allegedly found at the bottom were said to be ashes left by the fires that consumed the end of an aeon. The writers of these accounts contend that such an explanation would have been possible only after the introduction of Buddhism. Some Buddhist writers also argued that Chang Ch'ien, the Chinese envoy who travelled across Central Asia to Bactria in the second century BCE, heard about the Buddhist faith in his travels abroad and brought back to China some information concerning it. But only in Buddhist records of the T'ang Dynasty was it indicated that Chang Ch'ien brought back such information. In the earlier sources there is no record of his having mentioned the Buddha. When the Han general Ho

Ch'u-ping vanquished the Hsiung-nu in the northern frontier in 120 BCE, he found some golden statues of human forms, to which no sacrifices were offered, only the burning of incense and ceremonial bowing. These golden statues were once considered to be the images of the Buddha, and their introduction was said to mark the beginning of the spread of Buddhism in China. However, it is now well established that these golden statues were not images of the Buddha but were symbols of some local Hsiung-nu deities. We must conclude that all these accounts concerning the introduction are legendary or unreliable or are due to the religious zeal of s. After Buddhism has been introduced and established in China, Chinese critics often charged that the religion tended to shorten the duration of the ruling houses supporting it. As evidence of this, they pointed to the short-lived dynasties of Later Ch'in, Later Chao, Sung, and Ch'i, which lasted only 33, 24, 59 and 23 years, respectively. To counteract these criticisms, the Buddhists forged texts purporting to show that the religion was introduced into China during the early years of the Chou Dynasty (*circa* 1100-256 BCE). The motive for assigning the date of introduction to the early Chou Dynasty is very clear, for the Chou lasted over eight hundred years and provided just the answer needed to refute the anti-Buddhist critics. As fitting accompaniments of the birth and death of such a famous sage as the Buddha, many anomalies and unnatural events, such as earthquakes, violent winds, and a rainbow with twelve colour bands which did not vanish even at night, were listed in the forged texts and were said to have been observed by the Chou rulers.

Commenting strongly on the dream of Ming-ti (CE 58-75), K.S. Ch'en[8] remarks that if the story of Emperor Ming's dream and the subsequent mission lacks firm historical basis, then

8. Ibid., p. 31.

how did the legend arise? The following hypothesis has been advanced. During the Han Dynasty there were other centres of Buddhism in China besides the Lo-yang community, some of which antedated the Lo-yang group in origin. The members of the Lo-yang centre, in their desire to acquire prestige and authority, sometime during the second half of the second century CE, fabricated the story of the dream in order to claim priority over the others in the establishment of their church. However, this theory brings in its wake another question not so easily answerable. If the legend originated in Lo-yang, how can we account for its early inclusion in the Mo-tze, a text composed in south China at the end of second century by a Chinese Buddhist convert who had never been to Lo-yang? The most telling argument against this version of the introduction of Buddhism under Emperor Ming lies in the fact that Buddhism was already introduced into the country at the time of the purported dream.

We find the account of Emperor Ming-ti's dream in the legendary Buddhist chronicle, *Records of the Lineage of Buddha and Patriarchs* written by the priest Chih-pang in the Sung Dynasty (CE 1127-1280). This story of introduction of Buddhism is fabricated in such a way that it appears plausible because the number of envoys including their names and the name of the leader of the mission which Ming-ti had sent to India are also given in the account. The account runs as "The Chinese Emperor Ming-ti of the Eastern Han Dynasty (the latter Han Dynasty), in the seventh year of his reign once dreamt that a golden man came flying into the palace with the light of the sun shining upon his neck. The next morning the emperor enquired of his courtiers, what the message of that dream was. One of them, named Fu-i, immediately informed him that it was the sage of the Western world, named Buddha, who lived at the same time as the Chou Dynasty. Ming Ti was so much impressed by the dream that he sent as envoys

General Tsai-yin, the learned doctor Ch'ing-ching, Wang-tsun and other 18 members in all on a mission to India to bring Buddhist scriptures and the priests. After two years General Isai-yin and others met two Indian monks, named (in Chinese) Kia-yeh-mo-tan and Chu-fa-lan in the Yuch-chi country of Central Asia and received images of the Buddha and Sanskrit texts which contained more than six million words. These were brought to Lo-yang in CE 64, together with the two Indian monks riding on white horses. They paid their respects to the Chinese emperor and lived at Ho Lu monastery. The following year the emperor ordered the White Horse monastery to be built outside the west gate of the city of Lo-yang. Kia-yeh-mo-tan then started upon the translation the *Sūtras of the Fourty-two Sections*."

We are in full agreement with K.S. Ch'en that this version of the Buddhism into China cannot be accepted as authentic and reliable. It is improbable that some important event as the dispatch of envoys occurred as the result of a dream. The lack of unanimity in the different sources concerning such important items as the date of the mission, the destination, names of the envoys, and the foreign monks accompanying the return mission is a compelling argument against the reliability of the story. It appears that the episode became more and more embellished with details as time passed, so that by the fifth century it had become fully crystallized.

During Ming-ti's reign, says D.P. Singhal,[9] that many foreign monks, whose names have not been preserved, were in Lo-yang and Chan-gan. An imperial edict belonging to the emperor Ming dated CE 65 mentions Chinese terms for *śramaṇa* (monks) and *upāsaka* (lay disciples). From this time onward China began to receive a succession of Indian monks and texts. Around the middle of the first century, Buddhism, regardless

9. *Buddhism in East Asia*, pp. 54-55.

of its reception at the Chinese Court, had found acceptance in the region north of the river Huai, in the eastern Honan, southern Shantung, and northern Kiangsu. The most important city of this region was Peng Cheng (Hsu-chou), a flourishing centre of trade on an eastern extension of the Silk Highway. Some scholars have suggested that the "Church of Peng Cheng" in Tonkin, now in Vietnam but part of southern China at that time, was also a principal seat of Buddhism. This centre, however, was set up by monks who had arrived by sea, and were possibly in contact with the Buddhist centre of Peng Cheng in the north. From the middle of the second century the growth of Buddhism in China began to accelerate. Emperor Huan (CE 147-67), like Ch'u-wang-ying (Liu Yang, the Prince of Chu), enshrined the Buddha in his palace together with the Huang-ti (Yellow Emperor) and Lao-tzu. In 166, Siang-chieh of Shantung province came to the capital and presented the emperor with a letter admonishing him for his excesses, and reminded him of the teachings of the Buddha, which implies that Buddhism had already gained a widespread following in China.

Buddhism was introduced into China when Han Dynasty was in power. At first Buddhism flourished in China chiefly among the foreigners, including merchants, refugees, hostages and adventurers who had brought it from their own countries. To be precise, Buddhism was first officially introduced in China during the reign of Ming-ti of the Later Han Dynasty. In spite of recognition given to Buddhism by the Han Emperor Ming, there were many Chinese literati who opposed it because their own political, intellectual and social interests clearly would have suffered from its predominance. Hence, the Later Han official classes were hostile to the introduction of Buddhism, and since Confucianism continued to be a powerful factor in Chinese society. Buddhism has always been subject to the pressures of Confucian beliefs and politics and its fortunes have varied accordingly. Until Buddhism entered China, the rivalry between the Confucian and Taoist philosophies dominated Chinese thought. Confucianism, however, gained ground during the Han period, but not without incorporating some Taoist doctrines. Consequently, a culture based on the canonical writings, as edited and interpreted by Confucius and his school, had emerged. The former Han dynasty, in contrast to the active policy of its predecessors, encouraged scholarship and adopted Confucianism as the state religion. Confucian scholars were given higher positions, and a rationale for political, bureaucratic, and social relationships was sought in the Confucian classics. The intelligentsia and the ruling classes accepted the complete supremacy of these classics, and the government drew upon them as they were impregnated with legalistic notions for a standard code of morals and ritual rules regulating conduct of the rulers and the ruled. During the Later Han period rigid Confucian "ceremonialism" dominated the whole society. The Confucian classics had become highly formalized, verbose, and specialized. Li, or procedural rules, actually divided society into ranks of social positions. Even nations had come to be placed in hierarchial positions: China was "the Middle Kingdom" and other nations were "Barbarians." Within nations there were lords, aristocrats, officials, common people and slaves.

When Buddhism reached China, the Chinese were a frustrated and confused lot. Buddhism appeared to them as if it would provide them a healing-touch and solace and therefore they turned to Buddhism. D.P. Singhal[10] writes that disillusioned in Confucian thought, both the literati and the masses alike turned to Taoism and Buddhism, seeking an escape into spiritualism. The golden images of the Buddha, the burning of incense and the chanting of *sūtras* by the yellow-

10. Ibid., pp. 49-50.

robed Buddhist monks captivated the Chinese mind. Consequently, Buddhism was welcomed by all classes as a religion holding the promise of relief from misfortune. The chaos following the breakdown of the Han Empire encouraged the spread of Buddhism throughout the Chinese world. The mass alienation and revolt among the peasantry shook the very foundation of society and this was a promising seed-bed for the implantation of new ideas and institutions. The intellectuals began to seek some clue to their collective plight and turned to Taoism and Buddhism. Moreover, Buddhist worship was combined with a social programme for the whole community. In CE 191, a local Han official for the first time built a temple in north Kiangsu and instituted community welfare services designed to ameliorate some of the ills of an impoverished and demoralized peasantry.

The Later Han period is conspicuous for its political decadence, economic stress, and opulence in the urban area, which combined to add the general poverty of the common people. While the tax life led many of the rich to renounce worldly pleasure by turning to Buddhism, the peasants hoped for equality in the new faith. Chinese traditional thought had little left of its earlier vitality and intellectual curiosity to resist the influx of Buddhist ideas.

Throwing light on the further success and advancement of Buddhism in China, John Snelling[11] remarks that latterly plagued by revolt and court intrigue, the Han dynasty finally expired in CE 220 and for more than 350 years the middle kingdom was riven apart. At first it was divided into three competing kingdoms ruled by independent warlords; then followed a short-lived and precarious period of unity under Western Chin (CE 265-316) before war and chaos were again unleashed and eventually "barbarian" tribes took control of the north. The most powerful, the Toba, who originated in

11. *The Buddhist Handbook*, pp. 143-44.

Mongolia, established the Northern Wei dynasty and in time became thoroughly sinicized. Meanwhile, successions of native Chinese rulers held sway in the south. Ironically, it was the decline and fall of the centralized Han empire that created the right conditions for Buddhism to gain popularity and spread to other parts of China. For one thing, the official Confucianism lost prestige and credibility, and in particular the intellectual and aristocratic elite began to look elsewhere for spiritual inspiration. Taoism and a new mystical metaphysics called the Dark learning engaged their interest. But Buddhism with its profound teachings on suffering and impermanence had something particularly pertinent to offer amidst the prevailing chaos. The sophistication of its schools of thought probably also attracted many cultured people, as did the notion of withdrawing from the world to the seclusion of a remote temple (preferably set in idyllic pastoral surroundings) in order to quietly contemplate the deepest spiritual mysteries. Thus was born the gentlemanly scholar-devotee that is so characteristic of Chinese Buddhism. Many of these fled from the north as it was overrun by foreign invaders and found sanctuary in the Yangtse basin and in the south thus opening up those parts of the country. Gradually distinctive northern and southern types of Chinese Buddhism began to emerge from the resulting cleavage. Buddhism also now began to infiltrate court circles in many parts of the fragmented empire. Once it had fallen under the patronage of the mighty of the land its success was assured. It even found favour with some of the barbarian dynasties in the north. The reasons were not entirely spiritual. These very much wanted to undermine traditional Chinese culture and its dominant Confucianism; to advance a foreign religion was a good way of doing this. They may also have felt that the gentle teachings of the Buddha would produce a more tractable kind of subject — the Taoists, on the other hand, were always stirring up trouble. Most importantly however they welcomed Buddhist monks at first because of the magical benefits they thought would be able to bestow. Later, however, these monks assumed more dignified roles as wise counsellors. Under the Northern Wei dynasty, patronage of Buddhism soared and colossal schemes for building monasteries, temples, pagodas, and *stūpa*s were initiated. The impressive Yun-kang and Lung-men cave temples were begun at this time and still exist to bear witness to the vigour and dedication of the dynasty. Buddhism was also taken up by native Chinese rulers in the south, notably by the early sixth century Emperor Wu, who tried to make himself into a kind of Chinese Aśoka by suppressing Taoism and squeezing his nobility for substantial contributions towards the cost of building temples and monasteries. One enterprising fund-raising scheme that he devised was to reduce himself to the level of a temple servant . . . and then have his subjects "ransom" him. Needless to say, though acclaimed in Buddhist literature, the Confucians wrote him off as a feckless fanatic. One important result of this general success was the emergence of a native *Saṅgha* by the middle of the third century, when a Chinese version of the *Vinaya* (monastic code of discipline) was produced. Formerly monks and nuns had probably existed on a more ad hoc basis. As a period progressed and Buddhism attracted increasing patronage, the number of monasteries and temples as well as of ordained monks and nuns fairly soared. Zurcher quotes the following figures for the northern Wei empire alone:

CE 477: 6,500 monasteries; 77,000 monks and nuns.
CE 514: 30,000 monasteries; 2 million monks and nuns.

Edward Conze[12] records the history of success of Buddhism in China and says that at first it was a foreign religion of the non-Chinese population in China's outlying marches. In CE 148,

12. *A Short History of Buddhism*, pp. 64-65.

a Parthian, Ngan Che Kao, and in CE 170, an Indian, Tshou Chofo, and a Yuch-chi, Tchetsh'an, arrived in China from Central Asia and established a monastery in Lo-yang, the capital of the Han. It was only in the period of disunity (CE 221-589) which followed on the collapse of the Han, that Buddhism really became a major force in China itself. Only in CE 355, were Chinese for the first time permitted to become monks, at least in the realm of the Eastern Ts'in rulers. In the second century foreigners from Central Asia — Parthians, Sogdians, Indians, etc. — did some translation. In the third and fourth centuries Buddhism gained momentum among the people and at the Court, and some emperors clearly favoured it. By CE 400, 1300 works had been translated. Then came Kumārajīva, whose translations, made with the help of Chinese literati, were classical works and are still being read. By CE 500, Buddhism was firmly establised throughtout the whole of China and in a flourishing condition, with the sculptured grottoes for the monks.

Missionary Activities of Monk Scholars and Evangelization of the Chinese

Most of the Indian monks who migrated to China did so during the five centuries following the third century. During that time a stream of Chinese monks arrived in India to study Buddhism in its homeland, and to collect authentic Buddhist texts. Many of the records have perished, some are known only by their titles, while brief extracts or stray passages from others appear in China's vast literature. Only three records are preserved in full: Fa-Hien's *Fo-Ku-chi*, Hiuen Tsang's *Hsi-yu-chi*, and I-tsing's *Nan-hai-ki-kuei-nai-fa-chuan*. While nearly all the Chinese monks eventually returned home, most of the Indian monks who went to China remained there. Much less is known of the Indian monks who went to China than of the Chinese pilgrims who went to India. The Chinese had a deeper interest in objective observation and in recording history. Consequently, none of the numerous Indian monks who went to China has left a record of his experiences and impressions. Three Indian monks, Kumārajīva (*c.* CE 498-569), Paramārtha (*c.* CE 343-413) and Bodhidharma (CE 527), are held in particularly high esteem by Chinese Buddhists, and the School of Dhyāna Buddhism, which he founded and is known as Ch'an in China and Zen in Japan, is still alive in eastern Asia, especially in Japan where its main centre is Kyoto. There were many others who enjoyed local or regional fame and are mentioned in Chinese dynasties and histories. A host of others were absorbed in translating Sanskrit texts, working singly or jointly with Chinese scholars. Of the Indian scholars who visited China from the fourth to sixth centuries CE, the majority belonged to Kashmir; a few of them were collaborators of Kumārajīva. It must be mentioned here that following in the foot-steps of Hiuen Tsang's several bands of Chinese pilgrims poured into India during the seventh and eighth centuries; biographies of sixty monks including that of I-tsing have been preserved in Chinese texts. Several Indians also went to China at royal invitation. There were several Kashmiri scholars like Saṅghabhūti, Gautam Saṅghadeva, Puṇyavrat, Vimalākṣa and others who visited China between the years CE 380 and 450. Of other parts of India, including the south, who sent Buddhist missionaries, two south Indian monks who went to China in the sixth century CE, founded two schools of Buddhism. One of them was Bodhidharma, virtually a mythical figure of Buddhist China. So great was his fame that he was received by Emperor Wu on his arrival in China. It was he who introduced the meditative form of Mahāyāna Buddhism to China. The other south Indian who reached the Chinese capital in CE 582 was Vinitaruci who founded the Dhyāna School in Tonkin.

H. Sarkar[13] in his article, "Buddhist Contact of China," writes that with the unification of China under the T'ang Dynasty (CE 618-907), Buddhism entered its golden age. It was a period of close commercial and maritime activities also between the two countries. That the east coast countries took a leading role in the maritime activities is evident from the discovery of coins of the T'ang Dynasty in south India. It was again the period when the fame of the Nālandā University reached every corner of the Buddhist world. Of the leading members who helped in establishing a closer contact between the two countries, the name of Hiuen Tsang, the first Chinese traveller during the T'ang period, comes to our mind at once. He was treated as a royal guest by king Harṣavardhana, and on his return to China after a long period of fourteen years (CE 630-44) of sojourn, he likewise received a royal ovation; the emperor himself with his retinue came to receive the great traveller of the country. On his return, he founded a new school of Buddhist philosophy and translated about seventy-four texts. He rightly advised the emperor to establish political relations with the Indian kings because a new trend in the form of political relations between the neighbouring countries was then in the offing.

Here it is necessary to recall the first two Buddhist missionaries that came to China — one of Kaśayapamataṅga and Dharmarakṣa and the other of An Shih-Kao. An Shih-Kao was a Parthian of royal lineage. He is described as one who understood the language of birds and animals and was well versed in astronomy and medicine. Of the foreign monks living and working in Lo-yang, he was the most famous translator. Lo-yang monastery played a great role in propagation of Buddhism in China. J. Saunders[14] in his *Epochs in Buddhist History*

---

13. *India's Contribution to World Thought and Culture*, pp. 330-31.
14. p. 127.

writes that with these two missions at Lo-yang begins the first great epoch of Chinese Buddhism — an epoch of translation lasting for four centuries, during which leaders from foreign lands were patiently educating a Chinese church and forming Buddhist mind in China. Lo-yang continued its activity despite the indifference of the Wei rulers who came to power after the fall of the Han Dynasty in CE 220. At the request of Chinese monks, many Indian scholars undertook the translation of various Buddhist texts. For instance, Dharmakalā translated for the first time, the *Prātimokṣa*, while Saṅghavarman and Dharmasatya were responsible for producing Chinese renderings respectively of the *Karmavāca* and *Prātimokṣa* of the Dharmaguptaka School of Buddhism.

The list of translators and missionaries of monk scholars is very lengthy. We wanted to make one thing very clear that translation of Buddhist texts from Sanskrit into Chinese was an organized industry in India and there were two very important translation centres in China. One in northern and the other in southern China. These missionaries, monks, scholars and giant translators gave China such a sublime faith and wisdom that it changed the thoughts and minds of the Chinese people and it brought about a sea change in their ways of life and mode of thought. The royal patronage lent a great support in propagation and dissemination of Buddhist faith in China for many centuries.

Buddhist Imprint on Chinese Life

The advent of Buddhism in China was virtually the dawn of a great civilization. Inspired and enlightened by the ethico-spiritual ideals of Buddhism and its sublime culture, Chinese people got an opportunity to revamp their socio-religious life. We have already discussed in this chapter that the Chinese society at the time of introduction of Buddhism was a confused, frustrated and disturbed society. Confucianism and

Taoism could not satisfy their social and religious aspirations. More so, Buddhism was more developed religiously than Confucianism and more sophisticated philosophically than Taoism. It made no class distinctions and thus appealed to both the educated and uneducated, the rich and poor. Buddhism made a deep impression on the life of the Chinese people because it brought a message which indigenous thinkers could not provide. Both the ruling classes and the people supported this new religion.

Kenneth S. Ch'en[15] rightly remarks that it is in the religious life that Buddhism brought its greatest influence. This is as it should be, since it was as a religion that Buddhism was introduced to China. Through its pantheon of compassionate Buddhas and *bodhisattvas* who offered refuge to those in need, its promise of salvation to all, its emphasis on piety and silent meditation, the colourful pageantry of its rituals and festivals, its restraint of the passions, its universality and its tolerance, the religious life of the Chinese has been enriched, deepened, broadened, and made more meaningful in terms of human sympathy, love, and compassion for all living creatures. Its doctrine of *karma* brought spiritual consolation to countless numbers. Commenting on the impact of Buddhism on the Chinese people, D.P. Singhal[16] in his *Buddhism in East Asia* observes that the impact of Buddhism gave rise to a renaissance of Confucianism under the Śuṅga and Ming dynasties. Many Chinese scholars of traditional learning recognized the superiority of Buddhist teaching, especially in metaphysics and methodology. Hence, they were inspired to rejuvenate Confucianism, grafting onto it what they regarded as the merits of Buddhism. But the Chinese, deeply imbued with a sense of this-worldliness and social responsibility could

---

15. *Buddhism in China*, p. 484.

16. p. 109.

not completely reconcile with the other-worldliness of Buddhism. Therefore, the interaction between metaphysical Buddhist thought and Confucian ethics led to the emergence of a new philosophical movement, commonly known as Neo-Confucianism, during the Śuṅga period (CE 960-1279). Just as Buddhist interaction with Taoism gave rise to Chan, so with Confucianism it produced Neo-Confucianism or Li. Thus, Buddhism finally succeeded in stirring the Chinese intellect to respond in a positive way to the new stimuli. This Confucian response to Buddhism was characteristically Chinese — having failed to silence a critic, denounce him but act on his criticism. While Confucianism underwent drastic changes under the Buddhist impact, Buddhism itself, except in minor concepts, absorbed little of Confucianism.

P.C. Bagchi[17] writes: the influence of Buddhism on Chinese life and thought was tremendous. Besides certain forms of theistic religious beliefs, Buddhism introduced to China the doctrine of rebirth, the idea of causality, and the belief in reward and retribution. Buddhist philosophy, especially its conception of reality which permeates everything in nature and the notion of universal impermanence, had an abiding influence on the poets and artists and influenced China's aesthetic outlook. Buddhism also brought to the Chinese a deep religious feeling and a profound faith, which inspired the great works of art in China, such as we find in Yun-kang, Hung-men, Tun-Huang and other places.

D.P. Singhal[18] also identified areas of Chinese thought and culture which were influenced by Buddhism. He tells us that Buddhist elements are found in Chinese festivals, and local beliefs and practices. Certain features of the clan organizations, notably the idea and function of charitable estates for the

---

17. *2500 Years of Buddhism*, p. 60.
18. *Buddhism in East Asia*, pp. 116 ff.

benefit of the entire clan, are of Buddhist origin. Buddhist symbolism is seen in the ideologies and rituals of the secret societies, which have been so important in Chinese life and history. The concept of *karma* is to be found in all types of Chinese literature from poetry to popular tales. Buddhism made contributions from other areas of Indian culture than the philosophies — such as art, astronomy, mathematics, medicines and fables. The growth of Buddhism as a common faith was accompanied by a great increase in charitable works of all kinds. Buddhist monks had been the first to open free dispensaries and in times of epidemics they helped thousands of people in the stricken areas. They established free hospitals to which, by T'ang times, the state was contributing support. The great literary activity of the Buddhist scholars naturally had a permanent influence on Chinese literature, one of the oldest and richest in the World. While the antiquity of Chinese literature is apparent, its literary forms were slow-evolving. In fact, they did not begin to articulate and crystallize until after the impact of Buddhist translations, literary themes, and techniques. There is no epic poetry nor short story form until the T'ang period; no recorded dramas until the Mongol period; and no development of the novel until the Ming period. In a recent study, a Chinese scholar, Lai Ming, says that a significant feature in the development of Chinese literature has been the immense influence of Buddhist literature on the development of every sphere of Chinese literature since the Eastern Chin period (CE 317). We cannot say that without this influence Chinese literature would have remained static and only poetry and prose been its principal literary forms, but we can safely say that it certainly would have been different from what it is today. Buddhist influence on Chinese literature, as on other aspects of cultural life, was not a deliberately initiated and directed process, but a natural growth dictated by the needs of religious propaganda. The *sūtras* were written in combined prose and rhymed verse, a literary form unknown in China at that time. It was possible to communicate the meaning, but the tonal harmony and the beauty of the verses could not be translated. The Chinese language when pronounced in the Sanskrit polyphonic manner was likely to sound hurried and abrupt, and to chant the Sanskrit verses in monophthongal, Chinese prolonged the verses so much that the rhymes were lost. Hence, to make Chinese *sūtra*s pleasant to listen to, the Chinese language had to be modified to accommodate Sanskrit sounds, and greater attention paid to fan-chieh, the Chinese method of phonetic spelling, by joining the initial sound or consonant sound of a word to the end or vowel sound of another word. Consequently in CE 489, Yung Ming, Prince of Ching Ling, convened a conference of Buddhist monks at his capital to differentiate between, and define the tones of, the Chinese language for reading Buddhist *sūtra*s and for chanting the verses. Their deliberation improved and more accurately defined the sound of monophthongal Chinese, and a new theory, called the Theory of Four Tones was established: ping or "soft" tone; and three "hard" tones, shang or acute tone, chu or grave tone, and ju or abrupt tone.

Buddhist thought and culture exerted an influence over many facets of Chinese life — its thought, literature, language, art and science. Chou Hsiang Kuang in his book *History of Chinese Buddhism* has given a very good account of the impact of Buddhism on these aspects of Chinese life. P.C. Bagchi's book *India and China* and the eighteenth chapter of Kenneth Ch'en's book *Buddhism in China* have also furnished an account of the same.

Thus, we see that the greatest impact that Buddhist thought and culture had on the life of Chinese people was an educating, enlightening and civilizing one.

6

Impact of Buddhist Thought and Culture on Tibetan People

Brief History of Introduction of Buddhism in Tibet

IN the second chapter of this volume we have discussed in detail the socio-religious conditions that were prevailing in Tibet. We have mentioned that before the onset of Buddhism, *Bon*, an animist cult, was the dominant faith of Tibet. We are told in the recorded history of Tibet that it felt the first impact of Buddhism when the first Indian paṇḍit, Buddharakṣita, visited Tibet during the reign of Ha tho thori, the 25th king of Tibet (who was later on recognized as the earthly manifestation of Sāmantabhadra). B.L. Bansal[1] in his book, *Bon: Its Encounter with Buddhism in Tibet*, remarks that Buddhism was first established in Tibet, albeit on a small scale, during the reign of the mighty monarch, king Srong-btsang sgam-po born (CE 619) in the seventh century CE. It would appear that the Tibetans were aware of the existence of Buddhism in earlier times. According to one tradition, in the reign of king Ha tho thori, the fourth predecessor of Srong-btsang sgam-po, certain religious books fell from the sky down to the roof of his palace, but no one could understand them. These books were, therefore, kept in a separate room and worshipped in the belief that they had come from heaven. What must have happened

1. p. 78.

was that some itinerant Buddhist monks travelled from Nepal to Tibet, carrying a few books with them which were quite incomprehensible in that country. Probably later they came away leaving the books behind.

Before the seventh century CE, Buddhism was not known in Tibet and if known at all it was all a legendary gossip or mythical tales. There is a good evidence, write David Snellgrove and Hugh Richardson,[2] that Buddhism was first established in Tibet, albeit on a very small scale, during the reign of Srong-btsang sgam-po (Srong-btsang sgam-po) who died in CE 650. In later Buddhist tradition he was accounted as the first of the three great religious, i.e. Buddhist kings, the other two being Khi-srong lde-btsan (Trhi-sng-de-tsen) who ruled throughout the second half of the eighth century, and Ral-pa-can who ruled from CE 815 to 836. It is generally argued that Buddhism entered into Tibet during the reign of Naradeva (Mi-la) who ascended the throne when he was 13 years old. He was also known as Srong-btsang sgam-po (literally meaning: straightforward, strict and prompt) in Tibetan. Chenrezis, a Tibetan historian, states that the original name of the king was Khi-srong lde-btsan and he provides us with an interesting account of how the king came to be known as Srong-btsang sgam-po, and after this change, he like his father bred martial spirit and took delight in wars and campaigns. On his accession to the throne, he increased his military powers manifold and led an expedition against king Aṁśuvarman of Nepal in the south. Fearing defeat, the king Aṁśuvarman of Nepal thought it wise to establish matrimonial alliance with the king of Tibet who agreed, and accepted the princess as his queen. The princess of Nepal, Bhṛkuṭi, was a devout Buddhist and brought the images of Akṣobhya Buddha, Maitreya and Tārā as part of dowry. The king built a

2. *A Cultural History of Tibet*, p. 73.

temple in the middle of Lhasa to enshrine these images and it is called the Jokhang (House of the Lord). Two years later, Srong-btsang sgam-po, led a military campaign against the Chinese Emperor Seri-ge-bstan-po (Tai-tsung) and just like the king of Nepal, the king of China also decided to give his daughter, princess Wen-Ch'eng, in marriage to the king of Tibet. The princess of China, like the Nepalese princess, was a worshipper of the Buddha. She brought to Tibet, arts and crafts as well as an image of Śākyamuni, which is said to have been taken from Magadha by the Chinese about the first century BCE. This was also installed in a temple built by the king in Lhasa. Both the wives were further canonized as incarnations of Avalokita's consort, Tārā, the goddess of Mercy. The princess of China was glorified as the White Tārā, and the princess of Nepal as the Green Tārā. Thus, the king was converted to Buddhism by the persuasion of these two queens and the king himself felt the need to introduce Buddhism in Tibet and paid full attention on its propagation in Tibet. Srong-btsang sgam-po drew up a code of morals and customs and ruled over the kingdom on the basis of ten Golden Precepts which agree fairly with the ten rules of morality as recommended by Buddha for the observances of the Buddhist monks and the laity in their daily life. These Golden Precepts became the law of the king. A code of sixteen virtues was further formulated to convert his subjects in spirit, not just in name. These are sixteen general human laws and except for the section on monastic co-ordination, the remaining portions of the doctrine received great circulation and the kingdom of Tibet turned towards virtue. He sent young men to India, Nepal and China at the instance of his queens, for Buddhist works and acquiring knowledge of Buddhism. Thonmi Sambhota was sent to study in India with sixteen others to invent a script for the Tibetan language. They studied there with Ācārya Devavit Siṁha, paṇḍita Lipikāra and others noted for proficiency in the art of writing. His companions died due to heat and he stayed in India and studied both Buddhist and Brāhmanical texts thoroughly. There was no form of writing in Tibet at that time; the texts were memorized and translated orally. He reduced the Tibetan language to writing with the invented alphabetic script, consisting of 34 letters, 30 consonants and four vowel signs. This alphabet was an adoption of the central Indian script of the sixth-seventh centuries CE. With this, all historical events in Tibet and also sacred Buddhist works were translated and written down in this script. He is said to have written eight books on writing and grammar in Tibetan with the help of Ācārya Kusaka, Brāhmaṇa, Śankara, the Nepalese Ācārya Śila Mañju and the Chinese Ho-Sang. Two of his grammatical words were preserved in the Tibetan *Tanzur*, namely *Vyākaraṇamūlatriṁśakanāma* and *Vyākaraliṅgananāma*. The Karaṇḍavyūha, the hundred precepts and *Ratnameghasūtra* deserve mention. Thus, Thon-mi Sambhota is regarded as the father of Tibetan literature. The king obtained Buddhist texts from Nepal and got them translated into Tibetan. He also wrote a book dealing with the conjugation Bhairava, the Tāntric deity. The credit of ushering in a new Buddhist era in history of Tibet goes to the first monarch of Tibet, Srong-btsang sgam-po. The translation work continued steadily for several hundred years, till the closing of seventeenth century CE. As a result of this, several books dealing with Buddhism and applied subjects were rendered into Tibetan from Sanskrit and other Indian languages. Thus, he gave a strong impetus to the spread of Buddhist religion in Tibet and made Buddhism his state religion. He is revered as an incarnation of Avalokiteśvara, the patron deity of Tibet.[3]

In this context, the observations of V.V. Gokhle[4] are worth quoting. He writes that although Buddhism had come to Tibet

3. *Buddhism — A World Religion*, pp. 159-60.
4. *2500 Years of Buddhism* (ed.), p. 66.

under such favourable auspices, it did not take root in a foreign soil as easily or quickly as Srong-btsang sgam-po might have wished. It had to wage an incessant and arduous war for over three centuries against indigenous Bon beliefs. It had also to remove old superstitions, make compromises, adapt its own doctrines to the strange customs and traditions which had come down from time immemorial and suffer setbacks and banishment until the days of Atīśa in the eleventh century, when at last Buddhism may be said to have truly become the national religion of Tibet.

Whatever may have been the circumstances Buddhism could be introduced in Tibet as a state religion by Srong-btsang sgam-po on persuasion of his two wives. His Holiness the fourteenth Dalai Lama[5] in his article, "India: The Home of Tibetan Learning" writes that the sway of Buddhism became pronounced in the seventh century CE when the court minister, Thon-mi Sambhota, a brilliant intellectual, was sent to Indian paṇḍits in the various branches of learning. Thon-mi Sambhota returned to Tibet, and he not only innovated letters of Tibetan script, the first of its kind in Tibet, but also translated *Mdo-de-za-ma-tog* and *sPan-bKon-phyag-rgya-ma* into Tibetan. From then on, there grew up an extensive corpus of literature. A host of Indian and Tibetan paṇḍits and Lotsavas (translator scholars) translated into Tibetan the *Sūtra*s and *Tantra*s brought from India and Nepal. The *Kangyur* consisting of over one hundred bulky volumes and *Tangyur*, consisting of over two hundred volumes were all translated during this period.

V.V. Gokhle[6] lauding the missionary zeal of Srong-btsang sgam-po, writes that he built the famous temples of Romoche and Jokhang in Lhasa, and the grand architecture of the eleven-storeyed palace, called the Potala, which has also preserved

5. *India's Contribution to World Thought and Culture*, pp. 389-90.
6. *2500 Years of Buddhism* (ed.), p. 66.

to this day the remains of an original smaller structure, begun by him, in one of its lower apartments. Buddhism with some of its cultural advances and paraphernalia was thus brought to Tibet to replace the old animistic and *Bon* religious beliefs. The credit of ushering in a new Buddhistic era in Tibet thus goes to the first great monarch of Tibet, Srong-btsang sgam-po, who was a contemporary of Muhammad, the founder of Islam, Harṣa of Kanauj and the famous pilgrim-scholar, Yuan Chwang of China.

A very interesting and strange suspicion has been raised by Per Kverne[7] regarding the role of Srong-btsang sgam-po in the patronage of Buddhism. He writes that it is possible that Buddhism was introduced into Tibet during the reign of Srong-btsang sgam-po; for there are temples of that period like Jo Khang (which has been greatly enlarged and transformed over the centuries), dBu ru Ka tshal (east of Lhasa), Khra'bong (in the Yar lung Valley), and Ra mo che (in Lhasa itself). There is no evidence, however, that the king himself adopted Buddhism. Nor is there any mention of Buddhism in contemporary literary sources. On the other hand the king seems to have been loyal to his ancestral religion, Bon. While choosing Buddhist symbols for the Ra mo che Temple he consulted *Bon* priests as well. There was no conflict between Buddhism and the native religion of Tibet. Nor was there any opposition to a new or foreign religion. Srong-btsang sgam-po was buried in the traditional way in the Yar lung valley, where an enormous burial mound can still be seen. In introducing Buddhism into Tibet the king appears to have had political motives rather than religious. Through his conquest of a number of Central Asian states and his contacts with India, China and Nepal, which were all flourishing centres of Buddhist culture, he became acquainted with certain

---

7. *Tibet: The Rise and Fall of Monastic Tradition* (ed.), pp. 255-56.

elements of that culture, with its universalistic perspective and felt that Tibet would do well to imbibe those elements without inviting any foreign political influence. Secondly, he wanted to introduce the art of writing into Tibet. He finally chose Buddhism from India and with it many other aspects of Indian culture, especially a literary language. One cannot, however, tell that Buddhism was really present in Tibet during the reign of Srong-btsang sgam-po. It would appear that the king made use of the new religion for the advancement of culture. He did not establish any monastery; he only built a few temples. It is only in the following centuries, i.e. during the reign of king Khri-srong-lde-brtsan (CE 740-97), that one finds mention of Buddhism in official documents. king Khri-srong-lde-brtsan too was favourably inclined to Buddhism presumably from political considerations although later traditions hail him as the second king of the law and as an emanation of the Bodhisattva Mañjuśrī. In any case it is clear that Buddhism was established in Tibet under royal patronage and that it served to increase royal power. The native priests, who did not like the progress that the new religion was making in Tibet, made common cause with certain noble families against the king. After a bitter struggle, which seems to have taken the form of a palace intrigue, the king and the Buddhist party gained the upper hand, and the task of providing the law, *Dharma,* on a firm basis began.

Sangharakshita[8] in his *Tibetan Buddhism* has a different opinion about Srong-btsang sgam-po and his activities and achievements. He writes that the first religious king of Tibet was Srong-btsang sgam-po, who ruled in the seventh century, and seemed to be a remarkable man. His earliest achievements consisted of continuing the political and administrative reforms initiated by his father. Until that time, Tibet had been

8. pp. 18 ff.

split into a number of different feudal principalities, but Srong-btsang sgam-po — and his father before him — gradually brought them all together, centralizing the administration and establishing Tibet as a political unit with a military power which was greatly feared by all her neighbours. This was itself a great achievement, but it was not enough for Srong-btsang sgam-po. At that time Tibet was surrounded by a number of highly civilized states: Khotan to the north-west; Kashmir (then an independent kingdom) to the west; Nepal to the south-west (and beyond Nepal, of course, India); and the great empire of China, then under the T'ang emperor, to the east. All these states were Buddhist in those days, and all of them had attained a very high level of civilization and culture. Srong-btsang sgam-po could not help noticing this. He saw that although Tibet was politically united and in military terms a force to be reckoned with, where civilization and culture were concerned she very much lagged behind all her neighbours. So Srong-btsang sgam-po embarked on a programme of social reform and cultural development. First he redistributed the land that was in the possession of the nobles and the great landowners, to give the common people a bigger and better share. At the same time he encouraged agriculture, trying to persuade the wandering nomadic tribes to settle down and cultivate the soil. He introduced weaving, masonry, and carpentry. He also decided to prohibit blood sports, a step which hints at the beginning of his sympathy with Buddhism. Another old custom he prohibited was that of face-painting. Apparently Tibetans, men and women alike, had a custom of painting their faces bright red, but Srong-btsang sgam-po outlawed this, thinking it rather uncivilized. In the course of his travels and military campaigns Srong-btsang sgam-po had observed that the culture of the surrounding countries was very closely linked with Buddhism, and this led him to decide that Buddhism should be introduced in Tibet. He was supported in this mission by his two principal wives, the daughter of king of Nepal, and the daughter of king of China. What might have happened if the king's wives had followed religions other than Buddhism is an open question, but fortunately both were devout Buddhists. In Tibetan art they are often depicted on either side of Srong-btsang sgam-po. For his Nepalese wife, Srong-btsang sgam-po built the Jokhang, literally "Lord's House," in Lhasa. European writers often call it the "Cathedral of Lhasa." It is the oldest religious building in the Tibetan capital, and the one the Tibetan consider the most sacred. For his Chinese wife he built a smaller temple known as the Ramoche. In these temples were installed images of Akṣobhya and Śākyamuni brought from their respective countries by his wives. The temples were desecrated and demolished by the Chinese during the Cultural Revolution. Devout Tibetans later surreptitiously removed the battered heads of these two great images, which had been there for thirteen centuries, and brought them to India, where they presented them to the Dalai Lama. During the course of his reign, Srong-btsang sgam-po built many other temples, the first Buddhist temples to be built in Tibet. He also sent a group of young Tibetans to study Buddhism in Kashmir which in those days had a reputation of Buddhist learning. Thus Srong-btsang sgam-po practically created Tibetan culture, at least in its rudimentary form. Furthermore, he caused a new code of civil law to be drafted, and he ensured that the ethical precepts of Buddhism were widely taught throughout his domain. But as yet there were no Buddhist monks or monasteries in Tibet. In fact, Srong-btsang sgam-po's interest in Buddhism appears to have been more cultural than religious. This was inevitable, given the state of Tibet in those days. The spiritual life can be developed only when certain standard of culture — in the sense not of material improvement but of the refinement of one's whole way of life — has been attained. But even with this very important reservation, Srong-btsang sgam-po's work remains of the first importance. He laid the foundations of the Tibetan nation, of its culture and literature, and of Tibetan Buddhism itself — surely a very considerable achievement for one man. The Tibetans show their gratitude to Srong-btsang sgam-po even to this day by regarding him as a manifestation of the great *bodhisattva* of Compassion, Avalokiteśvara (the Dalai Lama being another, later, one).

Writing about the status of Buddhism during its early years in Tibet, David Snellgrove and Hugh Richardson[9] add that Buddhism during the reign of Srong-btsang sgam-po was probably restricted to the court, and its priests were Indian or Chinese. A few Tibetans may have studied the new faith and helped in the first translations of religious books, but even this is not certain. Srong-btsang sgam-po's next successors showed no great enthusiasm for Buddhism, although two of them, Dus-Srong (676–704) and Khi-srong lde-btsan (704-754), are credited in an eighth-century inscription with the foundation of chapels; the latter also had a Chinese wife, who presumably followed the faith, for thanks to her intercession a large number of refugee monks from Khotan were hospitably received and seven monasteries were built for them, where they stayed in peace for three years. When the queen died, they were driven away. Later Tibetan tradition makes great deal of the suppression of Buddhism in the later part or immediately after the reign of Khi-srong lde-btsan and of its trumphant restoration under his son Khi-srong lde-btsan (*c.* 740 to 798). That something of the sort took place is supported by ancient edicts preserved in the *History of dPa-bo gTsug-lag*, but the actions which are attributed in such later histories to irreligious ministers may have been instigated by practitioners of the indigenous Tibetan religion or may simply represent a

9. *A Cultural History of Tibet*, pp. 77-78.

spontaneous Tibetan reaction against the importation of foreign customs. At all events, the ban cannot have appeared so important to contemporary Tibetans as it did to the pious historian of later periods. The *Tibetan Annals* (from Tun-Huang) make no mention whatsoever of Buddhism, and the *Chronicles* has the scantiest allusion to it, while the Chinese records note no cataclysmic upheaval in Tibet at this time. In short, religious questions were not of primary concern during the early royal period. Nevertheless, compared with its first beginning during the reign of Srong-btsang sgam-po, Buddhism made rapid progress, both spiritual and material, thanks to the interest that Khi-srong lde-btsan showed in it.

After the death of Srong-btsang sgam-po in CE 650, Buddhism and the activities related with its promotion and propagation went into hibernation and during this period nothing worth recording about the progress of Buddhism happened. It is said that through the skilful guidance of Thon-mi Sambhota the Tibetans conquered practically the whole of Eastern Turkestan during the reign of Srong-btsang sgam-po's successor in CE 670. They found big monasteries, beautiful shrines and fine statues of the Buddhas and *bodhisattva*s in this region. They also came across a large number of *bodhisattva*s which created a stir in the religious world of Tibet, and ultimately paved the way for the foundation of Buddhism there.

The next great king was Khi-srong lde-btsan (CE 740-798). His rule marks the zenith of Tibetan power and the affirmation of Buddhism as the chief religion of the state. His great contribution was the foundation of the stately temple and monastery of bSam-yas (sam-ye) in which Tibetans were trained as monks for the first time. It was constructed as a great complex of buildings arranged around a central temple, said to be modelled on the great Indian Buddhist monastery of Odantapuri in Bihar.

It was during the reign of Khi-srong lde-btsan that Sāntarakṣita, Padmasambhava, and Kamalaśīla were brought to Tibet. He is regarded by the Tibetans as an incarnation of Bodhisattva Mañjuśrī even today. He was the son of the Chinese princess who was a devout Buddhist and from her he received a strong religious impulse for Buddhism in Tibet. He sent an envoy to China in search of Buddhist texts. He was also successful in persuading Saravāstivāda, the famous Buddhist teacher from India, to come to Tibet. On the advice of Śāntirakṣita, the king sent a messenger to bring Padmasambhava to Tibet.

Sangharakshita[10] in his *Tibetan Buddhism* writes about the contribution of this great king in the following words:

> "The second religious king of Tibet, Trisong Detsen, lived in the eighth century. He was an ardent supporter of Buddhism, but during the earlier part of his reign he was greatly hampered by the hostility of the followers of Bon. He invited to Tibet the Indian scholar and teacher Sāntarakṣita, best known nowadays as the author of a great work of Mahāyāna Buddhist philosophy called the Tattvasaṅgraha. But unfortunately Śāntirakṣita's mission was not very successful. He visited several places, he spoke on Buddhism, he gave a number of lectures, but then apparently an epidemic broke out all over the country. This gave the Bonists the opportunity they had been waiting for. They said, "You see what happens. In comes this Indian Buddhist teacher, and there is an epidemic! The demons are angry." Śāntirakṣita could find no answer for this, and knew another approach was needed. He advised the king to invite to Tibet the great Indian master Padmasambhava, who was then living at Nālandā University near Bodh-Gayā.

Another highly significant event during Trisong Detsen's reign was what Western scholars usually call the "Council of Lhasa,"

10. pp. 21 ff.

although it was in fact more of a debate than a council, and it took place at Samye. The debate was between Kamalaśīla, one of Śāntirakṣita's Indian disciples, and a Chinese monk who had turned up in Tibet and was preaching Ch'an (the Chinese forerunner of Japanese Zen) to the disapproval of some Tibetan Buddhists. So in CE 792 a discussion was arranged between Kamalaśīla and the Ch'an monk. We still have detailed records of this event, and the chief point of contention, apparently, was over the question of whether Enlightenment came gradually, little by little, or occurred all at once, in a great rush. Following the general Indian tradition, the Indian scholar held that it came gradually, step by step, by following the Eightfold Path, practising the ten *pāramitās*, and so on; while the Chinese monk argued that it happened all at once. The debate was adjudicated by king Trisong Detsen, and he decided in favour of Kamalaśīla. However, those who have studied the records believe that Chinese Ch'an master did pretty well too. Looking at it quite objectively and impartially, one might say that the point at issue between them is really a distinction without a difference. One does not attain Enlightenment either slowly or quickly; ultimately the question of time does not come into it at all. But the king said that Kamalaśīla had won, and that was that. Trisong Detsen further decreed that from then on Tibetan Buddhists should follow the Saravāstivāda School (one of the main Hīnayāna Schools) with respect to *Vinaya* or religious discipline, the Mādhyamika and Yogācāra Schools of the Mahāyāna for their philosophy and metaphysics, and the Tantra, the Vajrayāna, as far as meditation was concerned. In this way a synthesis of the three *yānas* was established. These three aspects of practice were also conceived of as constituting successive stages of the spiritual path. First you follow Sarvāstivāda discipline, then you study Mādhyamika and Yogācāra philosophy, and then you practise Tāntric meditation; in this way your spiritual life is complete. Thus the reign of Trisong Detsen saw three main developments: interest in Buddhism shifted from the cultural to the religious; the monastic order was established; and the *triyāna* character of Tibetan Buddhism was determined.

In our opinion, Khi-srong lde-btsan's greatest contribution to the cause of Buddhism was the establishment of stately temple and monastery of bSam-yas (Sam-ye). David Snellgrove and Hugh Richardson[11] say that the great bSam-yas temple has been severely damaged by fire more than once, but Tibetan devotion to traditional forms probably ensured that the original pattern and the original objects of worship were maintained in any restoration. Several of the outlying chapels which surround the great temple appear to be original, and unmistakable survivals are an inscribed pillar recording the foundation (but without any mention of the king), and a fine bell still hanging in the verandah and bearing a pleasing prayer for the king inscribed by one of his queens. It is gratifying to note that this monastery played a great role in propagation and dissemination of Buddhist faith in Tibet even in subsequent centuries. It was in this monastery that the first official initiation of the Tibetan novices in Buddhism took place under the priestly superintendence of Sāntarakṣita.

John Snelling[12] holds Trisong Detsen in very high esteem; he writes that all are agreed, however, that king Trisong Detsen was considerably more important than Songtsen Gampo. It was he who invited to Tibet the Indian master Śāntirakṣita, who in turn inaugurated the building of Samye, though as we have seen he ran into trouble and eventually had to be assisted by Padmasambhava. Other monasteries and temples were also established during Trisong Detsen's reign,

---

11. *A Cultural History of Tibet*, p. 78.
12. *The Buddhist Handbook*, p. 198.

and monks were favoured with royal patronage. Influential for the future too was the great Debate held at Samye between 792 to 794 under the sponsorship of the king himself. In this the Indian paṇḍit Kamalaśīla defended his convention, the Indian branch of gradualist ethically-oriented Buddhism against one Hvashang Mahāyāna, a representative of the Chinese Ch'an (Zen) school of sudden enlightenment. According to Tibetan account, the verdict went in favour of the Indian party and the Chinese departed. Thereafter Tibet took its Buddhism exclusively from India, though some residual Chinese influence did remain — in Dzogchen, for instance.

Khi-srong lde-btsan's grandson Ral-pa-can (CE 815-36) was another great religious king of Tibet. He proved to be another champion of Buddhism. His religious zeal was so great that he made his youngest son, a Buddhist monk. S.C. Das[13] writes that immediately after his succession he sent offerings to the different temples built by his ancestors. He built a new nine-storeyed temple, of which the three lower storeys were of stone, and three of wood. In the upper floors he kept the Buddhist scriptures, images and small shrines. In the middle floor he accommodated the paṇḍits and translators of the holy writings, and the ground floors he reserved for the use of his court and state affairs. Thinking that the propagation of religion depended much upon the predominance of the clergy, he organized many classes of priesthood. To each monk he assigned a small revenue derived from five tenants.

About his missionary achievements A.C. Banerjee[14] in his book *Aspects of Buddhist Culture from Tibetan Sources* writes that Ral-pa-can convened a meeting of the monks to give advice

---

13. *Journal of Asiatic Society of Bengal*, 1881, pp. 227-28.
14. pp. 29-30.

on the further propagation of Buddhism in Tibet. As a result, on his invitation many scholars came to Tibet from India. Prominent among them were Jinamitra, Śailendrabodhi, Surendrabodhi, Prajñāvarman, Jayarakṣita, Mañjuśrīvarman, Ratendraśīla and others who worked under them as Tibetan translators. They were entrusted with the work of translating the scriptures and commentaries of Nāgārjuna, Āryadeva, Vasubandhu and others. A considerable portion of the present canon was then translated into Tibetan at that time. According to Rockhill, at least half of the existing collections of *Tanjur* and *Kanjur* were done by these great teachers and translators. The newly built palace called On-chan-po with nine storeys was a centre of this translation activity. Monasteries were also built during his reign and monks of those monasteries could collect tithes of the lands assigned to the monasteries. It was during his reign that the history of Tibet came to be written for the first time. King Ral-pa-can is considered to be the incarnation of Vajrāpāṇi.

King Ral-pa-can was assassinated as a result of Bon conspiracy along with his chief minister in CE 836. He was succeeded by his brother Glang-dar-ma who was completely opposed to Buddhism. He was the apostate persecutor of Buddhism. A period of persecution ensued. Buddhist temples and monasteries were demolished, monks were killed or driven out, scriptures were destroyed, and the result was that Buddhism practically perished in Tibet, especially in Central Tibet, for nearly two centuries. Buddhism was revived in Tibet once again when Atīśa came to Tibet in CE 1042, from India. It must be reminded once again that glang-dar-ma was murdered in CE 842. Buddhism witnessed many ups and downs in Tibet from the death of Srong-btsang sgam-po in CE 650 until the murder of Glan-dar-ma about CE 842 during the successive reigns of eight Tibetan kings.

Role of Indian Paṇḍits in Establishing Buddhism in Tibet During Seventh and Eighth Centuries

After having discussed the role of royalty and the royal patronage extended to the introduction of Buddhism in Tibet, now we must discuss something about the Indian paṇḍits, who brought the seeds of Buddhism and inseminated the same in the Tibetan soil. Śāntirakṣita and Padmasambhava, both Indian teachers established Buddhism in Tibet in the eighth century CE. They represent two rather different forms of Buddhist practices, the one conventionally academic and monastic, and the other mystical and ritual. Both forms permeated the other to some extent, and it is significant that Padmasambhava was supposed to have been invited to Tibet on the suggestion of Śāntirakṣita, who found the country as a whole not so well disposed to the kind of teaching which he himself represented. Incidentally, it must be told that Padmasambhava was a saint and scholar of Kashmir, a sojourner in Tibet at the time, who was assisted in his missionary work in that country by two eminent scholars of Nālandā, Śāntirakṣita and his pupil Kamalaśīla. They instituted the Lamaist system in Tibet and established the first Buddhist monastery at bSam-yas, of which Śāntirakṣita was named the first abbot. But Buddhism thus established had to counter the native Bon cults and its final victory was achieved only through Dīpaṅkara's thirteen years missionary labour in Tibet.

Sangharakshita[15] compares these two stalwarts of Buddhism and remarks that Śāntirakṣita was a very great man, but he had his limitations. As a scholar, a philosopher, he could appeal to the conscious mind of the Tibetans, but they did not have the resources to overcome their unconscious resistance to Buddhist ideals. Padmasambhava, on the other hand, was not just a great scholar, not just an imminent philosopher, he

15. *Tibetan Buddhism*, p. 22.

was also a *yogī* and mystic which meant that he could breakthrough to a deeper level and make contact with the forces operating within the Tibetan collective unconscious. He was able to incorporate the Bon deities and the forces they represented into the framework of Buddhism, and even to use the energy contained in these archetypes in the interests of the spiritual life. The Bon demons having been "converted," Padmasambhava and Śāntirakṣita together founded the first monastery in Tibet, Samye, in CE 779. Built after the model of the famous Odantapuri monastery in India, Samye was completed in CE 787. Much of it was recently destroyed by the Chinese, but a film of it made by the Indian representative in Lhasa before the desiccation shows that it was a very beautiful place, reminiscent of what the great ancient Indian monastic universities must have looked like in their heyday. Śāntirakṣita and Padmasambhava also ordained seven Tibetans as monks, thus founding the Tibetan monastic *Saṅgha*. Padmasambhava left a permanent mark on Tibetan Buddhism, through the sheer force of his personality. Although he only stayed in Tibet for about eighteen months, the Tibetan accounts of his visit usually make out that it lasted for thirty-five years, presumably because he created such an impact in those eighteen months that it was as though he had been there for thirty-five years. He is traditionally regarded as the founder of Nyingma School, but he is greatly revered by the followers of all sects and schools of Tibetan Buddhism. It is ensured that in all Buddhist temples there is some picture of Guru Padmasambhava.

Per Kvaerne[16] writes that during the reign of the two immediate successors of Srong-btsang sgam-po, Buddhism made little progress. However, the political situation in the country was consolidated, and Tibet acquired a decisive voice in Asian politics. Khri-srong was favourably inclined to

16. *Tibet: The Rise and Fall of Monastic Tradition* (ed.), p. 256.

Buddhism, but two of his ministers were much opposed to it. They managed to get even a ban imposed on it when he was a minor. Khri-srong got rid of those ministers as soon as he came to age and invited the Indian scholar Śāntirakṣita to Tibet. He decided to set up a Buddhist monastery at bSam yas, south-east of Lhasa and on the northern bank of the gTsang po. This provoked opposition from the local priesthood and from some nobles, so much so that the king sent Sāntarakṣita back to India. After some time, seeing that the atmosphere was less hostile, he invited Śāntirakṣita again to Tibet, but Sāntarakṣita declined the offer. Instead he suggested the name of his brother-in-law Guru Padmasambhava, who was a tāntric master better equipped to tackle the situation which obtained in Tibet at that time. Padmasambhava was a native of Swāt in the extreme north-west of India. He played a crucial role in the introduction of Buddhism into Tibet. While Sāntarakṣita was a representative of the conventional *Vinaya*-based monasticism and the *Sūtra*-inspired philosophical tradition of the Mahāyāna, Padmasambhava was a *siddha*, an adept at magical rites and a master of techniques of subduing demonic forces. The influence of Padmasambhava and that of the Mahāyāna philosophical tradition as taught by Śāntirakṣita has been predominant in Tibet ever since.

Guru Padmasambhava, known as "Lotus Born," or "Rin po che," or "Precious Guru," or the "Second Buddha," in Tibet in the adjacent Himalayan regions of India was a unique personality in the eighth century. Around Padmasambhava are centred legends, mythologies, doctrinal systems, hierarchies of deities, and root teachings of Mahāyāna Buddhism embellished with all the glamour of Oriental imagery.

When Śāntirakṣita reached Tibet on a royal invitation by king Shri-srong-lde-btsan, Tibet was engulfed by all kinds of storms, epidemics, etc. The adherents of Bon with the active support of the king's uncle incited the people by alleging that this calamity was due to the wrath of the god at the introduction of this form of religion and also at the presence of the alien teacher in Tibet. This kind of propaganda caused a great setback for the spread of Buddhism. Śāntirakṣita had to flee to Nepal for the time being to evade the Bon-po's indignation. But, later on, he was invited back to Tibet by the king. Again, the people began to give bitter opposition to him and to his teachings. At this stage, Śāntirakṣita advised the king to invite the celebrated Buddhist teacher Padmasambhava to come to Tibet and subdue the Tibetan devils and demi-gods. Accordingly, Padmasambhava was invited to Tibet. He visited Tibet in CE 747. With his *siddhi* power he subdued all the local evil spirits of Tibet. The king built Samye monastery, the first Buddhist monastery in Tibet. Śāntirakṣita was appointed as the head of the monastery. He delivered many religious discourses to the Tibetans and the king. *The Blue Annals* records that "many Tibetan took up ordination and propagated the doctrine of the *Vinaya*." He conferred the monks vows first on the "Seven men on Trial" (Sad-mi-mi-dun). The three elder ones among them were: Mañjuśrī of dPa, Devendra of rTrans, and Kumudika of Bran; the three juniors were: Nāgendra, Ācārya, and Rin-chen-chog and an intermediate one was Katana. Bu ston also tells that "12 monks of the sect of the Sarvāstivādins were invited and it was put to the test, whether the Tibetans could become monks or not. After this, a few Indian teachers like Vimalamitra Buddhaghhya, Śāntīgarbha and Viśuddhasiṁha Buddhaghhya, were brought to Tibet. Thus, during the time of Sāntarakṣita, there commenced the systematic translation of the Buddhist works into Tibetan.

Padmasambhava was the founder of Lamaism in Tibet. He belonged to the then popular ritualistic and mystic *yoga* school at Nālandā, and he was skilled in Buddhist spells (*dhāraṇī*). He was a believer in Tāntric mysticism with its prayer to various Buddhist gods and goddesses. He is the reputed author of several manuals of worship (*sādhanās*) and propitiation of deities by means of repetition of spell (*dhāraṇī*). B.N. Puri[17] writes in his *Buddhism in Central Asia* that Padmasambhava also initiated an era of great literary activity and scholarship with the translation of Buddhist canons from Sanskrit. Several Tibetan scholars were sent to India to learn Sanskrit and Buddhist philosophy. Padmasambhava was one of the greatest exponents of tāntric Buddhism and was known as the *guru* or *mahācārya* in Tibet. His interest in tāntric ideas was probably the result of his association with Bengal which was no doubt a centre of Tantrism. When Padmasambhava vanished from Tibet, he left behind twenty-five disciples to propagate his teaching. Glang-dar-ma who ascended the throne in CE 836 attempted to extirpate Lamaism by destroying monasteries, burning books and driving Indian monks out of Tibet.

Evaluating the role and importance of Padmasambhava in Tibetan Buddhism, Helmut Hoffman[18] in his book *The Religions of Tibet* remarks that there can be no doubt about the historical importance of this strange Indian master, though those investigators who call him "the father of Lamaism" and leave it at that are probably going rather too far, because, as we have seen, at the time in question, other schools of Indian (Śāntirakṣita) and of Chinese Buddhism were also active in the formation of Tibetan religious life. However, Padmasambhava undoubtedly exercised a very powerful influence on this development and he founded a special religious tradition which has remained alive down to the present day, and has, despite the interacting relationships with other Lamaist sects, maintained its own specific features.

---

17. p. 150.
18. p. 50

Hoffman[19] seems to suggest foreign influence on Buddhism, particularly its Mahāyāna and Vajrayāna. He writes that Padmasambhava grew up in that centre of syncretism in north-west India which has always been the gateway for the entry of foreign people and foreign influence into this country. In fact, more than the political upheavals caused by the Greeks, the Kuṣāṇas, and others, it was the constant influx of outside spiritual and religious ideals which turned Eastern Iran, Udyana (near Swāt), Gandhāra, Bru sha, Shang-shung, and Kha che into a real cockpit of divergent religious beliefs — a circumstance which naturally had its effect on what was at that time the most influential and widespread Indian religion, viz. Buddhism. The major spiritual and religious influences operating in the days of Padmasambhava were Hellenism, the great scientific theories and the gnostic systems, the antique schools of mysticism, and Zoroastrianism in its orthodox and heretical forms beside Islam, the primitive beliefs of the West Himalayan districts and the Bon religion. Further, Manichaeanism, that world religion founded by the Babylonian Mani in the third century CE, appears to have spread eastwards and influenced Buddhism particularly its Mahāyāna and Vajrayāna forms.

Hoffman[20] writes that the Guru made an attempt to found a religion of his own in Tibet. He succeeded to some extent as his doctrine was adopted by the rNying-ma-pa sect, which honours him to this day. This sect has held a specific and independent place of its own in Tibet, its internal squabbles and other trends notwithstanding. Padmasambhava could not carry out his mission in its entirety. This is clear from his premature departure from Tibet in the face of opposition from the Bon priests and politically powerful ministers.

---

19. Ibid., pp. 50-51.
20. Ibid., p. 58.

Before we switch on to another great propagator of Buddhism in Tibet, Kamalaśīla, it would be worthwhile once again to tell something more about Śāntirakṣita. We know that he came to Tibet on a royal invitation for furthering the cause of Buddhism. At that time there was no institution in Tibet which could promote Buddhism. The founding of a monastery in Tibet was a challenge. Śāntirakṣita came to inaugurate the introduction of Buddhism in Tibet on an institutional basis. He did not know Tibetan. In order to assist and co-operate with him in his missionary work a paṇḍit from Kashmir named Ānanda who was proficient both in Sanskrit as well as in Tibetan came to Tibet. Śāntirakṣita has nothing to do with the disreputable magical practice of Nepal or with the obscene indulgences of the Vajrayāna. He was a thoroughly virtuous man. Śāntirakṣita had come to Tibet and spent four months in one of the royal palaces teaching the doctrines of Buddhism, and his choice of subjects throws some light on his mentality. It is reported that he preached on the ten moral injunctions (*daśaśīla*), the eighteen component parts of the individual (*aṣṭadaśa dhātvaḥ*), and the twelve parts of the *Pratītyasamutpāda*, the genesis in dependence; in other words, on matters of moral discipline and on fundamental philosophical question.

Hoffman[21] writes that this strange holy man and sorcerer (Śāntirakṣita), who was to place his own particular stamp on a certain aspect of Lamaism, and with whom we shall deal in greater detail later, was obviously far more capable of dealing with the demons of Tibet than was the gentle scholar Śāntirakṣita. According to legend on his journey from the frontier district of Gung-thang where he met the reception party sent by the king, to that spot on the northern bank of the Brahmaputra where he proposed to found a temple and a large monastery, Padmasambhava subjugated all the evil

21. p. 47.

spirits he met with. He was also obviously the right man to pick the most favourable astrological hour for the beginning of the building operation, to examine the site from the standpoint of its occult qualities, and to break the resistance of all the local hostile spirits. However, the laying of the foundation stone, the whole building plan, is said by Bu-ston and Padma-dkar-po to have been the work of Śāntirakṣita. It was he who decided to copy the most famous of the Buddhist holy places of the time, the Buddhist temple of Odantapuri built by the king of Bengal, Gopāla, in Magadha. The result was the famous first monastery of Tibet, the "incomparable, unchangeable holy place arisen through miraculous means," named bSam-yas for short. According to the most likely calculations it was probably completed in the year 787 after a building period of several years.

Now we come to Kamalaśīla who was an illustrious disciple of Śāntirakṣita and for some time a teacher of Tantra at Nālandā. He was invited to Tibet when the controversy arose over the interpretations of the Buddhist teacher among the followers of Śāntirakṣita and the pupils of the Chinese Hostang. He was particularly invited by the king to defend Śāntirakṣita's interpretations and "to pacify all strife and establish the true form of the teaching." Kamalaśīla and his disciples like Jñānendra, etc. advanced cogent reasons to refute the viewpoints of the Chinese Hva-can. The adherents of the Chinese Buddhist monks could not meet their point of view. Kamalaśīla came out victorious over the Chinese monks and the king appointed him as the head of the Buddhist *Saṅgha*, and ordered the Chinese Buddhist sage to leave Tibet. Ho-Shang's books were concealed and prohibited for propagation. This agitated the Chinese monks and his disciples and they arranged for Kamalaśīla's murder. Bu-ston writers thought the Chinese butchers subsequently killed the great teacher Kamalaśīla in a very cruel manner by squeezing his kidneys.

Kamalaśīla's victory in the debate was indeed a very important landmark in the history of religion of Tibet. He was the author of several works. There are 18 works attributed to Kamalaśīla which exist in Tibetan translations. The *Nyāyabindupūrvapakṣasaṁkṣipta* and the *Tattvasaṁgraha-pañjikā* deserve special mention. The former is a summary of criticisms on Dharmakīrti's *Nyāyabindu* while the latter is a commentary on Śāntirakṣita's *Tattvasaṁgraha*.[22]

Buddhist Sects of Tibet and their Founders

A.C. Banerjee[23] writes that the Tibetan sects came into existence with a view to preserving the purity of the Buddhist teachings and doing away with degrading practices, superstitions, beliefs and the like then prevalent prior to the Buddhist doctrines. Waddell[24] writes that the sects arose in revolt against the depraved Lamaism then prevalent which was little else than a priestly mixture of demonolatry and witchcraft. There were no sect in Tibet prior to the eleventh century CE. In the eleventh century CE, the king of Tibet to whom Buddhist renaissance owed much, invited Atīśa (Dīpaṅkara Śrījñāna) to come to Tibet from India to propagate Buddhism there. Since Atīśa came to Tibet he corrected, rectified and systematized the Buddhist teachings prevalent there. He reformed the *Saṅgha* in Tibet and brought a great renaissance in the religion. With his reformation originated the Kadam-pa sect, the first sect of Tibetan Buddhism as against the unreformed type of Buddhism called rNin-ma-pa "the old ones" founded by Padmasambhava, better known as Guru Rinpoche.

T.W.D. Shakapa[25] writes that "the teachings of Atīśa were subjected to a new school of Buddhism that came into being

22. *Buddhism in Tibet*, pp. 45-46.
23. *Aspects of Buddhist Culture from Tibetan Sources*, pp. 45-46.
24. *The Buddhism and Lamaism of Tibet*, pp. 74-75.
25. *Tibetan: A Political History*, pp. 59-60.

in Tibet. To distinguish themselves from the unreformed followers of Padmasambhava, the followers of Atīśa and Drom were called Kadam-pa (one of the doctrine) while the unreformed monks were called Nying-ma-pa (one of the old)."

Tibetan Buddhism got fractured into various sects from the time of Atīśa. Only a few of them are still surviving. There are five major sects or order of Tibetan Buddhism:

1. Nyingmapa (Sñin-ma-pa)
2. Sakyapa (Sa-sKya-pa)
3. Kargyupta (Bkaḥ-rgyud-pa)
4. Kadampa (Bkah-gdams-pa), and
5. Gelukpa (Dge-lugs-pa)

Nyingmapa Sect

This sect was founded by Guru Padmasambhava during the reign of Khri-sron-lde-btsan in the eighth century CE. This sect is also known as the "Red Cap" sect from the peculiar "Red Cap" worn by the Lamas. It is also known as the old "Translation" sect as its fundamental teachings are selected from the texts translated by Guru Padmasambhava, Ācārya Śāntirakṣita, Mahāpaṇḍita, Vimalamitra of Kashmir and others. This sect is subdivided into several sub-sects "based on the adoption of different revelations." Prominent among them are Dorje-tak-pa, Nindol-lin-pa, Kar-tok-pa and Na-dak-pa. The rNying-ma-pa sect divides the entire Buddha Dharma from the Sūtra to the Tantra into nine Yānas which are three Hetūlakṣanayānas (Yānas of cause) and six Phalavajrayānas (Vajrayāna of result). The three Hetūlakṣanayānas are Śrāvakayāna, Pratyekabudhayāna and Bodhisattvayāna. The six Phalavajrayānas are the three outer Tantras and the three inner Tantras. The three outer Tantras are Kriyāyoga, Caryāyoga and Yogatantra. The three inner Tantras are Mahāyoga, Anuyoga and Atiyoga.

Sangharakshita[26] in his book *Tibetan Buddhism* throws some light on the sectarian divisions of Tibetan Buddhism. It would be worthwhile to quote him "so if we ask ourselves what is meant by a "school" of Tibetan Buddhism, all we can say is that it is a particular lineage of teachers and disciples. A certain teacher teaches Buddhism to his disciples, they teach their disciples, and so on. This succession from master to pupils, is what we call the school. The line of transmission may have its own angle on the *Dharma*, it may stress a particular aspect of the doctrine or a particular practice, but the emphasis is no more than an emphasis, rarely, if ever, is it exclusive.

Eva. M. Dargay's[27] book *The Rise of Esoteric Buddhism in Tibet* throws light on a very important aspect of the rNying-ma-pa sect which was inaugurated by Guru Padmasambhava in Tibet. He writes that after the rNying-ma-pa were certain of their royal patronage, they had to include into their missionary efforts the reactionary and lower classes of the people. By this process the Bon religion and the popular belief were, as far as it was considered justifiable, incorporated into the frame of Buddhism in changed form. This is probably the explanation of the statement that Padmasambhava placed the native spirits under oath (*damcan*) to serve Buddhism in the future and that they fulfilled their oath. This assimilation of the Bon-religion and the popular belief continued, although scholars of the Old School fought against excessive assimilation. An overly close merging of the Old School ideas of the Bon and the popular belief, gave birth to the pseudo rNying-ma-pa; they devoted themselves to the fulfilment of the needs for magic of a society of farmers and cattle raisers. These pseudo rNying-ma-pa, unfortunately, often became more famous than the learned representatives of the school, who as true *yogīs*

26. p. 28.
27. p. 10.

remained silent and stayed in seclusion, and unlike the dGe-lugs-pa School, did not criticize these excesses in their own school. As transmitters of the textual tradition of the first monastery period (snga-dar), the Old School adheres to the "Teachings of the Earlier Translations" while the dGe-lugs-pa and bKa-gdams-pa schools recognize, above all, the translations of the second missionary period. Both traditions alternatingly polemicize against each other, yet, their respective philosophical systems were and are studied by members of the other branches.

Since the scope of our research extends from first century BCE to eighth century CE, we are not giving here the details of other sects, though we have referred to these schools in brief. It also must be made clear that when Guru Padmasambhava inaugurated a new phase of Buddhism it was never known as Nyingmpa. The reason is simple, Nyingmpa means "old ones." This epithet was coined at a time when Atīśa was on his *Dharma* Mission in Tibet in eleventh century CE.

Buddhist Influence on Tibetan Life and Culture

After having said so much about the introduction of a peculiar form of Buddhism in Tibet by the celebrated Indian paṇḍits like Sāntarakṣita, Padmasambhava, Kamalaśīla, etc. under the royal patronage of a series of eight kings right from Srong-btsang sgam-po to the infamous glang-dar-ma (CE 842), now it is an occasion to assess the impact of this new brand of Buddhism on the life and culture of the Tibetan people who were deeply wedded to an anomist faith called Bon.

The royalty in Tibet and the paṇḍits of India prepared the grounds for the establishment and propagation of Buddhist faith in Tibet. The establishment of a monastery (Samye) was decidedly a great factor in the Buddhist conquest over Tibet. When, in the beginning, Śāntirakṣita and Padmasambhava came to Tibet for introducing a new faith and philosophy, they had to face an aggressive and hostile wrath of the common masses as well as the nobles. It is very natural that an alien religion cannot make its way through at a stroke without convincing the natives. The Bon was the national religion of Tibet when Buddhism entered "The Land of snow." There was the system of Bon (Shamanism) religious practices in Tibet. Tibetans of the early seventh century were doing the sacrifices of animals and worshipping the spirits, the sun, the moon, mountains, trees, etc. Superstitions were ingrained in their thought, psyche, lifestyle and liturgies. The Tibetan royalty made efforts to change the minds of their subjects which gave rise to frequent revolts. If we closely scrutinize the early history of Buddhism in Tibet, we find that Buddhism had to make compromises with Bon religion and had to accommodate many rituals, practices and beliefs of the Bon religion. We also hear that there was a lull in Buddhist missionary activities for a hundred years after the death of Srong-btsang sgam-po. We also hear that Śāntirakṣita had to flee to Nepal when he first visited there. The Tibetans were apprehensive that Śāntirakṣita along with his new religion had brought a bad omen for the Tibetans. Not only that, even Padmasambhava's missionary sojourn to Tibet was also very short-lived. At every step and at all times during seventh, eighth and ninth century CE Buddhism had to face the hostility of the Tibetan masses and a few Tibetan kings. This opposition to the new Buddhist Order in Tibet was three-cornered — from the priest of the old native religion, from the nobles and from some belligerent kings.

Thus, we see that Buddhism could develop in Tibet in seventh and eighth centuries CE when there were internecine political conflicts. We also know that after the assassination of glang-dar-ma in CE 842 Buddhism eclipsed in Tibet for two centuries and it was revived there in CE 1042 when Atīśa reached there as a missionary propagator and propagandist.

In the seventh and eighth centuries Buddhism and its practices and beliefs could make headway only among the royalty and the converts who were indoctrinated and initiated in Buddhist lore and practices by the Indian and Chinese paṇḍits. Because of its geographical location, Tibet was frequented by a host of Buddhist scholars from India, China, Khotan, Kuchi, etc. All these scholars and paṇḍits tried their best to dish out to the Tibetans a sublime thought and a spiritually colourful culture.

It was through Buddhism that Tibetans got an immensely vast Buddhist literature which shaped their minds through culture and civilization. The greatest contribution of Buddhist thought and culture to the Tibetans was a "script" and a sublime religion with colourful pantheons and magical symbolisms. Not only that, Tibetans were gifted with art and craft and also a peculiar philosophy that supremely refined ethico-spiritual culture. The Tibetans deserve every appreciation and admiration for they preserved our philosophy and culture, in their thought and life. Every aspect of Tibetan life is deeply influenced by Buddhist thought and culture. There is sufficient evidence, both material and textual, to substantiate that Buddhist thoughts were the carbon copy of exalted Buddhist spirituality. Every structure, whether religious, regal, ceremonial or liturgical, exhibits and reflects the radiant spirituality and awe-inspiring serenity of Buddhist wisdom and its culture.

7

Religio-Cultural Transformation of Korea, Japan and Other South-East Asian Countries

THE impact of Buddhist thought and its ethico-spiritual culture on human civilization was so great that a large population of Central Asian and South-East Asian countries embraced this philanthropic religion and sublime faith. We have already discussed elaborately the history of introduction of Buddhism in Sri Lanka, China and Tibet. One thing which is worth noticing is the fact that Buddhism was brought to Sri Lanka, China and several Central Asian countries including Kashmir–Gandhāra and the kingdoms of the Himalayan region either by individual Buddhist devouts like Mahindra and Saṅghamitrā or by the royal missionaries comprising learned Indian paṇḍits. Kashmiri paṇḍits played a great role in dissemination and propagation of Buddhist faith in China and also in Java. Of the Indian paṇḍits who visited China from the fourth to sixth centuries CE, the majority belonged to Kashmir; a few of them were collaborators of Kumārajīva.

A great Kashmiri scholar who visited practically all Asian countries was Guṇavarman, born of a royal family. After the death of the Kashmir king he was offered the royal throne which he refused. He took active part in the missionary activities in Ceylon and Java; in fact the king of Java and his mother were converted to Buddhism by Guṇavarman. When

Java was attacked by a hostile army, the king sought his advice on the propriety of a Buddhist king getting involved in bloodshed. Guṇavarman's forthright reply was: "Every robber must be punished." It inspired the king who fought a great battle and attained victory. Guṇavarman's fame spread far and wide. The Chinese monks of Nanking made an appeal to the emperor for inviting him to China. Guṇavarman accepted the invitation and reached Nanking in CE 431 after visiting various places on the way in a vessel owned by the Indian merchant Nandin. He was received by the Chinese emperor himself who arranged his stay in the Jetavana Monastery in Nanking. This was his last reception, for Guṇavarman died within a year of his arrival there. So great was his diligence and erudition that within the brief period of his stay in China he translated not less than eleven Sanskrit texts into Chinese.

Buddhism was introduced to Korea, Japan and other countries of South-East Asia by the Buddhist missionaries which were not Indian. This was possible because of the physical distances and inaccessibility of these far-flung countries which were intercepted by seas and oceans. It may be said that the climatically hostile and geographically treacherous terrains of Central Asia through which the Silk Route passed to China were also not easy to tread. But as we know that Kashmir–Gandhāra region in north-west India was the stronghold of Buddhism and it was from here that Buddhism penetrated into Central Asia and China, it was not that difficult — though greatly dangerous — to brave the oddities of terrain and climate because it was all a caravan route which was frequented by the mercantile class of both China and the north-west India. The proximity of Kashmir to these neighbouring countries of Central Asia was also one of the reasons why Kashmiris could dare to go to these countries and to far-flung China as they were all connected by land routes. The Buddhism could reach and spread on such a vast tract of land due to the missionary commitment and unflinching dedication and determination of the paṇḍits of Kashmir. The best part of this missionary religious adventure was that these countries could receive the message of the Buddha from the Indians in its original brand and quality.

The other countries of Far-East Asia like Korea and Japan received the sublime gospel of the Buddha from the Chinese where Buddhism was fractured and fragmented into many sects and schools. When Buddhism came to China it successfully and amicably assimilated the native religion and beliefs of China within its fold in a short span of time but the Buddhism in China lost its virginity, and the forms and brands of Buddhism that came up in circulation and vogue were virtually an admixture or amalgam of native and foreign religion. In China the purity of Buddhism got adulterated as some missionaries from Central Asia also took an active part in the propagation of Buddhism in China.

Religio-Cultural Transformation of Korea

No Indian missionaries came to Korea and Japan for the propagation of Buddhist faith and dissemination of Buddhist wisdom but two or three Indian *ācārya*s did visit Korea. In his article "Cultural Relations of India and Korea" Raghuvira furnishes us brief details of the introduction of Buddhism to Korea by individual *ācārya*s but not the royal missionaries. Raghuvira writes,[1] "The history of Korea goes back to ancient times but her contacts with India commenced in the fourth century CE. It was during the era of three kingdoms. Of these, the kingdom of Kogooryuh was the nearest to China and, therefore, it was the first to receive the Indian religion from the Chinese mainland. In the second year of king Sosoorimwang, in CE 372, a *bhikṣu*, Soondo by name, came to

1. *India's Contribution to World Thought and Culture* (ed.).

Korea carrying with him the statues and message of the Buddha. The year CE 374 is specially memorable. In this, year, the second Indian *ācārya* came to Korea and in CE 375, two temples were erected. These temples of Ibullansa and Sungmoonsa were set up in the city of Pyongyang. It is not possible to ascertain the Sanskrit name of the Indian *ācārya*. In Korea he is popularly known as Ando. Ten years after the advent of Ācārya Ando, in the first year of king Chimryoowang, the second Indian *ācārya* came to Korea. His name was Mallananda. He came to another Korean kingdom of Paikje. After his arrival, the *Dharma* echoed in the kingdom of Paikje. A new religion, new ideas, a new art and a new cheer spread all round.

In CE 417 during the reign of king Noolchiwang, a third Indian *ācārya* visited the third kingdom of Korea, called Silla, via Koguryŭ. His precise Indian name is also not known. In Korea he is famous by the name of Mookhoja.

In his article "A short History of Ancient Korean Buddhism," Ahn kye-hyon writes[2] that when Buddhism was introduced to Korea in the fourth century during the period of three kingdoms, Koguryŭ was the first to receive the new teachings. However, even before this official introduction the Kao-seng chuan makes reference to the presence of Buddhism in Korea. The eastern Chin monk Chih-tao-lin (314–366) sent a letter to Koguryŭ monk, whose name is not given, praising another Chinese monk Chu-ch'ien (268–374). It was, however, only in the reign of King Sosurim (371–384) that Buddhism was officially recognized. The *Samguk sagi* (vol. 18) records that in the second year of his reign in year 372, Fu Chien, the king of the former Chin, sent a monk named Sundo with the images of the Buddha and copies of several texts from the canon, and in the fourteenth year in 384, another

2. *Introduction of Buddhism to Korea* (ed.).

monk named Ado came from China. In year 385, two monasteries, the Songmun Monastery and the Ibullan Monastery were founded for these two monks. This was the beginning of Korean Buddhism.

Regarding the introduction of Buddhism in Korea an interesting information of vital importance was furnished by Prof. Yong-kil Cho in his paper "Exchange of Buddhist Thought and Culture between India and Korea" presented in an international seminar organized in 2001 at Delhi. He alludes to a work known as *Samgookyusa* (*Records of Three kingdoms Book* 3, *Chapter* 4) written by Master Ilyeon of Goryo dynasty wherein it is recorded that an Indian princess from Ayodhyā, then a Buddhist stronghold in India, was married to king Suro (42–199) of Korea. She was given the name "Queen Heohwnagok." She went to Korea by sea and took with her a statue of the Buddha and material to build a stone *pagoḍā* which was constructed in Hogyesa Temple in Kimhae, then the capital of Gayā kingdom. The princess took Buddhist literature also along with her. S.R. Bhatt in his introduction to *Buddha and the Spread of Buddhism in India and Abroad,* vol. 2. rightly remarks[3] that the mode and time of introduction of Buddhism in Korea is shrouded in mystery and there are no definite historical records available in this respect, but according to one tradition it reached there by sea route around first century BCE. In ancient times Korea was divided into several small kingdoms. There was a kingdom by the name Gayā (or Garak) existing before Christian era which embraced Buddhism.

When Buddhism reached Korea for the first time in the latter half of the fourth century, Korea was then divided into three kingdoms Koguryŭ in the north, Pekche in the south-west, and Silla in the south-east. These states were continually engaged in warfare, and their boundaries constantly fluctuated.

3. *Buddha and Spread of Buddhism in India and Abroad* (ed.).

Regarding the introduction of Buddhism in Korea, D.P. Singhal writes[4] that Buddhism was brought to Koguryŭ in CE 372 — reportedly by royal invitation by a Chinese monk, Shun Tao (or Sundo), who came from a small kingdom of China at that time, divided into sixteen states on the upper borders of Korea. He was followed by another Chinese monk, A Tao, and in 375 the king built two temples, one for each monk. Buddhism came to Pekche in 384 from the south through an Indian or Tibetan monk named Marananda. It is said that the Pekche king came to the outskirts of the capital to receive him. Marananda was soon followed by other monks from China. Temples began to appear and Buddhism became the state religion. Silla was the last kingdom to receive Buddhism because of its isolated position; this happened more than thirty years after it had been introduced into Koguryŭ. According to tradition, a Buddhist priest, Mukocha, having cured the king's daughter of an illness by offering prayers to the Buddha, persuaded the king of Silla to send for monks from China.

It is vexingly controversial as to which of the three kingdoms of Korea first received Buddhism. Generally it is believed that Buddhism was first introduced to Koguryŭ and the plea given in support of this assumption is that it was nearest to China. Silla, it is said, could receive the light of this sublime faith in the last because of its isolated position. Regarding this controversy D.P. Singhal remarks[5] that it is quite possible that Buddhism reached Pekche by sea even before it was introduced to Koguryŭ, because Pekche had maritime links with southern China. Establishing this fact is difficult for very few Buddhist works of art have survived from this period in Pekche, as is also the case in Koguryŭ. In both kingdoms art works were destroyed during their dynastic

4. *Buddhism in East Asia.*

5. Ibid.

wars with Silla. The absence of definite information is particularly regrettable, since it was Pekche which established contact with Japan and in the middle of the sixth century, acted as a launching pad for Buddhist doctrine and art into Japan. Pekche admitted Buddhism in 384, 12 years later than Koguryŭ. The *Samyukyusa* says "In the first years of king Chi'mnyu's reign 384, an Indian monk, Maranant'a, came from Eastern China and was brought to the court where he received homage. In the next year 385, ten Buddhist monasteries were built in the new capital, Hansan, and monks were installed in them. This was the beginning of Pekche Buddhism. In the first year of King Asian's reign, in 392, the king ordered the people to believe in Buddhism and seek happiness.

Ahn Kye-hyŏn in his article, "A Short History of Ancient Korean Buddhism" writes[6] that the introduction of Buddhism in Pekche was similar to that in Koguryŭ. After this date there are no pertinent records in the *Samgukyusa* or the *Samguk sagi* until the reign of king Sŏng (523–554). During this reign it appears that Buddhism made great strides, activated in large part, by the return of the monk Kyŏmik from India in 527.

On the information provided by Ahn Ky-hyŏn culled from different sources we learn that during the reign of king Nulchi (417–457), a Koguryŭ monk, Mukhoja, came to Silla and stayed in a village in the north; there he propagated Buddhism in secret. At that time an enjoy from Liang China brought incense to Silla, but no one knew how to use it. Mukhoja instructed them in its use. He also cured the illness of a princess. Buddhism, though known at this time, had very little effect on Silla society. Later, however, during the reign of king Soji (479–499) another Koguryŭ monk, Ado, came to Silla and from this point on the number of followers increased. The name Ado, which was also the name of a monk who appeared in

6. Vol. 3, *Maranat's Open* Pekche.

Koguryŭ a century earlier, seems to have been used to mean a tonsured monk.

Buddhism gradually diffused among the general population, and the royal family sought to obtain official recognition for the new religion; this was opposed by aristocrats. Contrary to Silla society, the ancient tribal system remained strong. The clan was still an important social unit, and indigenous beliefs and customs were powerful and deep rooted; Buddhism could not gain acceptance among the people.

In spite of this, King Pŏphŭng (514-40) and his supporters tried to establish a more powerful monarchy by using the Buddhist *Dharma* as a spiritual prop and then identifying it with the king's order. This led to the promulgation of a new law by the king, reorganizing the administrative and bureaucratic system (in 520), and proclaiming official recognition for Buddhism (in 527), induced by the miraculous martyrdom of Ich'adon, a court official and a devout Buddhist. Buddhist belief and practice, initially, in Silla must have been similar to that in Koguryŭ and Pekche.

Rhi Ki-yong in his article, "Silla Buddhism: Its Special Features" writes[7] regarding the introduction and status of Buddhism in Korea. He writes that Buddhism from the period of its earliest introduction has exerted an enormous influence on Korea. It arrived during the period of the three kingdoms before the peninsula was united into a single nation. Buddhism helped bring people together, it was the spiritual support which united them. Officially adopted as the State religion in the sixth century, it remained so for nearly eight hundred years, up to the fourteenth century. Even after this time, during the Choson dynasty which favoured Confucianism, Buddhism remained a powerful religion in both belief and

7. *Introduction of Buddhism to Korea* (ed.).

moral principle.

Buddhism in the Silla dynasty had an especially significant place in the society, deeply influencing philosophy, art and literature. This chapter will examine the special features of Silla Buddhism which played an important role in unifying the kingdom.

The Buddhism which flourished in the three kingdoms of Korea was of a different form as is projected by Rhi Ki-yong. He observes[8] that there was a great difference in the form that Buddhism took in Silla as compared to the other two kingdoms, Koguryŭ and Pekche. At the time when the three kingdoms on the peninsula were in opposition to one another, Koguryŭ was the most advanced. Silla seems to have been least developed from all points of view, in part due to its geographical isolation from China, the centre of East-Asian civilization. Also, the Silla peoples were of a southern nature; they were pliable and made political decisions through consensus. This was quite different from the northern tough-minded military disposition found among the people of Koguryŭ. The kings of Koguryŭ and Pekche held absolute power and were in close cultural contact with China. Such tendencies were weak in Silla.

Dwelling upon this issue of difference, Rhi Ki-yong further tells us that in Silla, Buddhism was first officially recognized by King Pŏphŭng in 527, but this was not the result of his decision alone. In Koguryŭ and Pechke, on the other hand, official recognition followed immediately upon its introduction into their courts. The martyrdom of Ich'adon a kinsman and official at the court, and the consequent reorientation by the aristocrats made this recognition possible. Prior to this time, there were individuals in Silla who knew about Buddhism and the king himself was supportive of the new teachings. It

8. Ibid., p. 187.

was only the opposition by many aristocrats that delayed official acceptance. Ich'adon decided to offer his life for the cause. After committing the crime of starting to build a monastery on the pretext of following the king's command, his execution was demanded by the aristocrats who were in conflict with the throne. Ich'adon wanted, above all else, his sacrifice to aid in the propagation of the *Dharma* of the Buddha among the people of Silla. He was convinced that a miracle would occur because when his head was severed, the sky became dark, the earth rumbled and white milk flowed from his wound rather than blood. His head flew away to the summit of Mt. Kŭmgang (a mountain north of Kumgang). It is said that the aristocrats were astonished and, repenting for their action, prostrated themselves before the king. The king and aristocrats acting together, thus recognized Buddhism as state religion for the first time. Later King Pŏphŭng, whose name means "making the Buddha's *dharma* flourish," abdicated, relinquishing the throne to his young son, King Chinhung, and became a monk while his wife joined the order of the nuns. Thus they lived in retreat for the rest of their life.

The Buddhism had a great impact on the people of the three kingdoms in Korea. It would not be out of place to mention that Korean Buddhism tended broadly to follow the Chinese pattern with one important difference.

John Snelling[9] observes that being a small and politically vulnerable nation, the Koreans could not tolerate the same diversity of schools that proliferated in China. Various attempts, not entirely successful, were therefore made to syncretize and harmonize the teachings of the Buddhist schools, though at times the local form of Ch'an/Zen, called Son in Korea, was to prevail and has persisted to the present time despite the general rush towards Western type of

9. *The Buddhist Handbook*, p. 173.

modernization that has produced a concomitant explosion of Christianity.

It seems probable, as Rhi Ki-yong[10] puts, that until the unification in CE 668 under the Unified Silla, understanding of the texts remained at the elementary stage. According to extant historical records, a higher level of Mahāyāna thought was known in Koguryŭ than in the other two kingdoms, for example, Podŏk and his ten disciples gave lectures on the *Mahāpariṇirvānasūtra*. There were monasteries named after important doctrines and persons found in the texts: monasteries such as Yuma (Vimalakīrti) and Taesung (Mahāyāṇa); a monk called IIsŭng (*ekayāna* in Sanskrit, the One Vehicle). Uiyŏn, a Koguryŭ monk stayed in Ch'ang-an from 576–591 and brought back to Korea such texts as the *Shis-ti chin-lun* (*Daśabhūmikasūtraśāstra*), the *Ta-chih'tu lun* (*Mahāprajñāpāramitāsāśtra*), the *Pu-sa-ti ching* (*Vajracchedikaprajñāpāramitā* commentary). Hyeryang, a Koguryŭ monk who travelled to Silla and became the highest ranking cleric in King Chinhung's reign (540–576) seems to have been quite learned in the Mahāyāna texts.

About the compartive and formal influence of Buddhism on these three regions, Rhi Ki-yong observes[11] that in 643, Taoism which had been in Koguryŭ in 624, was raised to the level of the State religion with the support of a powerful minister of state Yŏn Kaesomun. In this northern kingdom some opposition to Buddhism probably began in the late sixth century, as evidenced by Hyeryang's move to Silla and the many Buddhist monks who went to Japan. The Japanese sources report on the large number of Koguryŭ monks teaching from the late sixth until the early seventh century: Hyep'yon, Hyeja, Sungnyung, Tamjing, Hyegwan, Tojung and

10. *Introduction of Buddhism to Korea* (ed.), p. 189.

11. Ibid.

Tosun. On the whole, Koguryŭ Buddhism seems to have been, dominated by a scholastic emphasis on Mahāyāna practices in a monastic setting; it does not seem to have reached a stage from where it could be practised or understood by the general population.

He goes on adding that the situation of Buddhism in Pekche was similar to that of Koguryŭ. There are few remaining literary sources, but those we have indicated an emphasis on ritual and the *Vinaya;* the theoretical studies of the doctrine may have lagged behind that of Koguryŭ. Although Buddhism was introduced in 384, none of our sources for a study of Pekche date before the sixth century; the oldest artefacts of Buddhism in this kingdom were found in the tomb of King Muryong (501–22). Among the items in that tomb are loths, patterned tiles and other artefacts of Buddhist origin, along with objects of other popular religious traditions. It was not until King Song's reign (523–553) that we find a record of attempts being made to achieve a more profound understanding of Buddhism. In 526, later historical sources report, Kyŏmik returned to Pekche after studying in India for five years. He brought with him texts such as the five recensions of the *Vinaya* (*Wu-pu-lu*) and the *Abhidharma* which he translated into Chinese. We are not sure about the exact nature of the texts which he brought since his name does not appear in the colophons of any of the translations of the *Vinaya* nor do we find it in Vich'on's catalogue, the *Sinp'yon chejong Kyojang ch'ongrok.* Early Pekche Buddhism may have been strongly influenced by that of Koguryŭ; the political events that resulted in monks from the northern kingdom moving to Japan of Silla, would have also caused them to travel to Pekche.

Korean Buddhism enjoyed its golden age during the Silla (668–935) and Koryŏ (935–1392) periods. It was then favoured by the intellectual elite and honoured with royal patronage.

In 668 Korea was united under the Silla dynasty which ruled until 935. Many Korean monks went to China to study Buddhist doctrines, and some even went to India. According to I-tsing, five Korean monks visited India during the seventh century. Prajñāvarman, a Korean monk, travelled by sea to Fukien in China and then, after learning Sanskrit and studying Buddhism for ten years at a monastery of Great Faith, he proceeded to India in the company of a Chinese monk. Of those who went to China to study, Yuan-tso (613–683) of the Fa Sian Sect and Yuanhiao (617–670) and Yi-siang (625–702) of the Huayen sect are best known. An outstanding monk of the period was Wohnyo, who laid the firm foundation of Korean Buddhism, and whose works are even now highly esteemed in China and Japan. However he did not go to China, which was under the T'ang dynasty at the time, although it was the fashion for scholars to do so. The Huayen doctrine, proclaiming the Buddha-nature of all beings without distinction, was first introduced to Korea in the latter part of the seventh century. As a result of the work of Yui-Shih, a Korean monk who had been actively associated with the learned circles of T'ang China, the "consciousness-only" doctrines of Yogācāra Buddhism spread in Korea. Korea borrowed profusely form the Chinese civilization, and this tendency helped to develop Buddhism at the time, even though Confucianism, its formidable rival, was also introduced in the early eighth century.[12]

In this context the observations of H. Hackmann[13] are worth quoting:

> In all three kingdoms the acceptance of Buddhism was associated with political intentions. They wanted the support of the powerful neighbouring kingdom. For this very reason Korea adopted, together with the new religion,

---

12. *Buddhism in East Asia*, pp. 140-41.
13. *Buddhism as a Religion*, p. 86.

much of the higher Chinese culture, for instance, the use of the Chinese written character.

H. Hackmann writes[14] that Buddhism had its golden age in this country at the time when a new Korean empire was formed after the destruction of the three older kingdoms. The soul of the movement which led to this result was a Buddhist monk, as he was murdered by a rival. The latter, who succeeded in placing himself on the throne of the newly united kingdom of Korea (with Songdo as its capital), founded a dynasty which lasted about 500 years (912–1392). He thoroughly supported Buddhism; monasteries and monks increased rapidly in numbers, and won a stronghold over the whole nation. There was a law at that time in existence urging that one out of three sons in a family should become a monk. During this epoch of its prosperity, Korean Buddhism on certain occasions even had some influence on China, its motherland. Important documents belonging to a noted Chinese school, which had been lost by the fate of war, were restored by an embassy sent from China to Korea, and this gave a new impetus to that school. It is equally worth noting that two systems of alphabetical writing invented for the Korean language show some connection with Buddhism. The first, the so-called Nido alphabet, an adaptation of Chinese characters employed for their phonetic value, was the work of a Buddhist monk and great scholar called Syel-chong, living toward the close of the eighth century CE. Some six centuries later the present Korean script, the Unmen alphabet, was invented under the auspices of King Jong (CE 1447). This alphabet was derived from the Tibetan (which itself is an offspring of Sanskrit), the knowledge of which was due to Buddhism. It is well known that the Korean Unmen is very likely the most simple and most perfect alphabet in the world.

14. Ibid., pp. 86-87.

During Koryŏ (935–1392) periods, Buddhism became the entire basis of Korea's religious life, affecting the ideology, customs and morals of the people as well as the political and economic life of the state. Festivals were celebrated by the Court with great splendour, and magnificent monasteries were founded. Many Buddhist monks even occupied high positions in the administration. Buddhist participation in politics, however, caused increased opposition which had begun to emerge during the latter part of the Koryŏ ascendancy.[15]

We are also told that Buddhism, hitherto the religion of the Korean aristocracy related to the Silla dynasty, became the faith of the common people through the efforts of such eminent monks as Pu-chao, who introduced Korea to Son (*Dhyāna* or Chan) Buddhism, and who is famous for his editing of the catalogue of the Chinese *Tripiṭaka,* known in Korean as the Tejang, published in 1010. Son Buddhism spread widely in Korea and during the twelfth century it became extremely popular as taught by Chinsul. Son Buddhism eventually assumed predominance in Korea, although, during the period of Mongol ascendancy in China, Lamaism was introduced to Korea.[16]

Regarding the brand and form of Buddhism that was introduced to Korea, S.R. Bhatt[17] observes that Korea has been an important Buddhist country practising Mahāyāna form of Buddhism but having Hīnayāna elements interspersed in it. It has reformulated Zen, Lamaism of Tibet and Mongolia, Tantrayāna (Vajrayāna), etc. to suit Korean indigenous culture. Introduced first from India and thereafter influenced by Chinese form of Buddhism, there has been tremendous impact of Buddhism on the Korean national life and culture for about two thousand years.

15. *Buddhism in East Asia,* p. 141.

16. Ibid.

17. *Buddha and Spread of Buddhism in India and Abroad,* introduction,p. xiv.

Raghuvira while writing on cultural relations of India and Korea says[18] that different sects were established in the three kingdoms of Korea. In Koguryŭ the Samnonjong sect, in Pekche the Yooljons or Vinaya sect, and in Silla the Yoosikjong sect flourished. The doctrine of *prajñā* was developed in Silla only. Everywhere temples and *vihāra*s were constructed. Both the king and the people erected them with faith and devotion. Images and paintings of the Buddha and other deities were done. The manufacture of sacred utensils used in worship and other works of art greatly contributed to the development of various fine arts.

Before this, art had not achieved a status in Korea. With the spread of Indian *Dharma*, architecture, sculpture, painting, woodcraft, metalcraft, reading, writing, philosophical thought and literature enriched the country.

Silla Buddhism which was everyway the face of Korean Buddhism displayed three very distinct periods of development. Rhi-Ki yong[19] puts them as under:

1. Early Period (From King Popjung [514–540] to the first half of King Munmu's reign [661–681]).
2. Prospering Period (after unification, the last half of king Munmu's time until king Hyegong [765–780]).
3. Declining Period (lasting untill the fall of the dynasty).

Elaborating the peculiarities and special features of these three, special characterstics of Silla Buddhism were prevalent in the Early Period but from the Prospering Period onward, there were major changes in the tradition. The *bodhisattva* ideals faded away and were replaced by a dependence on rituals and ceremonies which were performed by rote without the spirit of the Mahāyāna teachings. During the Declining Period,

18. *India's Contribution to World Thought and Culture* (ed.), p. 341.
19. *Introduction of Buddhism to Korea* (ed.), p. 192.

scholastic study of the *Dharma* had less support. During the Declining Period, a new form of Buddhism emerged based on the Ch'an (K. Son) from China. Nine divisions of this school developed in Korea and became known as the "Nine Mountains of Son." But the Son Buddhism was not easy for the masses to understand; if reflected more closely the tastes of the aristocracy. Social upheaval which marked the decline of the dynasty brought about a return to popular religious practices, and until the stability of the Koryŏ the ruling classes lost their role of leadership in the society. Silla Buddhism provided the spiritual basis for the kingdom during its time of greatest development and prosperity, and the decline of Buddhism also marked the decline of the kingdom.

We are told that the main philosophical leader of Silla Buddhism was Wohnyo who was both practical and original in his thinking. He was an outstanding scholar whose writings display a profound understanding of the important doctrine of Mahāyāna. An examination of his writings shows that he was deeply absorbed in the thought of the Ta-ch'eng ch'i-hsin lun (Awakening of Faith) and using this text as a basis showed a profound understanding of various Mahāyāna *sūtras*, such as the *Lotus-Sūtra*, the Chin-Kuang-ming, the Ta-sheng tong-hsing, the *Nirvāṇa-Sūtra*, the *Avataṁsaka-Sūtra*, the p'u-saying-luo pen yeh, the *Mahāprajñāpāramitā-Sūtra*, the Ta-chi, the Yao-shih pen-yuan, and *śāstras* such as the Chung-kuan, the Twelve-gate Treatise, the Yu-chia lun and *Mahāyānasaṁgraha*. Before becoming a monk, it is conceivable that he was a member of the hwarang youth organization which was so important for the aristocrats of Silla. In any case he became a teacher of these young men. A free spirit, he stood beyond the notion of sacred and profane. He made use of both sword and pen during his life and in following the principles of Mahāyāna at its most profound level, he is said to have remained unaffected by his surrounding and never made improper use of his status as a leader and teacher. He gave up the opportunity to study in T'ang China and turned away from a life course which could have led him to the highest posts of National Teacher or King's Teacher. He remained a man of the people and went out to wander among men of all classes. He had talent in music, writing and teaching, but was not confined by the words of the scripture or obsessive involvement with ritual and chanting. He responded to the desires of ordinary people who wished for a fortunate rebirth in the pure land. He also gave support to the beliefs in the *bodhisattvas* Maitreya, Avalokiteśvara and Kṣitigarbha and yet at the same time he taught that being concerned about rebirth in either paradise or hell was the result of inferior belief.

The story of religio-cultural transformation of Korean people would be left half-told if we do not mention the idea for which Wohnyo, Uisang and P'yohun strived dauntlessly with a missionary zeal. In his well researched article Rhi Ki-yong tells[20] us that Wohnyo's aim was the attainment of "oneness" that comes from the perfection of wisdom. In Korean this also mean "being large." His ideal was, in other words, the realization of a higher Self (tae-a). This "oneness" was to be understood within the context of the teachings found in the Buddhist texts, such as that of "one" (il) and "all-embracing circle" (won), the major doctrines of the *Avataṁsaka-Sūtra*. He described this as the "great" (tae) of the Ta-ch'eng ch'i-hsin lun. The "one" was conceived by Wohnyo as the integration of every kind of power and wisdom; we might even say it was the source of all values, the "source of the one mind" and as the source it brought about the extinction of all conflicts. The focus on "one" cannot be considered apart from the social situation of Silla before unification. This ideal of total harmony was taught to the political leaders and the young elite and

20. Ibid., p. 194.

served as a doctrine which could promise peace and prosperity through the uniting of the three kingdoms.

Uisang, an intimate friend of Wohnyo approached the problem of unity through the teaching of one vehicle (*ekayāna*), the major theme of the *Avataṁsaka-Sūtra*. Uisang had studied under Chih-yen in China and later held the title of National Teacher. His thought which was in agreement with the spirit of Wohnyo's teachings, was given a pictorial form: a meander design made up of a poem consisting of 210 Chinese characters entitled the Hwaom ilsung popkyedo. The meander begins with the word pop (*Dharma*) and the remaining characters weave their way until the final word near the centre which is pul (Buddha). The design is composed of 54 turns and is in the shape of the square. This poem taught one to go forward through the right path firmly holding the *Dharma*. "In one there is all, in all there is one; one is all, all is one." There is another famous meander made by a Silla monk, the Haein Sammaedo (The Ocean Seal Samādhi Meander), which follows this format used by Uisang.

The Koreans learned, particularly the people of Silla, from the teachings of these distinguished monks that these doctrines could be applied in the realm of social activity. The groups are not separated, but are interrelated to one another. The rulers and the people were also subject to the same notion of "being one" because there is no difference between self and others.

Because of her proximity to China, Korea owes a lot in language and ideology. In China, or in those neighbouring countries where Chinese wisdom and culture penetrated, learning was the prerogative of a few noble men and officials, who guarded it jealously from the masses. But Buddhism broke their barrier, and while the Confucian classics formed the basis of courtly and aristocratic education in Korea, Buddhism appealed to the intellectuals and to the common people, and formed the basis of popular education. Indeed, by purposely recruiting converts from the humbler classes, Buddhism made a significant contribution in the diffusion of culture. Wherever Buddhists went, religious literature was published in the local language. Even the statues, pictures and scrolls carried vernacular explanations.

Korea received from India and China all that is required for transfiguration of religion and culture for a civilized society. China gave her language and ideology to Korea. India contributed Sanskrit and phonetic letters from which syllabaries or alphabets were constructed, not only for vernacular writing and printing, but also as aids to the popularization of Confucian teachings. The Korean syllabary, called nido, was, like the Kana of the Japanese, a collection of syllables and not a true alphabet. The nido gave a phonetic value to some of the more common Chinese characters, although the idea of having a vernacular system of writing was probably suggested by Sanskrit letters, some of which represented Korean sounds accurately. The Korean alphabet, unmun (common language), was invented by a Buddhist monk named Syel-chong (or Sye-chong), one of the ablest scholars in Korean history. Incidentally, we should also mention the name of the priest known as Kyunik from Korea whose inquisitiveness attracted him to India, the source of supreme knowledge. From India he carried back scriptures relating to *Vinaya* and translated them into classical Chinese. He was a resident of the kingdom of Pekche.

As Buddhism spread along the Silk Route through Central Asia and into the East-Asian cultural sphere, it made its way into Korea. In this new cultural setting, the religious tradition was adopted by the court. Buddhism served as a culture carrier for the Chinese ideas that were spreading eastward and at the same time it still preserved much of the Indian heritage.

The richness of the religious expression to be found in Buddhist texts, rituals and institutions added much to the life of the Koreans.

Since our study is confined from first century BCE to eighth century CE, we shall not go beyond the scope of our inquiry. This much is sufficient to give a fair and panoramic picture of religio-cultural transformation of the Korean people under the impact of Buddhism.

Buddhism and Religio-Cultural Metamorphosis of Japan

From Korea, Buddhism made it further eastward, headway to Japan. The exact date and year of its introduction to Japan is still disputed. Regarding the introduction of Buddhism into Korea the account given by H. Hackmann[21] is worth quoting. According to him Japan owes the entrance of Buddhism to the missionary ardour of Korea. The south-western of the three above-mentioned ancient Korean kingdoms, Pekche (called by the Japanese Hiakusai or Kudara) was the starting-point of the mission. According to the account given in the old Japanese historical work *Nihongi*, in CE 552 a Korean king sent an envoy to the ruler of Japan to commend the new religion to him, and to convey to him objects for worship and sacred books. It is true that an unreliable Japanese authority speaks of an earlier advent of Buddhism in CE 522 (another authority says CE 534). It could at the most have been but an abortive attempt. Even after 552 Buddhism only advanced slowly and with many struggles. A party gathered about it, which the adherents of the native religion of Shintoism most strenuously opposed. A further importation of priests and sacred objects kept it in close connection with the land of its origin. The struggle about it resulted in its favour since CE 588. The greatest help to the rising Buddhism was Prince Shōtuku Daishi (he died

21. *Buddhism as a Religion*, pp. 88-89.

in 621), whose memory is still firmly cherished in history and the legends. The Buddhist monks and nuns who streamed into the country from Korea continued coming for a long time, and the influence of Korean art is still plainly visible at such places as Horiuji, or in the museum at Nara, in the most ancient Buddhist statues. As Korean Buddhism had adopted the Chinese form of the Mahāyāna school, so in like manner it transmitted and entered Japan as confirmed by some details in the old story of its introduction. Such is the nomenclature of certain divinities (Amitābha, Kwanvin, Tashihchi).

Kamata Shigeo in his article, "The Transmission of Pekche Buddhism to Japan" writes[22] that the official date of the transmission of Pekche Buddhism to Japan varies in different sources. The Nihon shoki, for example, gives the date as 552, while the Gankōji garan engi narabini ryūki shizaichō (History of the Gankōji monastery and ledger of property and income) and the jōgū Shōtuku, hoo teisetsu (Biography of Prince Shōtuku, king of the *Dharma*) claim that the transmission occurred in 538; the latter date is one most commonly accepted by modern scholars. All these documents agree that Pekche Buddhism came to Japan during the reign of King Sŏng (523–533), who sent Buddhist monks, images and scriptures to the royal court in Japan. While this is the official account, it is plausible that the first transmission of Buddhism to Japan occurred earlier. The lack of any corroborating literary evidence, however, prevents us from determining with any precision this date.

Early Japanese Buddhism was transmitted from Korea and the Chinese mainland. Kamata Shigeo writes[23] that Buddhism was transmitted from Pekche to Japan in 552, during the tenth month of the thirteenth year of Emperor Kimmei. At that time

22. *Introduction of Buddhism to Korea,* p. 143.

23. Ibid., p. 151.

King Sŏng of Pekche sent an envoy to Japan. This envoy carried with him a bronze image of Śākyamuni Buddha, as well as pennants, canopies, *sūtra*s and *śāstra*s. He also brought a proclamation from King Sŏng which told of the merit which would accrue to the court from the display and veneration of these objects. According to the Jōgū Shōtuku hōō teistsu, however, the date of transmission was earlier (538). Although it is not clear which of these dates is correct, the latter one seems more likely for the following reason. In 624, the thirty-second year of the Suiko, the Pekche monk Kwallŭk made a statement as follows: "It has not been even one hundred years since our king, having heard that Japanese emperor was wise, sent Buddhist images and scriptures to Japan."

If we were to accept the 538 date, it would mean that a period of 86 years would have elapsed from the time of Suiko until Kwallŭk's statement. In addition to this information, it should be noted that in 523 Pekche gave official recognition to Japan. With this evidence, the date of 538 for the transmission of Buddhism seems plausible.

Throwing further light on the history of transmission of Buddhism to Japan, Kamata Shigeo[24] goes on adding that there was, moreover, interaction between Japan and Pekche before the above-mentioned Buddhist gifts were sent. For example the Nihon Shoki relates that, in 283, "The Pekche king sent a seamstress named Chinmojin. She was the founder of tailoring in Japan." In the following year, Ajikki, who was an expert in both the Confucian classics and Buddhist scriptures arrived in Japan. He is perhaps best remembered because he brought along two very impressive horses. On his recommendation, scholar Wang arrived in Japan in 285. He became a tutor to the crown prince and introduced the Lunyu (Confucian Analects) and the Ch'ien-tsu wen (Thousand Character Classic)

24. Ibid.

to the court. These cultural contributions from Korea continued into the sixth century. In 513 Tanyangi, a master of the Five Classics arrived from Pekche followed in 516 by the Confucian scholar Han'goanmu.

This interesting history of Korean monks visiting Japan with a missionary zeal for disseminating Buddhism would be left incomplete if we do not tell that the flow of monks from Korea to Japan continued even after the introduction of Buddhism. In the fifteenth year of Emperor Kimmei (554), ten monks led by Tanhe came to Japan. Prior to the arrival of this group, we have a record that Taoism and seven other monks were already in residence there. Tanhe was housed in a newly constructed monastery and it was said, perhaps erroneously, that he was the first monk to reside in Japan. While we do not know with any certainty the type of Buddhism taught by these two masters, it is possible that they were students of the Mādhyamika and Tattvasiddhi schools. There are various theories about the number of monks who arrived from Pekche during this period. The records assert that not only Buddhist monks travelled to Japan but there were also specialists in the *I-Ching* (Book of Changes), and the classics and medicine. Judging from this account of the variety of specialists who served as the cultural guides, it can be assumed that some sort of educational institutions were established in Japan, where Confucian scholars, Buddhist monks and other adepts lived and taught. These Pekche scholars and monks served a tour of duty in Japan and then returned home.

This contact between Pekche and Japan increased, and in 577 in the sixth year of Emperor Bidatsu, Pekche sent a delegation of Buddhist scholars, teachers and meditation masters to Owakeno ōkimi-dera in Naniwa (present Osaka). The degree of veneration shown to these Buddhists is exemplified by Prince Shōtuku's regard for IIIa, who came in 583. The prince considered him to be a divine person and revered him as an incarnation of the Bodhisattva Avalokiteśvara. IIIa lived on mount Ken'o in Sesstu (present Osaka and Hyōgo) where he was assassinated by a Silla enemy. These Pekche monks, who were held in high regard, were true pioneers in the process of transplanting the seed of Buddha *Dharma* to Japan.

Lauding the role played by the Pekche monks in firmly establishing Buddha *Dharma* in Japan, Kamata Shigeo[25] tells that the sixth century was an active one for Buddhist missionary activity. In the second year of Emperor Yōmei (587), the Pekche monk P'ungguk was invited to teach the *Dharma* by the younger brother of the Emperor, Prince Anahobe. In order to give help to the ailing emperor, Kuratsukuri no Tasuna built Sakata Monastery and commissioned a Korean monk to construct a 6 ft. high image of the Buddha. The emperor's health continued to fail, however, and he died on the ninth day of the fourth month of that year. Fortunately, Prince Shōtuku and his supporters were able to defeat the group that called for the ouster of this alien religion. The culmination of this growing power of Buddhism in Japan came with the building of Shitennō Monastery and the invitation to the Pekche monk P'ungguk to conduct the rituals ceremony commemorating the completion of the building. Afterwards, he was installed as the first abbot of the monastery.

Dwelling more on the further history of propagation of Buddhism by the monks under royal patronage in Japan, Kamata Shigeo informs[26] us that the first year of Emperor Shunshūn (588), saw the arrival of the monk Hyech'ong who presented sacred relics of the Buddha to the throne. Hyech'ong was accompanied by architects, T'aeryang mal'tae and Mun'ga

25. Ibid., p. 153.

26. Ibid.

koja as well as by the painter Pekche and an anonymous tile expert. Besides these architects, carpenters, metal workers and other artisans were the monks Hyejung, Hyesuk, Toŏm, and Yŏnggae. These artisans and monks were associated with the building and completion of Hōkō Monastery and Hyech'ong became a resident in that site.

At the beginning of the seventh century, the tenth year of Empress Suiko (602), the Pekche Mādhyamika scholar Kwallŭk arrived. He brought with him documents on calendars, astronomy, geometry, divination and numerology, an indication of the breadth of interest among scholar monks. With the blessing of the emperor, he lived at Ganko Monastery and gathered around him a select group of thirty-four students. Among them were Yogonofubito no Oyatamafuru who studied calendrics and numerology and Yamashiro no Omihitate who was trained in numerology. The support which Kwallŭk had in the court was shown in the thirty-second year of Empress Suiko (624), when he was appointed to the office of "Bishop." At the same time a Koguryŭ monk Tŏkchŏk was made the "overseer of the *Saṅgha*." This was the inception of the Buddhist ecclesiastical hierarchy in Japan.

The transmission of Pekche Buddhism and culture to Japan continued until Pekche was conquered by Silla. During this period many Korean monks were granted permanent residence in Japan. In addition to the study of the Buddhist texts, they performed theurgic rites, such as those concerned with rain making and healing. The importance of these monks to the early development of Buddhism in Japan is made evident by the construction and naming of the Kudaradai Monastery (Great Pekche Monastery) during the eleventh year of Emperor Jōmei (639).

Not only monks but nuns also were involved in this process of bringing Buddhist practice from Pekche to Japan. Three

Japanese nuns Zenshin, Zensō and Eizen, travelled to Pekche in the second year of Emperor Yōmei (587) in order to study *Vinaya*. They carried on their study of the six sections of the *Vinaya* and the three returned to Japan and established the first formal study of the *Vinaya*. They were housed in Sakurai monastery where other nuns were later ordained.

For one hundred years after the first transmission of Buddhism to Japan, the relationship with Pekche was very close. And even after the defeat of Pekche in the second year of Emperor Tenchi (663), there were numerous refugees who sought safety in Japan. Among these refugees were many monks who exerted an influence even after the fall of the kingdom. Thus, we can say with certainty that Japanese Buddhism was started by Pekche monks.

The greatest name associated with the introduction of Buddhism in Japan is prince Shōtuku who became the Regent in 593. He is considered to be the founder of Japanese civilization as well as the unified Japanese nation. It was he who proclaimed Buddhism as the religion of the state and laid foundation of the Buddhist establishment consisting of learned and disciplined monks. By founding the temple of Tennoji near the sea on a hill of present-day Osaka he admitted embassies and missionaries and immigrants. The Tennoji Temple was probably the first attempt in Japan from where the social welfare owed its origin. During his regency (593–621), the state built the first Buddhist *pagoḍās*, seminaries, hospitals, dispensaries and homes for the aged and destitute. The Temple of Hokoji was built in 596 and the Temple of Horyuji in 607. At the latter, Prince Shōtuku himself gave lectures on the Mahāyāna *sūtras*, especially on the *Saddharmapuṇḍarīka* (The Lotus of the True Law) The *Vimalakīrtinirdeśa* and the *Śrīmālā Derisiṁhanada-Sūtra*. Later the Horyuji Temple became an important centre for the study of Buddhist idealism, of the Vijñaptimātratā or Yogācāra school. It must be mentioned here that Shōtuku became the Regent during the reign of his aunt, Empress Suiko (573–628) and was extremely popular with his people. He and other Japanese dignitaries adopted Buddhism because they believed it was the world trend of the time in philosophical thought. In February 594, he issued his first imperial ordinance as regent of the Empire, proclaiming Buddhism as the state religion and urging the development of the *Triratna*, the three basic tenets of Buddhism — the *Buddha*, the *Dharma* and the *Saṅgha*. They were to be the principal objects of faith and undivided devotion and were to constitute the fundamental basis of an upright life.

Shōtuku's father Emperor Yōmei who ascended the throne in 585 for a brief period, was the first Mikado to embrace Buddhism. He commissioned an image of Bhaiṣajyaguru, the Buddha of Healing, which was completed after his death and later installed in the world-renowned Horyuji Temple where it can still be seen. It was during his reign that the first Japanese, Tasuna, renounced the world to become a Buddhist monk.

Shōtuku dispatched envoys to China for fetching Buddhist texts and he himself wrote commentaries and expositions on available texts. The temples built by him and the art therein were the effective means of attracting the people's admiration of and reverence to Buddhist religion. The mural paintings, panel decorations, ceilings and pillars provided the settings for Buddhist worship and ceremonies, which were performed with musical accompaniment around the statue of the Buddha installed on a dais in the central part of the temple. Thus, all the fine arts were a part of Buddhist worship, which not only captivated the devotees, but also automatically and almost imperceptibly released and refined the aesthetic energies of its followers. The Japanese were fascinated by these temples, and by 624 there were 46 temples, 816 priests, and 569 nuns in Japan.

It would not be an exaggeration to say that the contributions of Shōtuku to Buddhism are perhaps as great as Aśoka's contributions in India. His political astuteness was really great. He set up direct diplomatic relations with China. He also provided the basis of national unity, guided and inspired the country with spiritual ideas of Buddhism and educate the people in arts and science.

A new phase in the history of Buddhism began with the establishment of a new capital at Nara (literary meaning "the abode of peace") in Buddhism in 710. Emperor Shomu (701–756) was the central figure of this phase who ruled for 25 years (724-749). He spent the last seven years of his life in monastic robes. Popularly known as the Era of the Heavenly Peace, Shomu's reign marks a climactic period in the development of religion and art, as well as in government administration. He built temples and monasteries throughout the country as centres of religious observance and discipline as well as of social work, especially medical care. He erected the impressive temple, Todaiji, at Nara which houses the imposing image of Roshana (or Vairocana Buddha) cast in a mood of calm reflection and superb dignity. The dedication ceremony of this statue took place in 752, with many Indian monks and visitors in attendance, and it is regarded as the most brilliant event in the history of Japanese Buddhism. Emperor Shomu also constructed the Daibutsu, the great bronze Buddha statue rising 49 ft. from the ground, which has come to be looked upon as a symbol of a united nation.

Regarding the Nara period D.P. Singhal's book *Buddhism in East Asia*[27] mentions that during that time Buddhist learning and culture greatly developed, coinciding with the introduction of the six Nara sects in politics and aristocratic society. For the Japanese these six sects brought together nearly all

27. Ibid., p. 150

the major elements of over one thousand years of Buddhist development in India and China. They were exposed to theology and their schools of philosophy were systematized for the first time. By the close of the Nara period very little of the knowledge contained in the six sects had reached the common man, but Japan had developed her own scholars and leaders. Examining the historical contribution of these sects, it is found that their major role was the introduction of the academic study of Buddhism into Japan; as centres of Buddhist propaganda among the masses they were unsuccessful. The government regarded their purpose in society still very much the same as what it was before. They were to conduct rites and services for the protection of the nation; the imperial family and aristocracy and to promote culture and study. From the historical development point of view, it is possible to regard the Nara period as merely representing the transfer of Buddhist institutions to Japanese soil. By the end of the era, the six Nara sects remained alien implants apparently exerting imperceptible and enormous influence upon Japanese thought and society. Certain basic Buddhist attitudes towards life were assimilated that left indelible marks upon succeeding generations. One such view was the nascent comprehension of the transitory and illusory nature of human life. Such views of impermanence represented a drastic change in Japanese thought.

We are also told there that the origin of Japanese educational system began in Buddhist temples, and the introduction of medicine, hospitals and dispensaries is similarly traced to Nara Buddhism. Even farm implements were improved under the patronage of travelling Buddhist priests; as well as on the vast temple holdings. Not only did they help to improve agriculture, thus the method of living, but they also brought about changes in methods of disposing of the dead. Cremation began to become popular. It well suited

Shinto concept of purification and also served the practical purpose of preserving scarce agricultural lands. Buddhist funeral rites gradually developed under indigenous influence and evolved into the cults of Jozo bosatsu (Kīrtigarbha) and Emma (Yama). But even more important were the gradual changes in social attitudes. The abandonment of hunting for pleasure and meat eating, along with the skilful development of vegetarian cooking, became Japanese characteristics.

Incidentally it would not be out of place to mention here that during the reign of Emperor Kōtoku (645–654) a scholarly Indian monk, Hodo (*Dharmamārga* or *Dharmapatha*), is said to have come to Japan from Rājagṛha, India. However, evidence supporting this visit is inconclusive. Japanese chronicles mentioned Bodhisena as the most prominent among a number of early Indian monks who came to Japan; while the details of his life in India are not known, he is much revered in Japan. Having received mystic inspiration from the Bodhisattva Mañjuśrī, he set out from India for China and arrived there in 730. Young in years but mature in wisdom, he was welcomed by both the clergy and laity. Impressed by his integrity and reputation, some Japanese monks and envoys who were on a mission in China at the time persuaded Bodhisena to come to Japan. Accompained by monks and musicians, including a Vietnamese monk, Fu-che, and a Chinese monk, Tao Hsuan, Boshisena arrived in Japan on 18 May in 736 after a stormy sea journey. By this time Japanese Buddhism was more than 200 years old, and visting monks were, as would be expected, accorded an honourable reception. Bodhisena settled in Japan and taught Sanskrit and preached Buddhism until he died in 760 at the age of 57. When the statue of Vairocana Buddha (Daibutsu), the biggest in the world, was cast and installed at Nara, it was Bodhisena who presided over the religious ceremony of dedication. A *stūpa* known as Baramon Soja (Brahmaṇa Archbishop) was built in his memory.

In the very beginnings of Heian period (794–1186), i.e. in 794, the capital was shifted from Nara to Heian (modern Kyoto). This effectively undermined the political power of the learned metropolitan *Saṅgha,* and thereafter the focus of Buddhism in Japan shifted from the political centre to the secluded mountain region where the important new movement chose to establish their headquarters. The Tendai and Shingon schools in particular came very much to the fore now, supplanting the other schools that had established themselves and laying the foundation for the future development of Buddhism in Japan. Esoteric ritualism became a particularly powerful force. A more characteristic form of Buddhism emerged during the Heian period. Buddhism during this period helped to improve the lot of women, but it did offer them equality beyond the confines of their society. Buddhism, tended by its Chinese parent, offered somewhat less equality than Indian Buddhism. By the late Heian period, the situation of women improved with the rise of Pure Land beliefs. Woman's place idealistically rose and the prostitute was promised the same hope of salvation as the pious monk.

We shall not go beyond this period because the scope of our study ranges from first century BCE to eighth century CE. But before we close this story, we must quote the observations of D.P. Singhal[28] in this regard. He writes that as Buddhism began to permeate Japanese society, its adherents began to show preference for one or the other of its several imported varieties, but later Buddhism in Japan began to develop its own distinctive local schools of thought. During the ninth century two new sects were founded: The Tendai by Saicho and the Shingon by Kukai. Their principal object was to present Buddhist doctrines in Japanese terms, and to discipline the monks. Both sects stressed not only spiritual salvation, but

---

28. *The Buddhist Handbook,* p. 132.

also its fulfilment in this world. It was through the efforts of the monks of these two sects that Buddhism became firmly and popularly nationalized. Saicho was one of the first to truly appreciate the situation. His pressure for the establishment of a Mahāyāna Kaidan, platform of ordination, was in fact an indictment of the corrupt practices of the Nara period but it was also a revolt against the government control of Buddhism. He believed that when the Buddhist institutions were free to set forth the goals of individual salvation, only then could they properly function as religious organization. Saicho's unceasing demand for the development of a Mahāyāna Kaidan ultimately provided the Buddhist order with a form of autonomy. The control of ordination granted the right to select and ordain monks for religious rather than secular goals. Gaining this privilege was one of the greatest accomplishments of the Heian era in terms of Buddhist development.

It would not be out of place to once again reiterate that, as John Snellings[29] puts it, that the great empire of China provided a useful model, and Chinese culture and institution began to be imported wholesale into Japan at that time. Chinese literary, artistic, architectural and technical forms were adopted, for example, and a governmental bureaucracy was set upon the lines of the Chinese pattern. The projected centralized state also needed a philosophical sub-structure to underpin it, and here Confucianism and Taoism had obvious advantages to offer. But most of all, Buddhism, which had been taken to a superlatively, high pitch of development in T'any dynasty China, enjoyed special favour at court. The Empress Suiko (reigned 592–628) was such a committed Buddhist that she retired to a nunnery shortly after her accession, and her nephew, the crown prince, Shōtuku (547–622), himself an enthusiastic Buddhist too, reigned as regent for more

29. Ibid., p. 177.

than 30 years, during which time the Buddhist cause was advanced considerably in the land.

Initially, the following six of the great Chinese schools of Buddhism were transplanted to Japanese soil in the early period, say the first three centuries.

Japanese name	Chinese name	Indian name
Sanron	San-lun	Mādhyamika
Jōjitsu	Ch'êng-shih	Satyasiddhi
Hossō	Fa-hsiang	Yogācāra
Kuṣa	Chü-shê	Abhidharmakośa
Kegon	Hua-yen	Avataṁsaka
Ritsu	Lü	Vinaya

These sects may be called as the ancient sects because they were established in Nara. At present there are 13 representative Buddhist sects in Japan:

1. Kegon (the Avataṁsaka school),
2. Ritsu (the Vinaya school),
3. Hossō (the Dharmalakṣaṇa school),
4. Tendai,
5. Shingon (Tāntric Buddhism),
6. Jodo,
7. Jodoshin,
8. Yuzunenbutsu,
9. Ji-shu,
10. Rinzai,
11. Soto,
12. Obaku, and
13. Nichiren

There were three others, the Sanron (the three *śāstra* school of Mādhyamika), the Kuṣa (the Abhidharmakośa school), and the Jojistu (the Satyasiddhiśāstra school) but they are more or less extinct and have little independent influence. Most of these sects originated in China. The Kegon, the Ritsu, and the Hossō have retained their Chinese character, while the others are Japanese creations. The three Chinese sects were influenced afterward as they were opposed to the new Buddhism. The Hossō sect is a type of Buddhist idealism, derived from the Yogācāra school, and regards everything as the manifestation of the fundamental mind-principle. The Kegon sect centres around the worship of the Vairocana Buddha. The 13 sects are generally grouped into five major sects Tendai, Shingon, Zen Buddhism, Pure Land or Jodo, and Nichiren. The Tendai sect, founded in 804 by Saicho (767–822), better known as Kengyo–Daishi, greatly influenced the cultural and spiritual life of the Japanese. Saicho sought to harmonize all beliefs with the teachings of the Hokke-Kyo (Lotus *sūtra*); he taught that all men can become Buddhas and urged them to attempt to do so. An off shoot of the Chinese T'ien-t'ai, the Tendai sect, absorbed the ideas and principles of other doctrines such as the Tāntric, the Dhyāna, and the Vinaya schools. It differs from the Chinese T'ien-t'ai in its practical approach but both base their teaching essentially on the Mahāyāna text, the *Saddharmapuṇḍarīka*, laying stress on the Ekayāna theory.

About these sects of Japanese Buddhism and the pedigree thereof, Edward Conze writes[30] that before 700, four "sects" were introduced, which were not however corporations pledged to support particular doctrines, but simply philosophical schools which expounded certain textbooks. They were the Jōjistu (625) based on Kumārajīva's translation of Harivarman's *Satyasiddhi;* the Sanron (625) which studies the three works of Nāgārjuna

30. *A Short History of Buddha*, pp. 94-95.

and Āryadeva which were the basis of the Chinese San-lun school; the Hossō (654) which has for its textbook the *Yuishiki*, which expounds the principles of Vijñānavāda after Yuan-tsang and Kuei-ki; and Kuṣa (658) which was devoted to the exposition of Vasubandhu's *Abhidharmakośa*. Then came the Hua-yen (730), now called Kegon, which lasted for many centuries, and worshipped Vairocana, as Roshana or Birushana, and also the *Vinaya* sect (753) which was called Risshū and which tried to introduce stricter rules of ordination, and declined soon. Much more substantial were the sects introduced during the Heian period (794–1186), which was dominated by the Tendai and Shingon who had their centres on two mountains. The one was founded by Dengyo Daishi (767–822) who had brought the T'ien-t'ai doctrine from China, the other by Kōbō Daishi (774–835) who had learned the mysteries of the Chēn-yen in Chang-an. The sacred Tendai mountain of Hieizan near the new capital of Kyoto was soon covered by not less than 3,000 temples or halls. The Tendai not only had a great influence on art, but all later sects arose from within it, in the sense that their founders had for a time belonged to this sect. Kōbō Daishi on his return from China not only became a great favourite at the imperial court, but also impressed the popular imagination more than any other Japanese teacher has done. For the people he is the hero of countless legends, for his followers a manifestation of Vairocana not yet dead, but awaiting within his tomb the coming of the future Buddha.

Paul Watt in his article, "Shinto and Buddhism: Wellspring of Japanese Spirituality"[31] rightly remarks that Shinto was the earliest Japanese religion, its obscure beginning dating back at least to the middle of the first millennium BCE until approximately the sixth century CE. When the Japanese began

31. *Asian Religions*, vol. II, pp. 21-23.

a period of rapid adoption of continental civilization, it existed as an amorphous mix of nature worship, fertility cults, divination techniques, hero worship, and Shamanism. Unlike Buddhism, Christianity, or Islam, it had no founder and it did not develop sacred scriptures, an explicit religious philosophy, or a specific moral code. Indeed, so un-self-conscious were the early Japanese about their religious life that they had no single term by which they could refer to it. The word Shinto, or "the way of the Kami (gods or spirits)" came into use only after the sixth century, when the Japanese sought to distinguish their own tradition from the foreign religions of Buddhism and Confucianism that they were then encountering. Thus, in its origins, Shinto was the religion of a pristine people who, above all, were sensitive to the spiritual forces that pervaded the world of nature in which they lived. As one ancient chronicle reports: In their world myriad spirits shone like fireflies and every tree and bush could speak.

Japanese culture is a refined fusion of Shinto, Confucianism and Buddhism. Japan is justifiably described as a storehouse of Eastern Asian culture. It is well known that Confucianism entered Japan 150 years earlier than the introduction of Buddhism, and it left a great impact on the socio-religious life of the people of Japan. Besides it gained popularity with the royal court, and was later to exercise a real influence on Japanese legal and institutional systems and contribute a systematic method of teaching morality. Taoist thought also had some influence on Japan, but it was never very significant.

H.R. Hackmann[32] observes that in Japan Buddhism had to find its way alongside with Shintoism, which was the indigenous religion of the country. Shintoism was a religion rich in legends, and full of fantastic worship of the powers of nature, amongst which the sun held a conspicuous position.

32. *Buddhism as a Religion*, pp. 90-91.

The tradition which derived the imperial dynasty from the sun-god had been the means of establishing the worship of the rulers, which, coupled with the ancient ancestor worship, was further developed into a kind of hero worship. It is to be observed that Shintoism possessed no dogmatic tenets or ethical system, and had not even established any formal religious observances; but its development had stopped at the early stage, where religion is only a free plug of the imagination. The imported Buddhism, as already shown, naturally appeared to Shintoism as an opposing force in the first instance. But the position of this vague and primitive nature worship was from the beginning a difficult one, when compared with the doctrine of the Indian thinker, a comprehensive system teeming with ideas, and reinforced by literature, art and ceremonies. Buddhism, indeed, achieved its master-stroke when it absorbed and completely incorporated its rival with itself, by means of a clever adaptation. The Shinto divinities were raised to the position of earlier incarnations of Buddhist *bodhisattva*s, and the boldness of Shinto worship and temple decoration was gilded by Buddhist splendours. Thus originated the so-called Ryobu-Shintoism — namely, the mixed Shintoism (also called Ryobu-Buddhism) — which was in reality only a variety of Buddhism. The man who was the principal promoter of this transformation was Kobo Daishi (as he is usually known with his posthumous honorary title), a remarkable leader of the eighth century, and down to the present day one of the most popular of Buddhist Japanese saints.

Highlighting the distinctions of Buddhism and the short-comings, Shinto Paul Watt[33] has observed that by the time Buddhism entered Japan in the sixth century CE, it had already

33. *Article on Asian Studies*, vol. II, pp. 21-23.

become a world religion with a history of a thousand years. The form of Buddhism that from the start was dominant in Japan is known as Mahāyāna, the Buddhism of the Greater Vehicle, and it brought with it an enormous canon of religious literature, an elaborate body of doctrines, a well-organized priesthood, and a dazzling tradition of religious art and architecture all of which Shinto lacked in the sixth century. Although its view of the world of mankind differed markedly from that of Shinto, it is important to understand that within the teaching of Mahāyāna Buddhism both differences from, and similarities to, the native tradition could be found. On the one hand, for example, Buddhism regarded the world as transient and saw it as a source of suffering for those who remained attached to it, a view that contrasts sharply with Shinto's ready acceptance of the world. On the other hand, however, there was an optimism in Mahāyāna Buddhism that meshed well with Shinto — an optimism about human nature, for it was committed to the belief that all human beings had the potential to attain the wisdom that brings an end to suffering, and an ultimate optimism about the world itself, since it taught that once human attachments are discarded, the world takes on a new and positive significance.

Buddhism weeded out all the preposterous ideas and imaginations of Shinto. Real advances in Japanese thought and culture were made only after the introduction of Buddhism. It was only after Japan had been exposed to Confucian ethics with a metaphysical background, as modified by Buddhist thought, that Chinese ideas made an impact on the Japanese mind.

Thus, we have seen how Buddhist thought and culture overshadowed Shinto and Confucianism on the soil of Japan. We have also shown how Buddhism and its sublime teachings altogether changed the religio-cultural countenance of Japan.

Religio-Cultural Transformation of Some Important South-Asian Countries

The ideals and teachings of Buddhism influenced the majority of people on a vast tract of land which was the part of Asian continent. It dominated the religio-cultural life of the inhabitants of not only India and Nepal but also converted the majority of inhabitants of Sri Lanka, China, Korea, Japan and several other countries of Central Asia and South-East Asia. The most important countries of South-East Asia where Buddhism firmly established itself were Sri Lanka, Burma, Siam (Thailand), Indonesian archipelago, Kampuchea (formerly Cambodia), Laos and Vietnam. We will briefly discuss here how Buddhist thought and culture gave these countries a most superior religion which inculcated in the minds of the people the basic lessons of exalted ethico-spiritual morality in the form of compassion, universal brotherhood, peace, non-violence, tolerance, sympathy and above all altruism.

In the earlier chapters we have discussed at length how Buddhist thought and culture influenced and shaped the socio-religious life of the people of Sri Lanka, China and Tibet and how it gifted them a system of their own thought and culture in a purged form. The impact of philosophy and wisdom of Buddhism was so great that the people voluntarily embraced this great religion which was completely free from any trace of dogmatism, conservativeness and superstitions. Rightly speaking, Buddhism, particularly its thought and culture, virtually salvaged the entire human race from the mire of false metaphysical speculations and primitive thoughts. It became the choice of the people who were rational and righteous.

Buddhism and Religio-Cultural Transformation of Burmese People

Lying immediately to the east of India, Burma is carved from north to south by the great river Irrawaddy. The original inhabitants were the Mon people, who also occupied parts of what is today Thailand. The Burmese themselves came down from the mountainous regions to the east of Tibet and established kingdoms in Central Burma by about the third century CE. It seems that Buddhism did not strengthen itself here until the fifth or sixth centuries BCE. Afterwards there is evidence of both Hīnayāna and Mahāyāna activities.[34]

R.C. Majumdar[35] tells us that according to the tradition preserved in the Ceylonese Chronicles, two Buddhist monks, named Sona and Uttara, were sent by Emperor Aśoka to preach Buddhism in Suvarṇabhūmi which is generally identified with Burma. This is, however, no reliable evidence to show that Sona and Uttara were actually sent as missionaries by Aśoka, and the location of Suvarṇabhūmi is also not beyond dispute. For, while some identify it with Burma, others place it in Siam or take it to denote broadly the whole of Indo-China. Barring the story of Sona and Uttara there is no other evidence that Buddhism flourished in Burma in the fifth century CE. Considering the close proximity of Burma to India, and the existence of not too difficult land routes between the two even before the Christian era, the possibility is not altogether excluded that Buddhism found its way to Burma even before, perhaps long before, the fifth century CE. But from this period onwards there are definite records to prove not only the existence but also the flourishing state of Theravāda Buddhism in the old kingdom of the Pyus known as Śrīkṣetra with its capital near Prome, the ruins of which lie in modern Hmawza. The archaeological remains at Hmawza, about five miles from modern Prome, and the Chinese account leave no doubt that the Theravāda form of Buddhism with Pāli canonical texts was introduced in the region

34. *The Buddhist Handbook,* pp. 126-27.

35. *2500 Years of Buddhism* (ed.), pp. 76-77.

around Prome not later than the fifth century CE by Indian missionaries who came from the eastern coast of the Deccan and south India. Besides, we also find traces of Mūlasarvāstivāda and Mahāyānism which probably came from eastern India.

We cannot resist the temptation of quoting Edward Conze.[36] He says:

> Buddhism reached South-East Asia as a result of the colonizing activities of Hindus, who not only founded trading stations, but also brought their cults and culture with them. From the third century onward the area, also known as "Further India," was increasingly ruled by the dynasties which could either claim Indian descent or which were at least motivated by the ideals of Hindu civilization. By the fifth and sixth century both Mahāyāna and Hīnayāna Buddhism had filtered into Burma. At first it came from the Pallava country to southern India (Magadha) and the Sarvāstivādins may well have established themselves for a time.

Buddhism in Burma changed the way of life of the inhabitants. H. Hackmann[37] endorses this fact that in Burma, Buddhism has penetrated more deeply than in Ceylon into the life of the people, and has given it more of its colour. Perhaps it is here that the religion of Gautama won its most real and attractive presentment, and the visitor to this country cannot fail in looking back on the religious life of the Burmese, to retain an impression of sunny brightness. Whoever is inclined to let himself fall under the spell of Buddhism finds here a certain inducement to do so, that is to say, if he penetrates into the country and does not confine his view to the semi-Europeanized city of Rangoon. As a whole it appears harmless

36. *Buddhism as a Religion.*
37. Ibid., pp. 142-43.

and antique, kindly and considerate, and it is only to a keen observer that its weakness and limitations soon become obvious. As in Ceylon the influence of Buddhism in Burma begins with the educational activity exhibited by the monks. Every village, every hamlet, without exception, possesses a temple, where at least one monk is in residence. Here in the Burmese Child's school it is customary for every child to receive a certain amount of instruction in the monk's abode. This training is indeed as limited and of the same quality as that of the young Sinhalese. It consists in reading and writing Burmese and little of the sacred language Pāli (here written in Burmese characters), learning by heart sacred formulae and prayers, the conduct of religions ceremonies, first acquaintance with the fantastic world of Buddhist legend and mythology, moral maxims, and something of popular poetry. By means of these teachings the individual is brought into early and friendly relationship with the religion of his country.

Regarding the influence of Buddhism on the life of the Burmese people, H. Hackmann[38] writes that in Burma the life of the people is in every way connected with Buddhism. So long as it existed as an independent kingdom, the influence of the monks extended even to the throne and made itself widely felt there. Direct access to the king, by means of petitions and audiences, was granted to the higher spiritual functionaries. They were allowed — and they frequently made use of the privilege — to criticize the action of the government when they considered it harmful to the people. They even possessed a jurisdiction of their own in context with the laity. Every monastery had a certain inviolability, so that it could afford shelter to a criminal when pursued by justice, and in times of danger it was resorted to by the laity to guard special treasures. Thus the monkhood became an important political

38. *A Short History of Buddhism,* p. 106.

factor, which in a certain sense served as an intermediary between the despotic monarchy and its subjects.

The impact that Buddhism left on religion and culture of Burma is beautifully summed up by Edward Conze[39] thus:

> Buddhism has been a great civilizing force in the life of Burma, has helped to tone down racial rivalries, fostered a democratic social life by minimizing the importance of wealth and caste, brought much beauty and knowledge with it, and above all, it has created a singularly cheerful, polite and likeable people.

It is interesting to note that 85 per cent population of Burma is Buddhist. The material culture, excessive industrialization and militarization in the world have also left their marks on the life and society of Burmese.

Religio-Cultural Transformation of Siam

On the testimony of R.C. Majumdar[40] and the archaeological findings, it can be said that Buddhism flourished in Siam (Thailand) from a very early period, about the first or second century CE, if not earlier. This is proved by archaeological finds at Pong Tuk and Phra Pathom. Phra Pathom is about 30 miles west. Remains of a religious structure, the image of the Buddha, inscribed terracottas and definite symbols of Buddhism like the *dharmacakra*, belonging probably to the first or second century CE, have been found in these places. To a somewhat later period belong the large number of ruined sanctuaries and some fine sculptures which indicate the strong influence of the Gupta period. These have been referred to as the Dvāravatī school. Dvāravatī was a flourishing kingdom at the time of Yuan Chwang, i.e. in the first half of the seventh century CE. About the eighth or ninth century CE, both Siam and Laos

39. *2500 Years of Buddhism* (ed.), p. 79.
40. *India's Contribution to World Thought and Culture* (ed.), p. 453.

formed part of Kambuja (Cambodia) politically and were influenced by the religious condition of that country. So both the Brāhmanical religion and Buddhism can be found flourishing side by side in all these regions.

The Siamese (Thai) people, though not themselves racially Chinese, originated in southern China, and it is therefore highly likely that their first encounter with Buddhism was with one of its Chinese forms. Siamese Buddhism is so similar to that of Ceylon and Burma in all its main features that it would be superfluous to describe it in detail.

To know how Buddhism brought about religio-cultural transformation, it is imperative to know the early history of Siam and its people. The geographical boundary of Siam in ancient times was not like that as it is today. Its political background is very interesting. By the end of seventh-eighth century CE, almost the whole of the northern part of Siam came under the Mon influence. The southern part under the kingdom of Kambuja has to its greatest extent included almost the whole of the country. It was only after the decline of this mighty empire in thirteenth century that Siam could become an independent political entity, that too not by the sons of the soil but by a new race — the Thais who dominated the history of Indo-China for nearly five centuries and overthrew the kingdoms of Kambuja and Campā. The Thais came from Yunnan in South China called Nan-Chao by the Chinese but known as Gandhāra by Indo-Chinese, one part of which was called Videharājya with its capital at Mithilā. It may be noted that the Thais of Yunnan had imbibed Hindu culture and civilization in their own mother country to a very large extent. The extinction of this great Thai State in Non-Chao in CE 1253 by the Mongol chief Kublai Khan probably accounts for the general movement of the Thais whose one branch, the Ahoms, proceeded north and conquered Assam; the second, the Shans, conquered

Burma; and the third branch came south and gradually conquered the whole of Siam and also Laos.[41]

Buddhism is traditionally said to have been the first among the Mon people, the original inhabitants, in the third century BCE brought by missionaries sent from India by the Emperor Aśoka. What exactly took place historically is unclear, though a fine Buddhist art evolved in Dvāravatī, a Mon kingdom that flourished from about the sixth century CE. A few centuries later however, the land fell under the sway of the Khmers of Kampuchea and its original life was influenced accordingly. There are traces of both Mahāyāna and Hindu influences from this time.

If we talk in the context of modern Thailand, we can say that Buddhism started the religio-cultural transformation on a large scale in a systematic way in the thirteenth century. The Thai conquest of the land in the thirteenth century gave Buddhism a further impetus. The Thai rulers were ardent followers of Hīnayāna Buddhism. Ram Kamheng who is said to have founded the Thai dynasty and the city of Sukhodaya probably about CE 1300 that "the court and inhabitants of Sukhodaya were devout Buddhists, they observed the season of *Vassa* and celebrated the festival of Kathina with processions, concerts and reading of scriptures. In the city were to be seen statues of the Buddha and the scenes carved in relief, as well as large monastery presented to a distinguished elder who came from Śrī Dharmarāja and had studied the entire *Tripiṭaka.*" The form of Buddhism described in this epigraph, in which stress is laid on the worship of the spirits and the *deva*s on which the prosperity of the kingdom is said to have depended, is a little different from Hīnayāna Buddhism found in Siam today.

---

41. *The Buddhist Handbook*, pp. 129-31.

Before the thirteenth century, the land was occupied by the dominant Khmers. The Thais ousted them and established themselves both as masters of parts of presently Thailand as well as of neighouring Laos and promoted the Sri Lankan brand of Theravāda Buddhism. About CE 1361, *bhikkhus*, including one Mahāsami Saṅgharāja, were brought over from Sri Lanka to "purify" local Buddhism, and the Pāli was established as the religious language. The Thais were able to return the compliment when in the mid-eighteenth century they sent monks to Sri Lanka to revive the ailing Sinhalese *Saṅgha*. This strong Theravāda tradition has survived in Thailand down to the present time. Today Buddhism is the state religion of Thailand and over 92 per cent of the population adhere to it. The king has to be a Buddhist, though his mandate as Defender of Religion means that his formal protection is extended to all personations: Hindu, Muslim, Christian, Confucian and whatever else; even the Communist party Buddhism is highly organized in modern Thailand and subject to a degree of state control. There is a supreme patriarch, appointed by the king, who is therefore nominally head of the Buddhist "church"; below ranges a pyramid of ecclesiastical hierarchy radiating outwards into the regions. In recent years, in common with other South-East Asian countries, Thailand has been launched through an accelerating pattern of disturbing change that has thrown up many complex social and political problems. The role of Buddhist monks within these changing patterns is obviously subject to different interpretations. The conservative *Saṅgha* has in fact come in for some criticism for its opposition to change and reform. Meanwhile, more radical elements in the *Saṅgha* have argued for a more activist stance.[42]

---

42. Ibid., p. 132

Even in this age of rapid industrialization and growing consumerism there is a living Buddhist tradition in the north-east of the country which is known as ascetic forest tradition. Here, a strong tradition of highly effective meditation and *Vinaya* practice has been preserved. Of particular importance has been the influence of Ajahn Cha, a disciple of Ajahn Mun, who has been responsible for training many notable Western *bhikkhu*s at Wat Nong Pah Pong in Ubon province. Ajahn Cha's foremost Western disciple is the American–born Ajahn Sumedho Thera, who firstly helped to establish the international Wat Pah Nanachat under Ajahn Cha's auspices and later Chithrust Forest Monastery in rural West Sussex, the first of a number of highly successful monasteries and centres in Britain.

Buddhism and its thought and culture brought about a marvellous religio-cultural change in the social and religious life of people in the countries surrounding Thailand and the Indonesian archipelago. About the middle of the thirteenth century CE, the Thais made themselves masters of Siam and Laos and put an end to the political supremacy of the Cambodians over them. Under the influence of the Thai rulers, Buddhism of the Theravāda school and the Pāli language flourished all over Siam and Laos. The Thai king Śrī Sūryavaṁsa Rāma Mahā-Dhārmikarājādhirāja was not only a great patron of Buddhism, but himself adopted the life of a Buddhist monk, preaching the doctrines of the Buddha all over his kingdom.

John Snelling writes[43] about Laos that it is a tiny landlocked country sandwiched between powerful neighbours: China, Burma, Thailand, Kampuchea, and Vietnam. Small wonder then that its history has been much marked by strife and foreign domination. During its early period, it fell under the

---

43. *2500 Years of Buddhism* (ed.), p. 80.

power of the Khmers, who probably introduced Buddhism — and Brāhmanism. Later it became virtually a province of Thailand and as a consequence Thai form of Sri Lankan Theravāda became dominant among the Laotians and survived until modern times.

Kampuchea and its Religio-Cultural Transformation

Kampuchea, formerly Cambodia, is situated in the Mekong valley between Thailand and Vietnam, though unlike Laos it enjoys access to the sea. The Khmer people are the dominant group here. During its early history, which is poorly documented, the area fell, like Burma and Thailand, under Indian cultural and religious influences. Both Brāhmanism and Mahāyāna Buddhism certainly enjoyed favour, and the Sanskrit language was used.[44]

The archaeological finds and the Chinese Chronicles prove that from the end of the fifth century CE, Buddhism flourished in Cambodia, though it did not occupy a dominant position, as it was less popular than some forms of Brāhmanical religion like Śaivism. The great emperor, Yaśovarman, who ruled at the end of the ninth century CE, established a Saugatāśrama which was specially meant for the Buddhist monks, and elaborate regulations were laid down for the guidance of this *āśrama* or hermitage.

Cambodia (Kambuja, Sanskrit) was the most thoroughly "Indianized" state in the whole of this region, i.e. it bore the deepest impression of Indian religion, culture, literature, art and architecture. Chinese account and a much later Campā (South Vietnam) inscription give us a very interesting account of the beginnings of the relations with India in this country. About the first century CE, a brāhmaṇa Kauṇḍinya arrived on the Cambodian coast, armed with a javelin presented to

44. *India's Contribution to World Thought and Culture* (ed.), pp. 493-94.

him by Aśvatthāman (the son of Droṇa), vanquished the native queen of this realm, married her and thus founded the kingdom of Fu-nan. Fu-nan seems to be a Chinese adaptation of the Khmer (the Cambodian language) word *bhnam* or *phnam* meaning a hill. It seems that the original Sanskrit name of the kingdom was Śrīśaila and that Kauṇḍinya's successors bore the title of Śailendras.[45]

The observations of B.R. Chatterji made in his article "Indian cultural Heritage in Cambodia" are worth quoting; he writes:[46] It is guessed that towards the end of the eighth century, probably during the early years the reign of Jayavarman II, Mahāyāna Buddhism made its entry into Kambuja. Jayavarman II had close relations with Śrīvijaya — a great maritime power which wielded sway over considerable portions of Sumatra, Malaya and Java — and which in this period had become a stronghold of Mahāyāna Buddhism in the archipelago. Borobudur in Central Java (the finest Buddhist *stūpa* in the world erected by command of Śailendra sovereign); the Nālandā copper-plate of the Pāla monarch Devapāla of Bengal afnd Magadha commemorating the gift of the Śailendra king of Śrīvijaya for a monastery at Nālandā; the visit of Atīśa to Śrīvijaya to study Buddhist text under the guidance of a renowned scholar there — all this evidence confirms the view that Mahāyāna Buddhism, emanating from Magadha and Bengal under the Pāla monarchs had crossed over to Sumatra and Java and at this time was entering Cambodia. The digraphic inscriptions of the illustrious Yaśovarman, the builder of Angkor, for centuries the capital of Kambuja, in which one of the two scripts employed in inscribing this series of inscriptions used letters of the north Indian type (not the usual Pallava characters of south India)

45. Ibid., pp. 496-97.

46. *The Buddhist Handbook*, p. 172.

generally used in South-East Asia. These letters are quite peculiar of the period and show features that directly link India and Cambodia.

From the sixth to thirteenth centuries, both Brāhmanism and Mahāyāna Buddhism flourished in Cambodia. As regards the history of Cambodia, the first important king was Bhāvavarman who was followed by Mahāvarman, Sanāvarman and Jayavarman. A clear history of Cambodia begins with Jayavarman II. Angkorthom was the capital of Kambuja, which was built by Jayavarman II. Both Hinduism and Buddhism left their deep impressions on Cambodia's socio-religious life and culture. While writing on Cambodia, we must mention its two grand architectural monuments — Angkor Vat and the Bayon. Angkor Vat is a wonder of the world always thronged by the visitors from the East and the West. It is a Viṣṇu temple on a gigantic scale.

The royal builder was Sūryavarman II and this most magnificent shrine was constructed about the middle of the twelfth century CE. Bayon was the work of Jayavarman VII. It is a Buddhist temple of colossal dimensions which has been very badly damaged by the iconoclastic zeal of his non-Buddhist successors to the Kambuja throne. It is in the form of a pyramid with three stages crowned by high tower. All the towers have human faces on the four sides. They represent Avalokiteśvara Bodhisattva who is the incarnation of mercy (*karuṇā*).

Buddhist Impress on Vietnam

John Snelling writes[46] that in ancient times the northern region, Annam, was for many centuries a province of the Chinese empire. To the south lay the Indianized states of Funan and Campā, which then overflowed beyond the present-day frontiers. The Vietnamese themselves originated in the north and in times came to dominate the whole of the land.

Independence from China was gained in the tenth century, but Chinese influence continued to exert a powerful effect, and in the long run this meant that the standard brand of Sri Lankan Theravāda that triumphed elsewhere in South-East Asia did not do so here. Instead Chinese forms of Mahāyāna Buddhsim, notably a successful amalgam of C'han and Pure Land prevailed, until the country fell to the Communists in 1975. Since then Buddhism had declined enormously and from time to time we hear reports of active persecution. It also must be added here that Buddhism probably entered Vietnam (Campā) in the third century CE. A Chinese Chronicle states that when the Chinese captured the capital of Campā in CE 605, they carried away 1350 Buddhist monasteries which later were discovered at a place called Ding Duang, built by King Jaya Indra-Varman in CE 875. This indicates that Buddhism must have flourished in the country for a long period before the seventh century CE. I-tsing remarks that in Campā the Buddhists generally belong to the Aryasammitiya school and that there are a few followers of the Sarvāstivāda school also. This would mean the prevalence of the Śrāvakayāna sect, but it appears from inscriptions of the eighth century CE or thereabouts, that the Mahāyāna sect of Buddhism was powerful in Vietnam (Campā), and possibly even the Tantric forms, later offshoots of the Mahāyāna, also prevailed there.

Religio-Cultural Transformation of Sumatra and Java

Buddhism left its indelible marks on the life, society and culture of Javanese. The island of Sumatra had become a stronghold of Buddhism as early as the seventh century CE. It appears from some inscriptions found there that king Sri Jayang who began to rule the Śrīvijaya kingdom in CE 684, was a Buddhist. In CE 686, he sent his army to conquer Java. Śrīvijaya, the capital of Sumatra, was a very important centre of Buddhist learning and culture. I-tsing, the famous Chinese pilgrim, who visited

India in the last quarter of the seventh century, studied here for seven years from CE 688-95. He had written glowingly about the popularity of Buddhism in the islands of Sumatra. In Sumatra, Sarvāstivādins were strong in the seventh century CE. Later on the Vajrayāna was brought in from the Pala University.

From Sumatra, Buddhism moved on to Java. Fa-Hien on his return from India to China via Sri Lanka, stayed in Java in CE 414-15 for five months and found Buddhism in a not very flourishing condition. Under the influence of Guṇavarman of Kashmir, the king and Queen of Java embraced Buddhism. On royal invitation Guṇavarman reached China in CE 439. It means Buddhism was introduced in Java about that time. A strong impetus to Buddhism was given by the Śailendra kings who ruled over the Malay Peninsula and a large part of Indonesia. The Śailendra kings had the same reverence and devotion to Buddhism as the Pāla kings of Bengal. The Śailendras established monasteries at Nālandā and gave generous donations for the maintenance of Nālandā institutions. Under the Śailendra dynasty, Buddhism progressed in Java from the eighth century onwards, although Śaivism always remained fairly strong. The Śailendras filled the Kedu plain with beautiful temples, adorned with exceptionally fine sculpture. The most famous of these is the gigantic Borobudur, a *stūpa* built in the sixth century, which is a *maṇḍala* in stone, and symbolizes the cosmos as well as the way to salvation. Those who walk in *pradakṣiṇā* through its galleries will thereby ritually undergo the process of moving out of *saṁsāra* into *nirvāṇa*, ascending through the three levels of the triple world to the supramundane transcendental realm. Some of the great Mahāyāna texts are here illustrated on bas-relief, i.e. the *Jātakamālā, Lalitavistara, Gaṇḍavyūha* and *Karmavibhaṅga.*

Borobudur is a marvel of architectural and sculptural beauty. It has about 1500 carvings which depict scenes from the life of the Buddha and from Jātakas. In the narration of scenes from the life-story of the Buddha as described in the *Lalitavistara*, the sculptor has created numerous masterpieces in addition to portraying various aspects of Indian culture.

Bali is another island east of Java. Both these islands are separated by a sea lane which is 177 km in length and 64 km in a breadth. Bali is first mentioned in the history of living rulers of China (CE 402-56). There it is said that when the king of Bali was asked about his ancestors, he replied that he can only say that, "The wife of Śuddhodana was a gırl of my country." This indicates that at that time the people of Bali professed Buddhism. The Chinese pilgrim I-tsing (seventh century CE) had come to Bali and he says that at that time Mūlasarvāstivāda Nikāya of Buddhism was prevalent in Bali.

Thus, we see that Buddhist thought and culture made its permanent impact on the socio-religious life and culture of the Asian people, particularly the people of Central and South-East Asia including Sri Lanka.

8

Contribution of Buddhist Thought and Culture to Literature, Art and Architecture of Asian Countries

THE contribution of Buddhist thought and culture to the treasure of literature, art and architecture of Asian countries has been immense and lasting. The peculiarity of Buddhism is that it is the religion which one man established. The entire Buddhist literature, art and architecture is only about the great saviour of humanity, i.e. the Buddha who was a staunch believer of *karma* theory and a discoverer of the Four Noble Truths as a final panacea for all sufferings with which the human race is afflicted.

P.N. Chopra in preface to his edited work, *Contribution of Buddhism to World Civilization and Culture* has rightly remarked that Buddhism made significant contributions in many other fields such as paintings, sculpture, art and architecture which is well evidenced by the impressive remains of Pagan and Prome (Burma), Borobudur (Indonesia), Anurādhapura and other sites in Sri Lanka, Angkor Vat (Cambodia) and Vat Benchamabopit (Thailand), Horyuji (Japan), Lung-men (China), Ajanta and Ellora (India), besides other massive structures more or less in ruins, and pieces of art discovered in India, China, Japan and other parts of Asia and Russia. It speaks volumes in favour of worldwide civilizing influences exercised by Buddhism in the past. Equally great has been Buddhist contribution in the field of logic and ethics, psychology and meditation, sociology and literature and the creative arts. Buddhist *Saṅghas* made an enormous contribution in the literary field and helped in the promotion of universal literacy. The Brāhmī script, which was used for Aśoka's inscriptions, travelled with Buddhism and became the base of Asian alphabets.

Prof. T.R.V. Murthy in preface to his book *The Central Philosophy of Buddhism* remarks that the vastness of Buddhism is surprisingly immense. An extensive and varied literature, canonical, exegetical and systematic, covering a period of more than fifteen centuries, is scattered in scores of Indian languages — Sanskrit, Pāli, Tibetan, Chinese and several Mongolian languages.

Contribution of Buddhism to Literature of Asian Countries

Where Buddhism — particularly its thought and culture — spread the first necessity that was felt was to create a literature in the language of that country. This ambitious mission could be achieved through a mass-scale translation of the Buddhist texts by very learned Buddhist scholars and also through the creation of a vast commentarial and exegetical literature. Keeping in view the Buddha's advice of *bahujana hitāya, bahujana sukhāya* the Buddhist literature was produced at a large scale in the *lingua franca*. For the first time the *Tripiṭaka*s were compiled and put in black and white in Sri Lanka during the reign of Vaṭṭagāmiṇī Abhaya in first century BCE. Thereafter, a vast exegetical/commentarial literature was produced by the monk scholar of Anurādhapura Mahāvihāra. The tradition of writing aṭṭhakathās was continued in Sri Lanka by the monk fraternity of both Anurādhapura and Abhayagiri. In these mahāvihāras the commentaries were written on *Tripiṭaka*s for a long time. It was at Anurādhapura that the illustrious commentator Buddhaghoṣa composed his *Viśuddhimagga* in order to interpret the *gāthās* of *Saṁyutta-Nikāya*. The Sri Lankan scholar made the greatest contribution to the treasure of early philosophical and post-canonical literature of Buddhism.

In chronological order, China comes next to Sri Lanka where a large part of Mahāyāna Sanskrit literature was translated into Chinese at the translation bureaus of Lo-yang and Nanking by Indian and Chinese Scholars under royal patronage. The exercise of translation of Buddhist *śāstras* into Chinese was carried out for centuries together and the most distinguished luminaries of this ambitious project were celebrated and formidable translators like Kumārajīva, Paramārtha and Hiuen Tsang. The share of Kashmiri paṇḍits in this missionary task was enormously great. From fourth to sixth centuries of the Christian era, a host of Kashmiri paṇḍits went to China and actively participated in the rendering of the Buddhist texṭs into Chinese language. Back home in India a vast literature on Buddhist philosophy was created besides Jātaka tales and Avadāna literature.

Richard A. Gard[1] in his article, "Buddhist contribution to Asian Cultural Arts," writes that as an example of Buddhist popular and written literature the Jātakas (birth-stories or tales of previous lives of the Buddha) have become the traditional basis for many Buddhist allegories, myths and stories and thereby have contributed immeasurably to the development of Asian folklore, both oral and written, especially in Theravāda, Vajrayāna, and, to a less extent Mahāyāna areas.

Kashmir happened to be a great seat of Sarvāstivāda literature. Many Śāstras and commentaries on logic and epistemology were created by the Kashmiri logicians.

---

1. *Contribution of Buddhism to World Civilization and Culture* (ed.), p. 176.

The contribution of Aśvaghoṣa to Buddhist literature is unique in the sense that he gifted us two excellent works — *Buddhacarita* and *Saundarānanda*. Here we find a sublime form of poetry saturated with an uncommon spirituality. Many biographies of the Buddha were also written.

We have a bewilderingly vast literature on Buddhism in Pāli and Sanskrit which is preserved even to this day in different languages like Sinhalese, Chinese, Tibetan, Mongolian, Burmese, Thai, Korean, etc. It is sad that a large part of original Buddhist Sanskrit literature is lost but happily it is preserved in their Chinese and Tibetan translations.

The number of Buddhist Sanskrit texts translated into Tibetan are comparatively less than those in Chinese. One fact is common to both China and Tibet that a great interest was shown by the royalty to procure the Buddhist Sanskrit text into their own scripts and languages and accordingly a concerted missionary effort was made to translate the original Buddhist Sanskrit Śāstras into Chinese and Tibetan.

There were three major forms of Buddhism — Hīnayāna (Early Buddhism/Pāli Buddhism), Mahāyāna Buddhism (Sanskrit Buddhism) and Tāntric Buddhism. The literature pertaining to early Buddhism is available in Pāli, Sinhalese, Burmese and Thai. And the literature pertaining to Mahāyāna and Tāntric Buddhism were created, preserved and translated from Sanskrit into Chinese and Tibetan. It must be pointed out here that wherever Buddhism spread, those nations got created their own literature in addition to the imported ones. Thus we see a vast variety of Buddhist literature in all the Buddhist countries of Asia.

It was only in Sri Lanka that the process of creation of Buddhist literature never stopped. Even it continued till the last century. One thing which is very typical about Buddhist literature is this that it is related exclusively with the life and teachings of the Buddha.

Buddhism gave the finest religious books to the world like *Dhammapada, Bodhicaryāvatāra* and *Śikṣāsamuccaya*. The Mahāyāna literature known by the name *Vaipulya-Sūtra* was the greatest contribution of Buddhism to religio-philosophical and ethico-spiritual literature of Buddhism. *Prajñāpāramitā* literature is also an extensive philosophical literature of the Mahāyāna line of thought. Among the *Vaipulya-Sūtras, Saddharmapuṇḍarīka* occupies a great position. Among all the Buddhist literature of the Mahāyāna group, *Bodhicaryāvatāra* of Śāntideva is very spiritual and didactic and it gives a lot of inspiration and guidance for the cultivation of *bodhi* which ultimately leads to the attainment of *prajñā*.

The versified history of India and Sri Lanka is furnished in the *Dīpavaṁsa* and *Mahāvaṁsa*. The most important Buddhist classic *Milindapañha* contains within its pages a lot of historical information and didactic maxims for leading a virtuous practical life. The aṭṭhakathās are replete with a lot of information regarding history, politics and society of that time. The Buddhist thought and culture brought a vast literature on philosophy, mysticism, symbolism, occult practices and ethics. The literature which was created in the name of Buddha and his *Dhamma* inspired the humanity for generations and will continue to inspire and enlighten the posterity. If we talk about the literary contribution of Buddhism, we can be justly proud of Aśvaghoṣa's *Buddhacarita*. It must be pointed out here that in poetic excellence Aśvaghoṣa has excelled even the Great Kālidāsa. *Theragāthā* and *Therīgāthā* are also the most outstanding contributions of Buddhism.

Contribution of Buddhism to the Art and Architecture of Asian Countries

Venerable Rewata Dhamma in his article, "The Contribution of Buddhism to the World of Art and Architecture," has rightly remarked that what Buddhism has given to the world is not only a profound analysis of, and the practical solution for, the problem of human suffering but also a monumental and rich legacy to the world of art and architecture. Much of this legacy is visible even today in its homeland of India and in the much of the Eastern World.

In order to give vent to his religious feelings and sentiments man has resorted to many ways, the chief among which are: art, architecture, painting and poetry. During his lifetime, the Buddha always discouraged idolatry. The Buddha did not appoint his successor to look after the affairs of his *Dhamma* and *Saṅgha*. He had clearly briefed Ānanda that after his *mahāparinirvāṇa,* his teachings (*Dharmakāya*) would lead the way. But after the Buddha's *mahāparinirvāṇa,* his disciples and followers ignored his instructions and out of sheer reverence for him started erecting *stūpas, caityas* and *vihāras*. In the beginning, the reliquary memorials of the Buddha — *bodhi* tree, alm-bowl and his foot prints — were the objects of veneration for his followers. After the Buddha's *mahāparinirvāṇa* there was a row over the distribution of his *sarīra-dhātu*. Since then the *caityas* came into existence. The word *caitya* is derived from word *cita* or funeral pile, and denotes anything connected with funeral pile, e.g. the tumulus raised over the bones of a dead saint. Although generally speaking *caitya* means a relic shrine or temple or any place of worship, technically it means a mound.

It also must be clear that *caitya* is a religious term, while *stūpa* is an architectural term for a relic mound. The *stūpa* is often identified with the *dagobā*, but incorrectly so, since a *dagobā* is only part of the *stūpa*. The *stūpa* is the whole monument, while *dagobā* is only the area where the relic is deposited. As most of the *stūpas* are erected over relics, they may also be called *dagobās*. Not all *stūpas*, however, contain relics, since many were built on spots where some memorable events connected either with the life of the Buddha or his Jātakas had taken place.

We have already told that after the passing away of the Buddha, *caityas*, *stūpas* and *dagobās* were venerated as if they were the embodiment of the Buddha. How these religious structures came to be venerated has a different history.

T.N. Ramachandran[2] in his write-up throws sufficient light on this issue. He writes that the highest objects of worship for the Buddhist are the *Triratna* or the three jewels: (1) The Buddha, (2) The *Dharma* and (3) The *Saṅgha*. There are also other objects of worship which, when compared with the *Triratna*, can only be described as material or formal, but which appealed more forcibly to the layman than all the percepts, parables and sayings of the Buddha, the *pratyeka–buddhas*, the *arhats*, and the *cakravartin*, over which great monument were erected by a "grateful posterity." In the majority of cases, these relics are what are called *dhātus* which can be conveniently grouped into three classes, namely, *śārīrika* or corporeal relics, *uddeśika* or memorials and *pāribhogika* or objects having been of use to the Buddha, sacred spots, holy trees, and the like. According to tradition, the oldest corporeal relics are the hairs of the Buddha which were given to the merchants Tapusa and Bhalliko, and later deposited by them in a shrine built in their native city in Orissa. The chief corporeal relics are "those which are properly called *śarīras*, i.e. the remains of a corpse after cremation." The Buddha died in the land of the Mallas who did honour to his bones with dancing, music, garlands and perfumes. Ajātaśatru from Rājagṛha, the Licchavīs of Vaiśālī, the Śākyas of Kapilavastu, the Bulis of Allakappa, the Mallas of Pāvā, the Koliyas of Rāmagrāma and the brāhmaṇas from Vethadīpa — all claimed their share in the division of the relics. It appears that after the division had

2. *2500 Years of Buddhism* (ed.), p. 245.

been made, a messenger of the Mauryas of Pippalivana came for a portion of the relics. As there was nothing left, he took pieces of coal which the Mauryas began to revere and placed in a *stūpa*. Thus, originally there were eight *stūpa*s: in Rājagṛha, Vaiśālī, Kapilavastu, Allakappa, Rāmagrāma, Vethadīpa, Pāvā and Kuśinagara, besides those erected by brāhmaṇa Droṇa and the Mauryas of Pippalivana.

In the three centuries before and after the birth of Christ, India witnessed a phenomenal growth of Buddhist art and culture. A large number of *stūpa*s and *caitya*s were built during this period richly carved with scenes from the life of the Buddha and his previous births. The inspiration of Buddhist art came from religion, and the sculptural wealth of Buddhist edifices goes to prove that religion did not necessarily mean ritual or doctrine, but that latent spiritual quality which finds "tongues in trees, books in running brooks, sermons in stones and good in everything." In the north-west owing to the impact of Greece and Rome hybrid art developed and a complete Buddhist imagery called Gandhāra was elaborated.

It is said that Emperor Aśoka had built 84,000 *stūpa*s all over his vast empire in the seventh century CE. Hiuen Tsang has seen several thousand *stūpa*s and *caitya*s in India in the eleventh century CE. Alberuni saw the remains of a great *stūpa* built by king Kaniṣka near Peshawar. The tradition of *stūpa* architecture continued to flourish in Sri Lanka, Burma, Java and North Asian lands. Special mention may be made of the great *stūpa* of Borobudur in Java, *Svayambhū caitya* in Kathmandu (Nepal) and the great *stūpa* in Anurādhapura (Sri Lanka). Burma has also preserved a number of magnificent *pagoḍā*s dating from the thirteenth century onward.[3]

---

3. *Contribution of Buddhism to World Civilization and Culture* (ed.), p. 164.

Buddhist art and architecture made its conspicuous presence and developed to perfection with all subtle nuances wherever Buddhism was taken. In Sri Lanka an artistic intense activity was carried on throughout the first millennium of the Christian era. The sculpture of the Anurādhapura period was inspired by the Indian models of Buddhist art. L.M. Joshi[4] writes that Indian Buddhist images in stone, ivory and bronze were frequently imported by the Buddhists of South Asian countries. The bronze of Nālandā were especially popular in these countries. The sculptures which decorate the great *stūpa* of Borobudur were made following the guidelines given in Buddhist holy books of Indian origin. In Burma, Siam (Thailand) and Cambodia were found the simultaneous growth of Buddhist and Brāhmanical sculptures. The iconographic features of these images show contacts with the sculptures from Tamil region, Orissa, Bihar and Bengal. Tibet and Nepal produced a vast amount of sculpture in stone and in metal connected with Mahāyāna and Tāntrika forms of Buddhism. Statues of the Buddhas and *bodhisattva*s in pure gold and silver, often inset with gems and pearls, have been discovered in all countries of Asia. One of the reasons of Turkish and Mongol inroads in South Asian countries was the lure of gold and precious stones treasured in Buddhist and Brāhmanical temples. Tibet was the only fortunate country which succeeded in preserving huge quantities of gold in images and sanctuaries. Thousands of Buddhist images and sacred emblems have been discovered in Bamiyan and Central Asia. The largest Buddha figure ever made in stone was at Bamiyan.

The Buddhist Sculpture of Central Asia and China

The contents of this great art are Buddhist. Regional elements are found in costumes, jewellery, etc. and physical features.

4. Ibid.

This is true of the sculpture found in Khotan and Tun-Huang also. Buddhism had dominated the architecture and sculpture of China and Japan since the time of its introduction in those countries. Besides stone and metal statues, wooden sculptures of excellent quality were produced in ancient and medieval centuries in China and Japan. As in the areas of architecture and sculpture so in that of painting, the range of Buddhist contribution has been massive and extensive. The oldest examples of Buddhist painting are preserved on the walls of a few of the rock-cut halls of Ajantā. Some of these murals are masterpieces of the first order. It is the personality of the Buddha which had endless charm for the painter as much as for the sculptor. The artist successfully conveyed by means of brush and paint the austere simplicity and dignified serenity born of inner peace that characterized the attitudes of the Enlightened One. The paintings of Ajantā are in water-colours. The earliest of them date from the second century BCE. The life of the Buddha is painted in epic details. Scenes from the Jātakas form the subject matter of several paintings executed in a narrative manner. Buddhist painting reached its maturity during the fifth and sixth centuries CE. Besides Ajantā, another centre of painting was Bāgh near Gwalior.

Buddhism produced a mass of wonderful rock-cut architecture in western India and Deccan between second century BCE and sixth century CE. Beautiful sanctuaries and large monastic halls, adorned with marvellous sculptures and paintings, were hewn out of rocks and mountains. The main centres of this rock-cut art are Kārle, Bhaja, Kanheri, Kondane, Junnār, Nasik, Pital-Khora, Aurangabad, Ellorā and Ajantā. Outside India, rock-cut architecture of Buddhist monasteries and sanctuaries, is found in Sigiya (Sri Lanka), Bamiyan (Afghanistan) and several places in Central Asia and China. Special notice may be taken here of the Hall of Thousand Buddhas in Tun-Huang.

Chronologically, some of the most important and earliest surviving Buddhist monuments in India are Sāñcī (150 BCE to 50 BCE), Bodh-Gayā (75 BCE), cave temples of western India — Kārle (150 BCE), Bhaja (second century BCE) and early Ajantā caves (second and first centuries BCE), etc. followed by Sārnāth (first to sixth century CE), later Ajantā caves (fifth to seventh century CE) and Nālandā (sixth to seventh century CE). Sāñcī, near Bhopal, the oldest Buddhist stone monument was originally a brick *stūpa* erected by Aśoka in which the relics of the Buddha were enshrined. In course of time, the Śuṇgas encased it in stone and provided a stone railing around with four gates at the cardinal points, in imitation of wooden railing and gateways. The gates are elaborately carved with episodes from the life of the Buddha and the Jātakas. Bharhut and Amarāvatī had similar *stūpa*s, railings and gateways. At Sāñcī, Bodh-Gayā, Bharhut and Amarāvatī, the surviving relics of the Buddha are not represented in human form. His presence are indicated only symbolically; a riderless horse in motion with an umbrella held over the seat under the *pīpal* tree, the Enlightenment at Bodh-Gayā, an empty seat with a wheel, indicating *dharmacakra,* set between two deers on either side indicating the First Sermons in the Deer Park at Sārnāth; and a *stūpa* indicating the Great Decease at Kuśinagara. It is evident that in the early Buddhist art, it was uncanonical to represent the Buddha in human form. It eschewed idolatry perhaps in line with the Vedic tradition.[5]

The Buddhist art and architecture spread with the teachings of the Buddha and made its conspicuous presence. Y. Krishan[6] in his article "The Buddhist Art of India" had rightly remarked that the expansion of Buddhism outside India carried its art forms to those countries. Thus the *dagobā*s of

---

5. Ibid., pp. 186-87.
6. Ibid., p. 182.

Ceylon, the *pagoḍā*s of Burma, the *wat*s of Thailand and Cambodia, the *chorten*s of Tibet, the *stūpa*s of Central Asia, the *bagoda*s of China and Japan, are all derived from the *stūpa* in India. The Gautama Buddha with their peculiar *uṣṇīṣa*s and *mudrā*s became the classical models for the art of all Asia. The technique, style and content of the art of paintings of different countries of Asia was also deeply influenced and moulded by Buddhist paintings of Gandhāra (Bamiyan) and Ajantā. The wall paintings of Sigriya and Pelorunnava in Ceylon, the fragmentary paintings of western Turkestan, the wall paintings discovered in oasis colonies in the Eastern Turkestan along the northern Silk Route — Kucha (Kizil) and Turfan — and along the southern silk routes — Miran, Khotan — of Tun-Huang in China, of Horyuji, Nara and Kyoto in Japan, on the walls of monasteries and *thanka*s of Tibet are a testimony of Indian Buddhist inspiration. Some of the masterpieces of world art, Borobudur in Java, the Khmer Buddha heads from Cambodia and the Buddha Amitābha from Nara in Japan, derive their inspiration and expression from art forms, symbols and styles evolved in India. Thus the art and architecture of South-East Asia, Central Asia and Far-East were deeply influenced and stimulated by the Indian prototypes.

The Buddhist art in its varied forms is largely and essentially religious in content. The Buddhist architecture too is exclusively religious in its appearance and context. Whenever one talks of Buddhist architecture, we are instantly reminded of *stūpa, caitya* and *vihāra;* all three indicate forms of religious architecture. In Sri Lanka a *stūpa* is called *dagoba* (Sanskrit *dhātū-garbha*) because it houses the sacred relics (such as tooth, bone, nail or ashes) of the Buddha's body or of any other great Buddhist saint. In Burma and other East Asian countries the *stūpa* is now called *pagoḍā*s (perhaps a Portuguese word).

With the emergence of Mahāyāna and the introduction of *bhakti*, precisely Buddha *bhakti*, a great exercise was done to carve the Buddha image in different postures. If we closely look at the history of development of Buddhism, through all its phases — Hīnayāna, Mahāyāna and Tantrayāna — we shall find that contribution of Buddhism to iconography was enormously great. In this context the observations of Rewata Dhamma are also worth quoting: The Mahāyāna School recognized the historical Buddha Gotama, the Śākyamuni, but raised him to the level of a god. He then became but one of many, many divine Buddhas and was eventually regarded as a powerful emanation of the Supreme Essence. It was these celestial Buddhas that were portrayed in Mahāyānist art and very beautifully too in countries such as China, Vietnam, Japan and Korea and of course Tibet where the Mahāyāna tradition is followed.

One very important point that needs to be mentioned here according to Rewata Dhamma is that the very earliest examples of the Buddhist art are not iconic but aniconic images and were popular in India after the death of the Buddha. This is because the Buddha himself did not sanction personal worship or the making of images of the *tathāgata*, as to have done so would have contradicted his message to mankind. He taught and encouraged people to heed his examples and be self-reliant in striving to put an end to human suffering and endless rebirth in *saṁsāra* and realize *nirvāṇa* for themselves. He was the living proof that this was possible and promised this was attainable by anyone through renouncing worldly and ego-centric desires and by making earnest efforts at mental development and purification, as this would help one to eradicate the causes of suffering, greed, hatred and delusion and ultimately result in the attainment of Arhatship and *nirvāṇa*. Siddhārtha Gautama was a Buddha, a self-perfected, self-enlightened human being and not a saviour of man. He was a human role-model to be followed but not idolized. Of himself he said, "Buddhas only point the way." So this is why the earliest artistic tributes to the Buddha Gautama are abstract symbols indicative of major events and achievements in his last life and in some cases his previous lives.

With the passage of time and the fracture in Buddhist Order, Buddhist art became iconic and Buddha-*bhakti* found its expression in religious structures like *stūpa, caitya* and *vihāra.* The Buddhist art also found its expression in wall paintings, scrolls, frescoes and wood-carved religious structures besides the religious craft. In all their forms Buddhist art, architecture and paintings were truly a tribute to the Compassionate Buddha who was Śāstā *par excellence.* We should be proud that the Buddha was born in our land and he bequeathed us a sublime culture and enlightening thought. And it is our greatness that we disseminated his wisdom to the world to save the humanity from the mire and fire of this *saṁsāra.* In a nutshell, this was the contribution of Buddhist thought and culture to the art and architecture of Asian countries. These religious structures, icons and paintings are an eloquent testimony of that Great Saviour of Humanity. Like the lighthouses these religious structures will continue to radiate and illuminate the hopes of the future generations of the Asian people.

Conclusion

CONCLUSION is the last main division of a subject, usually containing a summing up of the points and a statement of opinion or decisions reached. After having said so much about the impact of Buddhist thought and culture on socio-religious life of the Asian people with special reference to Sri Lanka, China and Tibet in eight well-planned chapters we are now in a position to establish our own opinion. We have already said in the main body of the volume that Buddhism was a tremendous civilizing force as well as movement not only in its homeland but also in a number of countries which were spread over a large tract of Asian Continent ranging from Bactria in the west to Japan in the east and from Mongolia in the north to Sri Lanka in south and Java and Sumatra in the south east.

After the advent of the Buddha and Buddhism, the Asian people got a fresh spiritual breeze and they were inspired to cultivate an altruistic culture which would unite and integrate the entire humanity into a bond of universal fraternity. Buddhism came forward with an enlightened thought and philanthropic culture and dished out for the ailing humanity a remedial prescription of universal brotherhood, compassion and eternal peace. Through whatever routes the message and culture of the Buddha travelled, they all got saturated with Buddhist thought and overshadowed by highly refined Buddhist culture. We have discussed in the opening chapter of the book what routes did Buddhism take in the early years of its expansion to the far-flung areas of Central Asia and the Far-East. Its overseas expansion to Sri Lanka, Java, Indonesia and Japan was also discussed. In this chapter we tried to project the cultural geography of Buddhist Asia and also indicated the land and sea routes through which Buddhism spread under the royal patronage by the royal missionaries. We also hinted at the expanse of cultural territories of Buddhist Asia during the first eight centuries of the Christian era and even some centuries before the Christian era.

In the second chapter we have concentrated our attention on discussing the state of society and religion of the pre-Buddhist Asian countries. All important countries of Asia, which subsequently adopted Buddhism as their faith were practising different religions before the advent of Buddhism. We have particularly discussed the religions of Sri Lanka, China and Tibet when they were not converted into Buddhist lands.

The third chapter deals with Buddhism and the cultural transformation of Asian people by devout royalty. Here we have discussed elaborately the role and contribution of royalty in bringing about a cultural transformation in many Asian countries under the direct impact of Buddhist thought and culture. It must be emphasized here that Buddhism gave us both thought as well as culture. So wherever Buddhism spread, it transformed the thought and culture of that land and when thought and culture was changed then society and religion was automatically changed.

The fourth chapter is devoted to the study of impact of Buddhist thought and culture on Sri Lankan people. Chronologically, it was here in Sri Lanka that Buddhist thought and culture left its lasting impression on the socio-religious life of Sri Lankan people which continues even to this day.

In the fifth chapter we have discussed in detail how the royalty and the Buddhist scholars implanted a new thought and culture in China by translating a large number of Buddhist Sanskrit texts into Chinese and gifting a great spiritual treasure of wisdom. The missionary programme of the royalty and the scholars brought forth a perceptible change in the socio-religious life of the Chinese people.

In the sixth chapter once again we showed how the teachings of the Buddha, his thought and his culture influenced the life of the Tibetan people.

In the seventh chapter we have discussed how religio-cultural transformation could take place in Korea, Japan and other South-East Asian countries under the impact of Buddhism. Here too, we have discussed at large the role and contribution of the royalty and monk scholars in bringing about a sea change in the socio-religious life of the people of these Buddhist countries.

In the last chapter of this volume we have tried to tell briefly the most important contributions of Buddhist thought and culture to literature, art and architecture of Asian countries.

We know that the influence of Buddhist thought and culture on socio-religious life of the Asian people was so great that they completely divorced their native religions, beliefs and customs. Instead Buddhism had to compromise with the native beliefs and customs and had to accommodate them in its embrace. This is the reason why we find a tinge of Bon in Tibetan Buddhism, a tinge of Confucianism and Taoism in Chinese Buddhism, and a tinge of Shinto in Japanese Buddhism. The recorded history of the Buddhist Asian countries tells us that there were many ups and downs in the fate of Buddhism in these countries but ultimately Buddhism remained victorious. Now with rapid industrialization and growing consumerism, and in an atmosphere where there is a rat race for material prosperity, Buddhism and its influence are declining though an attempt is being made to propagate the glory of Buddhism, its thought and culture. Despite all these facts, there is no doubt that Buddhism has in its store a message of peace, sympathy, tolerance, friendliness and universal brotherhood. Its teachings are really capable of civilizing any barbaric race. We are of the considered opinion that Buddhism influenced the thought and culture of several nations and made them civilized and properly understood. Buddhism will continue to exercise its ethico-spiritual influence even on modern societies of the world.

Bibliography

Adikaram, E.W., *Early History of Buddhism in Ceylon*, Colombo, 1946.

Aggarwal, R.C., *Life of Buddhist Monks in Chinese Turkestan.*

Ahir, D.C., *Buddhism in North India*, Delhi: Classical Indian Publication, 1989.

———, *Heritage of Buddhism*, Delhi: B.R. Publishing Corporation, 1989.

Ahir, D.H., *Buddhism in South-East Asia*, Delhi: Sri Satguru Publications.

———, *Buddhism Sites and Shrines in Indian History, Architecture*, Delhi: Sri Satguru Publications.

———, *Glimpses of Sri Lankan Buddhism*, Delhi: Sri Satguru Publications.

Altekar, A.S., *Education in Ancient India*, Banaras, 1957.

Anand, Mulk Raj, *Tibetan Art.*

Anesaki, M., *History of Japanese Religion*, 1963.

Bagchi, P.C., *India and Central Asia.*

———, *India and China*, Calcutta, 1944.

———, *Le Canon Bouddhiaue China*, 2 vols., Paris, 1927.

———, *She-Kia-Fang-Che*, Santineketan, 1959.

Bajpai, K.D. (ed.), *Cultural History of India*, Delhi: Prajna Prakashan, 1985.

Bamjai, P.N.K., *A History of Kashmir*, Delhi: Metropolitan Book Company, 1980.

———, *Kashmir and Central Asia*, Delhi: Life and Light Publication, 1980.

Banerjee, A.C., *Aspects of Buddhist Culture from Tibetan Sources*, Calcutta: Firma KLM, 1984.

———, *Buddhism in India and Abroad*, Calcutta: The World Press Pvt. Ltd., 1979.

———, *Sarvāstivāda Literature*, Calcutta: The World Press Pvt. Ltd., 1979.

———, *Studies in Chinese Buddhism*, Calcutta: Firma KLM, 1977.

———, *The Splendour of Buddhism*, Delhi: Motilal Banarsidass, 1991.

Banerjee, P., *Early Indian Religion*, Delhi: Munshiram Manoharlal, 1991.

Bansal, B.L., *Bon its Encounter with Buddhism in Tibet*, Delhi: Eastern Book Linkers, 1994.

Bapat, P.V., (ed.), *2500 Years of Buddhism*, Delhi: The Publication Division, Ministry of Information and Broadcasting, Govt. of India, 1959.

Barthelmy, J., *Buddhism in India and Sri Lanka*.

Barua, B.M., *History of pre-Buddhistic Indian Philosophy*, Delhi, 1970.

———, *Inscription of Aśoka II*, Calcutta, 1943.

Barua D.K., *Buddhist Art of Central Asia*, International Institute of Pali and Prakrit Studies, Calcutta, 1981.

Barua and Sinha, *Bharhut Inscription*, Calcutta, 1926.

Basham, A.L., *The Wonder That Was India*, New York: Grove Press, 1959.

Batchelor, S., *The Jewel in the Lotus : A Guide to the Buddhist Traditions of Tibet*, London: Wisdom Publication, 1987.

Beal, Samuel, *Abstract of Four Lectures on Buddhist Literature in China*, London, 1982.

———, *Indian Travels of Chinese Buddhists*, Bombay: *Indian Antiquary*, 1881.

———, *Si-Yu-Ki Buddhist Record of the Western World*, 2 vols., Delhi: Motilal Banansidass, 1981.

———, *Travels of Fa-Hien and Sung-Yun, Buddhist Pilgrims from China to India*, (400-518 AD), Translation from the Chinese, London, 1869.

Bell, Sir Charles, *Religion of Tibet*, Calcutta: Clarendon Press, 1967.

———, *The People of Tibet*, Oxford: Clarendon Press, 1931.

———, *The Religion of Tibet*, Oxford: Clarendon Press, 1931.

Berbal, R. De, *Buddhism in Sri Lanka and South-East Asia*.

Berlin, E.S., *The Buddhist Sects of Japan*, London, 1938.

Bhagwat, N.K. (ed.), *Mahāvaṁsa*, University of Bombay, 1936.

Bhandarkar, D.R., *Carmichael Lectures*, 1918.

Bhattacharya, A., *History of Ancient India*, Delhi: Sterling Publishers Pvt. Ltd., 1982.

Bhattacharya, B., *The Indian Buddhist Iconography*, Delhi: Firma KLM, 1987.

Bhattacharya, N.N., *History of Researches on Indian Buddhism*, Delhi: Munshiram Manoharlal, 1981.

Bingham, *The Founding of the T'ang Dynasty, Baltimore*, 1942.

Bird, G.W., *Wandering in Burma*, London, 1897.

Bishop, H.D. (ed.), *Chinese Thought, An Introduction*, Delhi: Motilal Banarsidass, 1978.

———, *Indian Teachers in China*, Madras 1923.

Bu Ston, *History of Buddhism*, (2 vols.) trans., E. Obermiller, Heidelberg, 1931-1932.

Buswell, R.E. Jr., *Buddhism in Korea,* New York: Macmillan & Co., 1987.

Buswell, S.W., *Chinese Art,* 2 vols, London, 1904.

Byron, E., *The Religion of Japan,* Harper and Row, San Francisco, 1984.

Cave, H.W., *The Ruined Cities of Ceylon,* London, 1900.

Chakravarti, N.P., *India and Central Asia,* Calcutta, 1927.

Chandra, Lokesh (ed.), *India's Contribution to World Thought and Culture,* Chennai: Kendra Prakashan Trust (Reprint), 2003.

Chandler, D.P., *A History of Cambodia,* Westview Boulder, 1990.

Chang, B., *Religions in Korea,* Seoul: Korean Overseas Information Services, 1984.

Chattopadhyaya, Alka, *Atīśa and Tibet,* Delhi: Motilal Banarsidass, 1981.

Chattopadhyaya, D. (ed.), *Tarnath's History of Buddhism in India,* Shimla: Indian Institute of Advanced Study, 1970.

Chattopadhyaya, S., *Early History of North India,* Delhi: Motilal Banarsidass, 1976.

Chatterji, B.R., *Indian Cultural Influence in Cambodia,* 1964.

Chaudhary, B.N., *Buddhist Centres in Ancient India,* Calcutta: Sanskrit College, 1969.

Chau, Pu Chu, *Buddhism in China,* Peking, 1960.

Chauly, G.C., *Early Buddhist Art in India,* Delhi: Sundeep Prakashan, 1998.

Chen, Shin Yu, *Introduction of Buddhism to Korea,* Berkeley: Asian Humanities Press, 1989.

Chau, Thick M., *Hiuen Tsang: The Pilgrim and Scholar,* Nha Trang.

Chii-Luch-Lo, *Chinese Sources of Indian History,* Proceeding of the Indian Historical Records Commission, 1948.

Chen, Kenneth, *Buddhism in China,* Princeton University Press, 1964.

———, *Buddhism in China History.*

———, *Buddhism, the Light of Asia.*

———, *The Chinese Transformation of Buddhism,* Princeton N.J.: Princeton University Press, 1973.

Chopra, P.N., *Contribution of Buddhism to World Civilization and Culture,* Delhi: S. Chand and Co., 1988.

Chun, Shin Yong (ed.), *Buddhist Culture in Korea,* Seoul: Si-Sa-Yong-Sa Publishers, 1982.

Clark, C.A., *Religions of Old Korea,* New York: Garland, 1981.

Codrington, H.W., *A Short History of Ceylon,* Macmillan and Co., 1926.

———, *The Indianized States of South-East Asia,* Australian National University, 1975.

Conze, Edward, *A Short History of Buddhism,* George Allen and Unwin, 1980.

———, *Buddhism, its Essence and Development,* New York: Harper Torchbooks, 1965.

———, *Buddhist Scriptures,* New York: Garland, 1982.

Coomaraswamy, A., *Buddha and Gospel of Buddhism,* Delhi: Munshiram Manoharlal, 1964.

———, *History of Indian and Indonesian Art,* Delhi: Munshiram Manoharlal, 1972.

———, *The Elements of Buddhist Iconography,* Cambridge, Mass: Harvard University Press, 1965.

Cunningham, A., *The Ancient Geography of India,* Delhi: Low Price Publication, 1871.

Damrong, Princes, *Indo-Tibetan Buddhism,* London, 1987.

Dragay, Eva. M., *Rise of Esoteric Buddhism in Tibet,* Delhi: Motilal Banarsidass, 1977.

Das, S.C., *Contribution of Religious History of Tibet,* Delhi: Munshiram Manoharlal, 1970.

———, *Indian Paṇḍits in the Land of Snow,* Calcutta: Firma KLM, 1965.

———, *The Religion and History of Tibet,* New Delhi: Cosmo Publications, 1980.

———, *Tibetan Buddhist Historical Glossary,* New Delhi: Sri Satguru Publications.

David, T.W. Rhys, *Buddhist India,* New Delhi: Indological Book House, 1970.

Davy, *Travels in Ceylon,* London, 1821.

Deambi, B.K. Kaul, *Corpus of Sharda Inscriptions of Kashmir,* Delhi: Agam Kala Prakashan, 1982.

———, *History and Culture of Ancient Gandhāra and Eastern Himalayas,* New Delhi: Ariana Publishing House, 1985.

De, V.M.W., *Ancient Buddhism in Japan,* 2 vols, 1928.

Douglas, R.K., *Buddhism in China,* London: Society for Promoting Chiristian Knowledge.

Dowman, K., *The Sacred Life of Tibet,* London: Thorsons, 1997.

Dutt, N., *Early Monastic Buddhism,* Calcutta: Firma KLM, 1981.

———, *Gilgit Manuscripts.*

———, *Mahāyāna Buddhism,* Delhi: Motilal Banarsidass, 1978.

———, *The Spread of Buddhism and Buddhist Scholars,* Delhi: Rajesh Publication, 1980.

Dutt, R.C., *A History and Civilization of Ancient India,* Delhi: Seema Publication, 1972.

———, *Buddhism and Buddhist Civilization In India,* Delhi: Seema Publication, 1933.

Dutt, Sukumar, *Buddhism in East Asia,* Delhi: Indian Council for Cultural Relations, 1966.

———, *Buddhist Monks and Monasteries in India,* Delhi: Motilal Banarsidass, 1988.

———, *The Buddha and Five After-Centuries,* Calcutta: Sahitya Samsad.

Havell, E.B., *Indian Scriptures and Paintings,* London, 1933.

Thomas, E.J., *History of Buddhist Thought,* London, 1933.

Edkin, Joseph, *Chinese Buddhism : Historical, Descriptive and Critical,* Delhi: Aryan Books International, 1996.

Edwin, Arnold, *Light of Asia.*

Eliot Charles, *Japanese Buddhism,* London, 1935.

———, *Hinduism and Buddhism,* 3 vols., London, 1921.

Elizabeth, R.S., *The Buddhist Art of Nagarjunakonda.*

Ekval, E. Robert., *Religious Observances in Tibet,* Chicago III, 1964.

Farker, E.H., *China and Religion,* New York, 1905.

Fisher, R.E., *Buddhist Art and Architecture,* London: Thames and Hudson, 1993.

Fitzerald, C.P., *China : A Short Cultural History,* London, 1942.

———, *Finding out About Imperial China,* London: Frederick Müller Ltd.

Foucher, A., *The Beginning of Buddhist Art and Other Essays on Indian and Central Asian Archaeology,* London, 1917.

Miton, G.E., *The Lost Cities of Ceylon,* London, 1916.

Ganhar, J.N. and P.N. Ganhar, *Buddhism in Kashmir and Ladakh,* Delhi, 1956.

Gaulier, S., J. Robert and M. Monique, *Buddhism in Afghanistan and Central Asia,* Leiden, 1976.

Getty, A., *The Gods of Northern Buddhism,* Oxford, 1988.

Ghosal, U.N., *Ancient Indian Culture in Afghanistan,* 1928.

Giles, H.A., *The Travels of Fa-Hien (399-414 AD) Or Record of the Buddhist kingdom,* Cambridge, 1923.

Ghosal, U.N., *Ancient Indian Culture in Afghanistan,* 1982.

Gode, P.K., *Studies in Indian Culture.*

Goodrich, L.C., *A Short History of Chinese People,* New York, 1959.

Goswami, Jaya, *Cultural History of Ancient India (A Socio-economic & Religious Culture Survey of Kapisa & Gandhāra),* Delhi: Agam Kala Prakashan, 1979.

Goyal, S.R., *A History of Indian Buddhism.*

———, *A Religious History of Ancient India (up to 1200* AD*)*, vol. I, Meerut: Kusumanjali Prakashan, 1984.

Grante, M., *Chinese Civilization*, London, 1930.

Greyson, J.H., *Korea, A Religious History*, Oxford: Clarendon, 1989.

Griffis, W.E., *The Religions of Japan*, New York, 1896.

Grunwedal, *Buddhist Art in India*, London, 1901.

Gupta, S.P. (ed.), *Aspects of India's History and Culture*, New Delhi: Life and Light Publication.

Hackin, J., *Buddhist Art in Central Asia*, London, 1931.

Hackmann, H., *Buddhism as a Religion*, New Delhi: Sharda Publishing House, 1994.

Haldar, S.M., *Buddhism in India and Sri Lanka*, New Delhi: Om Publication, 2001.

Hall, D.G.E., *A History of South-East Asia*, London: Macmillan, 1981.

Hallade, M., *Gandhāra and Evolution of Buddhist Art*, London: Thames and Hudson, 1968.

Hamilton, C.H., *Buddhism in India, Ceylon, China and Japan*, Chicago: A Reading Guide, 1931.

Han, Woo-keun, *The History of Korea*, Honolulu: University of Hawaii, 1971.

Hanayama, Shinsho, *A History of Japanese Buddhism*, 1916.

———, *Bibliography of Buddhism*, Tokyo: Hokusedo Press, 1961.

Hassnain, F.M., *Buddhist Kashmir*, New Delhi: Life and Light Publication, 1973.

Havell, E.B., *Handbook of Indian Art*.

Harichandra, B.W., *The Sacred City of Anurādhapura*, New Delhi: Asian Educational Services, 1985.

Hazra, K.L., *Buddhism in India as described by Chinese Pilgrim*, Delhi: Munshiram Manoharlal, 1983.

———, *Royal Patronage of Buddhism in Ancient India*, New Delhi: D.K. Publications, 1984.

Heber, A.R. & M.K. Heber, *Himalayan Tibet and Ladakh*, New Delhi: S.S. Publication, 1976.

Herman, Oldenberg, *Buddha: His Life, His Doctrine, His Order*, London, 1888.

Hettiarchi, S.B., *Social and Cultural History of Ancient Sri Lanka*, New Delhi: Sri Satguru Publications.

Hoffman, Helmut, *The Religions of Tibet*, London: Allen and Unwin.

Hsiang, Kuan Chau, *The History of Chinese Buddhism*, Allahabad: Munshiram Monoharlal, 1955.

Hu-shih, *The Indianization of China : A Study in Cultural Borrowing*, Cambridge,

1937.

Griffiths, J., *The Paintings in the Buddhist Cave Temples at Ajanta*, 2 vols., London, 1896.

Smitter, J.G., *Architectual Remains in Anurādhapura*, London: Ceylon, 1896.

Ferguson, J., and J. Burger, *The Cave Temples of India*, London, 1880.

Joshi, Jagat Pati, *Facets of Indian Civilization*, Delhi: Motilal Banarsidass, 1997.

Joshi, Mani Lal, *Studies in the Buddhistic Culture of India*, Delhi: Motilal Banarsidass, 1987.

Jumsai, M.L., *History of Laos*, Bangkok, 1971.

Codrington, K. de B. *Ancient India*, London, 1926.

Rama., K., *Buddhism : A World Religion*, New Delhi: Vedams Books Pvt. Ltd.

Kang, Yun., *The Buddhist Cave Temples of Fifth Century* AD *in North China.*

Kaul, Advaitavadini, *Buddhist Savants of Kashmir*, Srinagar: Utpal Publication, 1987.

Koul, B.K., *History & Culture of Ancient Gandhāra and Western Himalayas*, New Delhi: Asian Publishing House, 1985.

Keith, Arthur B., *Buddhist Philosphy in India and Ceylon*, 1979.

Kern, H., *Manual of Indian Buddhism*, Delhi: Motilal Banarsidass, 1989.

Khosla, Romi, *Buddhist Monasteries in the Western Himalayas*, Kathmandu: Ratna Pustak Bhandar, 1979.

Khosla, Sarla, *History of Buddhism in Kashmir.*

Kingtom, William, *The History of Ceylon*, New Delhi: Sri Satguru Publications.

Knox, G.W., *The Development of Religion in Japan*, New York, 1907.

Kosambi, D.D., *The Culture and Civilization of Ancient India in Historical Outline*, New Delhi: Vikas Publishing House Pvt. Ltd., 1981.

Justine, L., *Buddhism and Lamaism in Tibet*, New Delhi: Gaurav Publishing House.

King, L., *Buddhism in Contemporary Burma.*

Lobsang, L., *The Religious Culture of Tibet.*

Herringhan, Lady, *The Ajanta Frescoes*, London, 1915.

Lahiri, Latika, *Chinese Monks in India*, New Delhi: Motilal Banarsidas, 1986.

Lama, Anagarika G., *Foundation of Tibetan Mysticism*, Rider, London, 1960.

Lancaster, L & C.S. Yu. *Introduction of Buddhism to Korea*, California: Asian Humanities Press, 1989.

Law, B.C., *Geography of Early Buddhism*, New Delhi: Bhartiya Publishing House, 1973.

———, *On the Chronicles of Ceylon*, Calcutta, 1947.

———, *History of Buddha's Religion*, New Delhi: Sri Satguru Publications, 1986.

Legge, James, *Travels of Fa-Hien*, Oxford, 1886.

Lillie, Arthur, *Buddha and Buddhism*, New Delhi: ESS ESS Publication, 1975.

Ling, Trevor, *Buddhist Trends in South-East Asia*, Singapore: Institute of South-East Asian Studies, 1993.

———, *The Buddha : Buddhist Civilization in India and Ceylon*, 1973.

Litvinsky, B.A., *Outline History of Buddhism in Central Asia*, Calcutta, 1970.

Liu, Xinru, *Ancient India & Ancient China : Trade & Religious Exchanges*, Oxford University Press, 1988.

———, *Silk and Religion*, Mumbai, 1998.

Majumdar, R.C., *Ancient India*, Delhi: Motilal Banarsidass, 1987.

———, *History and Culture of Indian People*, New Delhi: Bhartiya Vidya Bhawan.

Mahindra and Mittal, P., *Buddha and Spread of Buddhism in India & Abroad*, New Delhi: Low Price Publication, 2002.

Malalgoda, Kitsiri, *Buddhism in Sinhalese Society*, London: University of California Press, 1976.

Malalasekera, G.P., *Pāli Literature of Ceylon*, 1940.

Marshall, Sir John, *Buddhist Art of Gandhāra*, Cambridge University Press.

Masahar, A., *Religious History of Japan*, Tokyo, 1907.

Matsunga, D., *Foundation of Japanese Buddhism*, 2 vols., 1976.

Mendis, G.C., *Early History of Ceylon*, 1940.

Mitra, Debala, *Buddhist Monuments*, Calculta: Sahitya Samsad, 1980.

Mittal, P. and Mahendra, *Buddha and Spread of Buddhism in India and Abroad*, Collection of Articles from the Indian Historical Summary Quarterly, vol. 2, New Delhi.

Mookerji, P.K., *Indian Literature in China and Far East*, Bombay, 1949.

Mookerji, Radha K., *Ancient Indian Education*, London, 1947.

Murthy, K.K., *Buddhism in South-East Asia*, New Delhi: Classical Publishing Company, 1990.

———, *Buddhism in Japan*, New Delhi: Sundeep Prakashan, 1989.

———, *Buddhism in Tibet*, New Delhi: Sundeep Prakashan, 1989.

Müller, Max, *Origin of Religion*.

Krom, N.J., *The Life of Buddha in the Stūpa of Borobudur According to Lalitavistara Text*, The Hague, 1926.

Nakamura, H., *Ways of Thinking of Eastern People: India-China-Tibet-Japan*, 1964.

Nanjio, B., *A Catalogue of the Chinese Translation of the Buddhist Tripitaka*, Oxford, 1883.

Narada, M. Thera, *Buddhism in Nutshell*, Colombo, 1982.

Narain, A.K. (ed.), *Studies in the History of Buddhism*, New Delhi: B.R. Publishing Corporation. 1980.

Neilsen, C. Neils., *Religions of the World*, New York: Saint Martin's Press, 1998.

Nigosian, S.A., *World Religions*, London: Edward Arnold, 1975.

Noble, J., *Central Asia : The Connecting Link Between East and West*, Nagpur, 1952.

Norbuj, J. and C. Turnbell, *Tibet, Its History Origin and People*, New Delhi: Allied, 1984.

Oberlin, S., *The Buddhist Sects of Japan*, 1938.

Obermiller, E., *History of Buddhism*, 2 vols, Heidelberg, 1931.

The History of Buddhism in India and Tibet, New Delhi: Sri Satguru Publications, 1996.

Osgood, C., *The Korean and their Culture*, 1951.

Paine, R.T. and A. Soper, *The Art and Architecture of Japan*, Harmondsworth, 1955.

Pande, G.C., *Studies in the Origin of Buddhism*, Delhi: Motilal Banarsidass, 1975.

Pandeya, R.C., *Buddhist Studies in India*, Delhi: Motilal Banarsidass, 1975.

Pannikar, K.M., *Studies in Indian History*, Bombay: Asia Publishing House, 1963.

Parker, H., *Ancient Ceylon*, London, 1909.

Pathak, R.K., *Historical Survey of Indian Buddhism*, Delhi: Ramananda Vidya Bhawan, 1989.

Petch, L., *A Study of Chronicles of Ladakh*.

Powers, J., *Introduction to Tibetan Buddhism*, U.S.A.: Snow Lion Publication, 1995.

Pratt, J.B., *The Pilgrimage of Buddhism*, 1928.

Prince, D.H., *A History of Buddhism in Siam*.

Puri, B.N., *Buddhism in Central Asia*, New Delhi: Motilal Banarsidass, 1975.

Ram, Rajendra, *A History of Buddhism in Nepal*, New Delhi: Motilal Banarsidass, 1978.

Ram, Rahula, *Central Asia: An Outline History*, Delhi: Concept Publishing Company, 1997.

Rahul, Walpola, *History of Buddhism in Ceylon, Anurādhapura Period*, Sri Lanka: The Buddhist Cultural Centre, 1956.

Rahula, Walpola, *The Heritage of a Bhikkhu*, New York: Grove Press, 1974.

Richardson, H.E., *Tibet and its History*, London: Oxford University Press, 1962.

Richardson, H.E and David Snellgrove, *A Cultural History of Tibet*, 1968.

Reichelt, K.L., *Truth & Tradition in Chinese Buddhism*, Shanghai, 1927.

Reischaufer, K.A., *Studies in Japanese Buddhism,* 1970.

Ridley, Michaels, *The Art of the World Religion Buddhism,* New Delhi: Heritage Publication, 1978.

Robert, B.D., *Religious Observances in Tibet,* Chicago: University of Chicago Press, 1964.

Robinson, H., *The Buddhist Religion,* 1970.

Rockhill, W.W., *Life of Buddha,* London, 1884.

———, *The Land of the Lamas,* New York, 1891.

Roerich, G.N., *Art and Architecture of India,* Delhi: Abhinav Publication, 1978.

———, *Tibetan Paintings,* Paris, 1925.

———, *The Blue Annals,* New Delhi: Motilal Banarsidass, 1979.

Rowland, Thomas, *The Art and Architecture of India.*

Saha, Kaniska, *Buddhism in Central Asia,* Calcutta: Firma KLM, 1970.

Saloman, R., *Ancient Buddhist Scroll from Gandhāra.*

Samten, G.K., *A General Introduction to the History and Doctrines of Bon,* Tokyo: Toyo Bunto, 1975.

Sagharakshita, *Tibetan Buddhism,* Birmingham, U.K.: Windhorse Publication, 1996.

Sansom, G.B., *Japan: A Short Cultural History,* London, 1931.

Saunders, E.D., *Buddhism in Japan, With an Outline of its Origin in India,* Greenwood Press, 1977.

Saunders, J.K., *Buddhism and Buddhists in Southern Asia,* 1923.

———, *Epochs in Buddhist History,* New Delhi: Bharatiya Book Corporation, 1985.

Schlagint Weit, *Buddhism in Tibet,* London, 1968.

Seckel, D., *The Art of Buddhism (Bibliography),* 1963.

Sein, K. Taw, *The Introduction of Buddhism in Burma.*

Sengupta, Sudha, *Buddhism in the Classical Age* (BCE *400*-CE *750*), New Delhi: Sundeep Prakashan, 1985.

Sen, S.N., *India Through Chinese Eyes,* Madras, 1956.

Sharma, J.B. and S.P., *Buddhist Culture,* New Delhi: Sublime Publication, 1994.

Sharma, I.K., *Buddhist Monuments in China and South-East Asia,* New Delhi: Sundeep Prakashan, 1955.

Shastri, M.N., *Buddha: His Life, His Teachings, His Order.*

Shastri, Nalikanta, *Aspects of Indian History & Culture.*

———, *Life of Hiuen Tsang.*

Shakya, M.N., *A Short History of Buddhism in Nepal*, Kathmandu, 1984.

Sickman, L. and A. Soper, *The Art and Architecture of China*, 1971.

Singhal, D.P., *Buddhism in East Asia*, Delhi: Books & Books Publishers, 1984

Sircar, D.C., *Inscription of Aśoka*, Delhi: Publication Division, Govt. of India, 1975.

Smith, Huston, *The World's Religion*, New Delhi: Harper Collins Publishers, 1997.

Snellgrove, D.L., and E.R. Huge, *A Cultural History of Tibet*, Boulden, 1980.

———, *Buddhist Himalayas*, Oxford, 1957.

———, (ed.), *Images of the Buddha*, Tokyo: Kodansha International, 1978.

———, *Indo-Tibetan Buddhism*, Boulden, 1980.

———, and S. Tadensz, *The Cultural Heritage of Ladakh*, New Delhi: Vikas Publishing House Pvt. Ltd., 1977.

Snelling, John, *The Buddhist Handbook*, London: Rider, 1987.

Soothhill. E.W., *Three Religions of China*, London, 1929.

Solomon, Richard, *Ancient Buddhist Scrolls From Gandhāra*, University of Washington Press.

Starr, Fredrick, *Korean Buddhism*, 1978.

Strin, Aurel, *Archaeological Exploration in Chinese Turkestan.*

———, *On Ancient Central Asian Track*, London: Macmillian and Co. Ltd., 1933.

———, *Tibetan Civilization*, London, 1972.

Stone, R.E., *The Buddhist Art of Nagarjunakonda.*

Susan, W., *Life Along the Silk Road.*

Suzuki, *Zen Buddhism and its Influence on Japanese Culture.*

Suzuki, B.L., *Mahāyāna Buddhism*, London: George Allen & Unwin, 1981.

Suzuki, D.T., *Zen and Japanese Buddhism*, Tokyo: Japan Tourist Bureau, 1970.

———, *Zen and Japanese Culture*, New York: Pantheon Books, 1959.

Suzuki, Kakichi, *Early Buddhist Architecure in Japan*, 1980.

Takakusu, J., *The Essential of Buddhist Philosophy*, Delhi: Motilal Banarsidass, 1978.

Tchicadzumi, *Buddhist in Japan.*

Tennent, E.J., *Ceylon*, 2 vols, London, 1860.

Than Tun (ed.), *Essay on the History of Buddhism of Burma*, Scotland: Kiscadale Publication, 1988.

Thomas, E.J., *History of Buddhist Thought.*

———, *The Life of the Buddha as Legend and History*, 1927.

Thomas, F.W., *Tibetan Literary Texts and Documents concerning Chinese Turkestan*, vol. I., London, 1935.

Thomas, L.A., *Beginning of Buddhist Art*, London, 1917.

Thapar, Romila, *A History of India*, vol. I., London: Penguin Books, 1986.

Toki, *Buddhism in Japan*.

Tripathi, Ram, *Sautrāntika Darsanam*, Sarnath: CIHTS, 1990.

Tripathi, R.S.S., *History of Ancient India*, Delhi: Motilal Banarsidass, 1987.

Tsering, N., *Buddhism in Ladakh*, New Delhi: Sterling Publishers, 1979.

Tucci, G., *The Religion of Tibet*, London: Routledge and Kegan Paul.

———, *Tibetan Painted Scrolls*, 3 vols., Rome, 1949.

Upasak, C.S., *History of Buddhism in Afghanistan*, Sarnath: CIHTS.

Verma, S.K., *Art and Inconography of Buddha Images*.

Vincent, A.S., *A History of Fine Art in India and Ceylon from Earliest Times to the Past Day*, Oxford, 1930.

Vogel, J.P., *Buddhist Art in India, Ceylon and Java*, Oxford: Clarendon Press, 1977.

Waddell, L.A., *Buddhism in Tibet*, London, 1895.

———, *Buddhism and Lamaism of Tibet*, New Delhi, 1979.

———, *Lhasa and its Mysteries*.

Wales, H.G.Q., *The Indianization of China and South-East Asia*, London, 1967.

Warder, A.K., *Indian Buddhism*, Delhi: Motilal Banarsidass, 1980.

Warren, *The Religions of the World & World Religion*.

Watter, T. (ed.), *On Yuan Chwang's Travels in India*, 2 vols., Delhi: Munshiram Manoharlal.

Weber, Max, *The Religion of China: Confucianism & Taoism*, 1951.

Weiger, *A History of Religious Belief & Philosophical Opinion in China*.

Welch, H., *The Practice of Chinese Buddhism*, 1950.

Wells, K., *Thai Buddhism, its Rites and Activities*, Bangkok: Christian Bookstore, 1960.

Winternitz, M., *A History of Indian Literature*.

Wright, A.F., *Buddhism in Chinese History*, Stanford: Stanford University Press, 1959.

Yu, Lan Fung, *A History of Chinese Philosophy*, vol. II, 1953.

Zurcher, E., *The Buddhist Conquest of China*, New York: E.J. Brill, 1959.

Index